GAṆEŚA

GAṆEŚA
Lord of Obstacles, Lord of Beginnings

Paul B. Courtright

OXFORD UNIVERSITY PRESS
New York Oxford

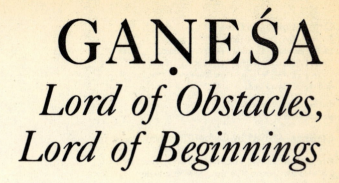

Oxford University Press
Oxford New York Toronto
Delhi Bombay Calcutta Madras Karachi
Kuala Lumpur Singapore Hong Kong Tokyo
Nairobi Dar es Salaam Cape Town
Melbourne Auckland

and associated companies in
Berlin Ibadan

First published in 1985 by Oxford University Press, Inc.,
200 Madison Avenue, New York, New York 10016

First issued as an Oxford University Press paperback, 1989

Library of Congress Cataloging in Publication Data

Courtright, Paul B.
Gaṇeśa: lord of obstacles, lord of beginnings.

Bibliography: p.
Includes index.
1. Gaṇeśa (Hindu deity) I. Title.
BL1225.G34C7 1985 294.5'211 84-25399
ISBN 0-19-505742-2 (PBK)

Grateful acknowledgment is made to the following for permission to reprint excerpts:
From *An Anthology of Sanskrit Court Poetry*, trans. Daniel H. H. Ingalls, 1965. Harvard Oriental Series 44. Reprinted by permission of Harvard University Press.
From *The Hermit and the Love Thief: Sanskrit Poems of Bhartrihari and Bilhana*, trans. Barbara Stoler Miller, 1978. Reprinted by permission of Columbia University Press.
From *The Inner World* by Sudhir Kakar, 1978. Reprinted by permission of Oxford University Press.
From *The Jnaneshvari*, Vol. 1, trans. V. G. Pradhan, ed. H. M. Lambert, 1969. Reprinted by permission of George Allen & Unwin Publishers, Ltd.
From *The Rig Veda*, trans., Wendy Doniger O'Flaherty, 1981. Reprinted by permission of Penguin Books, Ltd.

Cover: Dancing Ganesa. Tenth or Eleventh Century. Near Ahichattra (Uttar Pradesh) White Sandstone 58.5 x 34.8 cm (23 x 13 11/16") The Ackland Art Museum, The Universsity of North Carolina at Chapel Hill. Gift of Clara T. and Gilbert J. Yager in honor of Dr. Charles Morrow and his wife Mary Morrow, for their many contributions to the University and to the Ackland Art Museum during his term as provost.

9 8 7 6 5 4 3 2 1

Printed in the United States of America

For Peggy, Benjamin, Jonathan,
Rachel, and David,
who taught me about beginnings

Foreword

This is a book that I would have loved to have written. From the very moment when Paul Courtright told me he was working on it, years ago, I envied him. A book about Gaṇeśa! What fun that would be! What a wonderful book it would *have* to be. And it *is* a wonderful subject for a book; Gaṇeśa has everything that is fascinating to anyone who is interested in religion or India or both: charm, mystery, popularity, sexual problems, moral ambivalence, political importance, the works. One can start from Gaṇeśa and work from there in an unbroken line to almost any aspect of Indian culture. Although in an ideal sense this is true of any aspect of any culture—dig deep enough on any spot on the earth and you will reach the earth's center . . . and then out again to any other spot—some subjects offer a more immediate and more powerful network of routes to the nerve center, and Gaṇeśa is such a subject.

And Courtright has traveled on *all* of these roads. This is a superb example of what Clifford Geertz has called "thick description": it shines lights on the bulky figure of Gaṇeśa from so many different directions that something very like a three-dimensional figure does truly emerge at the end. I cannot think of anything that one would need to know about Gaṇeśa that this book does *not* tell one; nor, on the other hand, does it commit the sin of telling one more about Gaṇeśa than one wants to know. Very few gods have had such deep academic devotion accorded to them; of South Indian divinities, only Pattini has been so blessed (by Gananath

Obeyesekere). It seems appropriate that this god of scribes should be the one to have this book-offering made to him.

The route that Courtright travels is basically the philological trunk-route with major diversions. He gives us *all* the texts, from the thin, murky origins through the jungle growth of medieval and contemporary folklore, and he supplements them with a great deal of information about how people actually live with Gaṇeśa. The mythology is treated fairly; each of a number of reasonable interpretations is given its due, and none is insisted on. The episode of beheading by the father cries out for (and has been given by others) a party-line Freudian analysis; Courtright does, indeed, sail through this particular strait, but though he listens with unwaxed ears to the song of the psychoanalytic sirens, he is not seduced. He offsets the Freudian analysis with his own striking model of the parallels between the Gaṇeśa story and the Hindu ritual of the initiation of a young boy. This ritual is in turn set in its own context between the ancient Vedic rituals (to which other parts of the Gaṇeśa corpus also refer) and the contemporary ritual of *pūjā* to Gaṇeśa, as Courtright has witnessed and participated in it in Maharashtra. The aspect of Gaṇeśa's mythology that deals with his ambivalent relationship with the demonic powers of evil or, more particularly, with the battle between the powers of good and the powers of evil is then given a most illuminating new context by Courtright's description of the part played by Gaṇeśa in contemporary Indian politics.

The reader is thus given an *embarras de richesses* of reliable primary materials that Courtright himself has organized, transmitted, and presented with his own thoughtful suggestions for interpretation. The reader may or may not accept these interpretations, but in any case one is invited to place one's own map over the terrain presented here, to ask one's own questions of the god, to write one's own book about Gaṇeśa in one's head even as one reads the one that Courtright has published. For, as we learn from the *Mahābhārata* tale in which Vyāsa dictates the epic to Gaṇeśa, every great book exists in toto in the mind of the elephant-headed god, and we scribes merely scramble to scribble down those bits of it that we can grasp, including the "knots," the obstacles to full comprehension, that the god of obstacles throws in on purpose to keep us on our toes and to keep us in awe of him.

WENDY O'FLAHERTY

Acknowledgments

This book has grown from seeds planted during my first visit to India twenty years ago, when I was privileged to enjoy the hospitality of many Hindu friends and acquaintances who shared their lives with me and taught me about their Lord Gaṇeśa. I hope what I have written here about Gaṇeśa will be at least a recognizable portrait of their beloved deity.

Many colleagues and friends have contributed enormously to making this book possible. In India, M. D. Chaudhari, M. N. Bopardikar, D. K. Kharwandikar, and P. S. Jacob gave generously of their time and knowledge while I collected materials and observed religious practices in and around Ahmadnagar. In Pune, S. G. Tulpule and Gudrun Bühnemann read portions of the manuscript and corrected numerous errors. I spent many enjoyable hours reading Purāṇic stories of Gaṇeśa with the late Mrs. Maitreyi Vinod. Her love of Gaṇeśa and Sanskrit literature inspired my work.

A special word of gratitude goes to Wendy Doniger O'Flaherty, who not only shared her vast knowledge of Purāṇic literature and Hindu mythology and made many valuable suggestions on several drafts of this book, but also graced this undertaking with her inexhaustible enthusiasm and confidence in its value.

To my colleagues and friends who read all or portions of the book and made helpful suggestions—especially Harvey Alper, Alan B. Anderson, Richard Brubaker, David McL. Crosby, Anne

Feldhaus, Janet Varner Gunn, John S. Hawley, Norvin Hein, Alf Hiltebeitel, Henry Samuel Levinson, Charles H. Long, Charles D. Orzech, and Mary K. Wakeman—I extend my deepest thanks.

These splendid individuals deserve whatever merit may accrue from this book. However, they are absolved of any consequences resulting from its defects; those are mine alone. Unless indicated otherwise, all translations from the Sanskrit and Marathi are mine. I am deeply grateful to Job Thomas, who provided me with several photographs for the book, and to Jeffrey Patton, who drew the map.

Earlier versions of parts of this book have been published in the *Journal of Religious Studies* [Patiala], *Purāṇa* [Benāres], and *Gods of Flesh, Gods of Stone: The Embodiment of Divinity in India,* edited by Joanne Waghorne and Norman Cutler in association with Vasudha Narayanan (Chambersburg, Pa: Anima Books, 1985). Thanks of another sort are due to the American Council of Learned Societies, the National Endowment for the Humanities, the Excellence Fund, and the Research Council of the University of North Carolina at Greensboro for providing financial resources at various stages in the research and writing of this book. My father and mother, Harold and Norma Courtright, generously gave moral and financial support at many critical moments. I am grateful to Cynthia A. Read of Oxford University Press for seeing the manuscript through the publishing process with such sustaining humor and goodwill.

Finally, special words of gratitude belong to Peggy, my wife, who lived with Gaṇeśa and me through many obstacles and beginnings, and helped in a thousand ways to give birth and life to this book.

Greensboro, North Carolina P.B.C.
January 1985

Contents

Abbreviations

TEXTS

AB	*Aitareya Brāhmaṇa*
AP	*Agni Purāṇa*
ĀŚS	*Āśvalāyana Śrauta Sūtra*
AV	*Atharva Veda*
BĀU	*Bṛhadāraṇyaka Upaniṣad*
BDP	*Bṛhaddharma Purāṇa*
BGS	*Baudhāyana Gṛhya Sūtra*
BGpS	*Baudhāyana Gṛhyapariśiṣṭa Sūtra*
BhG	*Bhagavad Gītā*
BhP	*Bhāgavata Purāṇa*
BhavP	*Bhaviṣya Purāṇa*
BrP	*Brahmāṇḍa Purāṇa*
BVP	*Brahmavaivarta Purāṇa*
ChU	*Chāndogya Upaniṣad*
DP	*Devī Purāṇa*
DBP	*Devībhāgavata Purāṇa*
GB	*Gopatha Brāhmaṇa*
GG	*Gaṇeśa Gītā*, Yoroi's Translation
GP	*Gaṇeśa Purāṇa*
GarP	*Garuḍa Purāṇa*
H	*Harivaṃśa*
J	*Jātaka*
JB	*Jaiminīya Brāhmaṇa, (Talavakāra)*
KP	*Kūrma Purāṇa*
KSS	*Kathāsaritsāgara*
LP	*Liṅga Purāṇa*
Manu	*Mānavadharmaśāstra*
MatsyaP	*Matsya Purāṇa*
MudP	*Mudgala Purāṇa*
MBh	*Mahābhārata*, Critical Edition
MBh 1862	*Mahābhārata*, Bombay Edition
MBhP	*Mahābhāgavata Purāṇa*
MGS	*Mānavagṛhyasūtra*, Dresden's Translation
ML	*Mātaṅgalīlā*, Edgerton's Translation
MP	*Mārkaṇḍeya Purāṇa*
MS	*Maitrāyaṇī Saṃhitā*
P	*Purāṇa*
PGS	*Pāraskaragṛhyasūtra*

PP	*Padma Purāṇa*
R	*Rāmāyaṇa*
ṚV	*Ṛg Veda*
ŚB	*Śatapatha Brāhmaṇa*
SkP	*Skanda Purāṇa*
ŚP	*Śiva Purāṇa*
ŚP Dh	*Śiva Purāṇa, Dharmasaṃhitā*
SRK	*Subhāṣitaratnakoṣa,* Ingalls' Translation
ŚV	*Śaṅkaravijaya* of Ānandagiri
TĀ	*Taittirīya Āraṇyaka*
Tāṇḍya	*Tāṇḍya Mahābrāhmaṇa (Pañcaviṃśa)*
TB	*Taittirīya Brāhmaṇa*
U	*Upaniṣad*
VāmP	*Vāmana Purāṇa*
VarP	*Varāha Purāṇa*
VayuP	*Vāyu Purāṇa*
VP	*Viṣṇu Purāṇa*
YS	*Yājñavalkyasmṛti*

PERIODICALS AND SERIES

AA	*American Anthropologist*
ASS	Ānandāśrama Sanskrit Series
Bib. Ind.	Bibliotheca Indica
ERE	*Encyclopedia of Religion and Ethics*
HOS	Harvard Oriental Series
HR	*History of Religions*
JAAR	*Journal of the American Academy of Religion*
JAOS	*Journal of the American Oriental Society*
JAS	*Journal of Asian Studies*
JGJhRI	*Journal of the Ganganatha Jha Research Institute*
JRAS	*Journal of the Royal Asiatic Society*
WZKSO	*Wiener Zeitschrift zur Kunde des Süd- und Ostasiens*

Guide to Pronunciation

Sanskrit and Marathi vowels are pronounced as in Italian, except for the short *a,* which is pronounced like the *u* in the English word "but"; the long *ā* is pronounced like the *a* in "father"; *e* and *o* are always long; *ṛ* in Sanskrit is a vowel and should be pronounced like the *ri* in "ring." Consonants are pronounced as in English, with the following cases being noted: *c* as in "church" for words in Sanskrit and Marathi, although there are some exceptions in Marathi, such as *Cincvad* and *caurang,* in which the *c* is pronounced *ts;* the *j* is pronounced as in "joy"; and *ś* and *ṣ* are similar to the sound *sh* in "shine." The aspirated consonants should be pronounced distinctly: *th* as in "hothouse"; *ph* as in "top hat"; *gh* as in "doghouse"; and *bh* in "clubhouse." For Sanskrit and Marathi terms, which may be important to specialists, I have used standard diacritical notations (e.g., Gaṇeśa instead of Ganesha). To avoid needless confusion, the names of places and historical persons are used without diacritical marks and follow commonly recognized spellings (e.g., Bombay instead of Mumbaī and Tilak rather than Ṭiḷak). I have adopted the now common spelling for the city of Pune, formerly spelled Poona, although the latter form appears in quoted materials using that spelling and in the Bibliography, where the old spelling was used.

GAṆEŚA

1

The Making of a Deity

> Another had the head of an Elephant, and was call'd Ganescio. They say, he is the Son of Mahadeu, who finding him one day with Parveti, his wife, but his own Father, and not knowing who he was, kill'd him out of jealousie, cutting off his Head; but afterwards understanding that he was his own Son, he repented him of his error, and resolv'd to bring him to life again. Wherefore meeting with an Elephant (as he had purpos'd to do with what he first happen'd upon) he cut off his Head, and plac'd it on the dead Son's Shoulders. Whereupon Ganescio reviv'd, and thenceforward liv'd immortal with an elephant Head.
>
> But I doubt not that, under the veil of these Fables, their ancient Sages have hid from the vulgar many secrets, either of Natural or Moral Philosophy, and perhaps also of History: and I hold for certain that all of these so monstrous figures have secretly some more rational significations, though express'd in this uncouth manner. (Della Valle, Vol. 2, pp. 73–74)

This description of the Hindu god Gaṇeśa was written by the Italian traveler Pietro Della Valle in 1624. Della Valle, like most other Westerners who would come to India in subsequent generations, was astonished that people conceived of a deity who took the form of a being with the body of a man and the head of an elephant. The appearance of this and other deities seemed beyond Della Valle's comprehension; yet, he made an important concession in the midst of his astonishment. He admitted that these "monstrous figures" concealed more "rational significations."

Repulsion at the form of the deity with an elephant head and suspicion that there may be more going on than meets the (Western) eye, is a good starting point for our inquiry into this unusual deity. What is our reaction to be when we learn that for Hindus this particular deity is the most popular and universally adored of the reputed 330 million deities that make up the Hindu pantheon? Pictures and statues of Gaṇeśa are everywhere in India: in shops, on family altars, beside the roads, at intersections, in shrines at the entrances of villages and temples, inside the covers of books. He is praised at the beginning of ceremonies of worship and at marriages and other important rites of passage, and songs of devotion to him break the silence as the dawn of a new day begins.

Who Is Gaṇeśa?

Of the legions of Hindu gods and goddesses whose images adorn the walls of temples, shops, and homes, Gaṇeśa is the easiest to recognize. He is the one with the elephant head. Although there are some variations in his iconographic representation, which may be of interest to historians of Indian art, he is usually depicted either in a standing, sitting, or dancing posture with his face looking directly forward. His elephant head is missing one tusk, a piece of which he sometimes holds in one of his four hands. In one hand he may hold a hatchet [*paraśu*]; it is said that Paraśurāma used it to cut off the tusk when Gaṇeśa refused to allow him inside his parents' bedroom, but it is also a symbol for the cutting away of illusion and false teaching. In another hand he holds a goad [*aṅkuśa*], like that used by an elephant trainer, symbolizing the logic that cuts through illusion; in another a noose [*pāśa*] used to restrain the wild elephant and representing the restraint of passions and desires. Sometimes one hand gestures fearlessness and reassurance [*varadahastamudrā*] and another holds one of the sweetmeats [*modaka*] for which Gaṇeśa is said to have a gluttonous fondness. Around his potbelly he wears a serpent as a sacred thread. His torso is masculine but sufficiently pneumatic in appearance to suggest the lower limbs of a child or a *yakṣa*, one of the dwarfish guardian troops that protect and serve the gods and their shrines. The overall impression one gets from this image is comic. His manner suggests benevolence behind the obvious strength and stamina conveyed by the elephant head (see *Bṛhatsaṃhitā* 57.58; Banerjea, pp. 354–61; Getty, pp. 10–66; T. A. Gopinatha Rao, vol. 1/1, pp. 35–37; A. M. Shastri, pp. 173–174; see also pls. 1, 2).

There are many myths of Gaṇeśa's origins and exploits to be found in ancient and contemporary sources. No single version of the myth of Gaṇeśa contains all the elements found in all the variants. For our purposes, however, we may summarize the most frequently attested aspects of his story as follows:

> Once when Śiva had left his wife Pārvatī for a long time in order to meditate on Mt. Kailāsa, she became lonely and longed to have a son who would give her love and protection. She rubbed the unguents on the surface of her limbs and out of this material she rubbed forth a being in the shape of a young man. She breathed him to life and placed him at the doorway of her bath, instructing him to admit no one.
>
> Meanwhile, Śiva returned from his long meditations and arrived at Pārvatī's private chamber, but the young man blocked the way and refused to let him in. Not knowing that this guard was Pārvatī's creation, Śiva became angry and, after a battle, cut off the guard's head. Overhearing the commotion outside, Pārvatī came out. When she saw what had happened, she was overcome with grief and anger at what Śiva had done. She told him that unless he restored her son with a new head she would bring the universe to destruction. So Śiva sent his servants in search of a new head. As they traveled north, the auspicious direction, they found an elephant and cut off its head and returned to place it on the vacant shoulders of Pārvatī's guardian son. As the son revived, Śiva praised him and gave him the name of Gaṇeśa, made him lord of his (Śiva's) own group of devotees [*gaṇas*], and adopted him as his own son.
>
> Śiva then told all the gods and goddesses who had assembled there that Gaṇeśa must be worshipped before all undertakings or these will come to ruin. Gaṇeśa then became the Lord of Obstacles and placed barriers against all who neglected to worship him; he became the Lord of Beginnings and brought success to all who remembered him. From that time on, Gaṇeśa has placed and removed obstacles from the paths of gods, demons, and humans.

In mythology and iconography Gaṇeśa finds his place initially within the world of Śiva and Pārvatī, the erotic-ascetic lord and his benign-fearsome wife. Gaṇeśa is said to be Śiva's son, although his sonship is of a peculiar sort. Like Śiva, Gaṇeśa is a dancer, a destroyer of demons, the one wrapped in serpents. His elephant head is like that of the demon elephant Gajāsura, whom Śiva slew and made its skin into a garment as he danced on its head. Gaṇeśa is the leader of Śiva's *gaṇas,* the dwarfish denizens of the twilight—comic, horrible, and erotic, like the *maruts* of the Vedic Indra.

Gaṇeśa is also said to be Pāvatī's son, molded by her from the substance on the surface of her limbs and fashioned into the shape of a manchild. He is the guardian of her private chamber, her shrine. Most of the myths about Gaṇeśa tell the circumstances of his birth, his change of heads, and how he became the lord of Śiva's *gaṇas.* From these beginnings, Gaṇeśa moves out of the shadow of his illustrious parents and gains his own unique identity. He is the creator and remover of obstacles, the guardian at the entrances to all actions and places, whose presence can avert evil influences that would bring undertakings to ruin. He is the god to be worshipped first, before all others, in ceremonies both private and public. He is the Lord of Beginnings, the guarantor of success. Indeed, in Marathi, an idiomatic expression for making a beginning is *śrīgaṇeśa karṇe,* literally, "to make Lord Gaṇeśa," and *gaṇapatīce keḷe,* "to conceive a child."

Like other Hindu deities, Gaṇeśa has many names, at least a thousand. Among his more commonly known names, many describe his appearance: Gajamukha or Gajānana—the elephant-headed one; Ekadanta—the single-tusked one; Vakratuṇḍa—the one having the twisted trunk; Lambodara—the potbellied one. Other names refer to his role or function in the divine scheme of things: Siddhadāta—the bestower of success; Vighnarāja—the Lord of Obstacles; Vināyaka—the remover; Gaṇeśa, Gaṇapati, or Gaṇādhipa—the lord of Śiva's *gaṇas.* In South India, he is most widely recognied by his Tamil name, Piḷḷaiyār—the son or the young elephant.

In contemporary India, Hindus generally regard Gaṇeśa as a benign and helpful deity, one who brings success and assures worldly well-being. Yet, whatever success he contributes to human undertakings is understood to come in response to the honor paid him by his devotees. Beneath this strong and helpful guise, there lies a more ambivalent tendency; if he is not worshipped, he may withdraw his support and cause undertakings to fail. In Sri Lanka Gaṇeśa is worshipped in extraordinary modes of ecstatic experience. As one contemporary anthropologist describes him, he is the "fierce captain of wild elephants. He possesses mediums and inflicts severe punishments on any who dare ignore his immanent manifestations" (Pfaffenberger, p. 107).

One would expect a ubiquitous and popular deity of such unique appearance to have received a good deal of attention from both Indian and Western scholars of religion and mythology. But, except for some attention paid him in general studies on Hindu mythology, ritual practice, and iconography and some specialized works dealing with Śiva, only a modest handful of monographs and articles have been devoted specifically to Gaṇeśa and his significance within the Hindu universe. The reasons for this lacuna are probably several. Gaṇeśa makes his initial appearance in the Hindu pantheon relatively late, during the early Purāṇic period (c. fifth century A.D.), and this fact has led many Indologists to conclude that he is too derivative of other deities, particularly Śiva, to merit special inquiry. Lacking the clear aura of Vedic roots, Gaṇeśa has languished on the sidelines. To some, his theriomorphic form suggests that he is too "primitive," emerging from lower classes or aboriginal communities into reluctant Brāhmaṇical recognition, and therefore lacking the mythological richness or iconographic sophistication to be a worthwhile focus of sustained study. For others Gaṇeśa is simply too mundane; he is merely a god concerned with worldly success and material well-being. Except in the eyes of a small group of devotees for whom he is the embodiment of transcendental reality [*brahman*], Gaṇeśa has his feet planted firmly on the ground in the midst of this world. To those who look to Hinduism primarily for its mysticism and spirituality, Gaṇeśa does not seem to embody profound religious significance; rather, he appears tainted, trivial, perhaps even vulgar. Gaṇeśa lacks the erotic and lyrical appeal of Kṛṣṇa, the ascetic and cosmic ferocity of Śiva, the heroic majesty of Rāma, or the primeval creative and destructive power of the Goddess. In short, Gaṇeśa is too ordinary. Scholars have tended to ignore his obvious popularity among Hindus and failed to look beyond the material benefits he is believed to bestow for the sources of his appeal. In this study I hope to redress some of this imbalance. Gaṇeśa deserves more attention than he has received.

There are some brief discussions of Gaṇeśa in most anthologies of Hindu myths and decriptions of Hindu beliefs and practices. Gaṇeśa's iconography has received the most sustained attention from authors writing in English (P. K. Agrawala 1978, Banerjea, Getty, T. A. Gopinatha Rao, H. K. Sastri, 1978). Some Indian scholars have tended to concentrate more on the history of various forms of Gaṇeśa worship (Aravamuthan; Bhandarkar; Ghurye; Heras; Kane—vols. 2/1, 5/1; Mitra; Ramasubramaniam; U. V. Rao). However, important preliminary work has been done on the myths and texts devoted to Gaṇeśa (e.g., Bühnemann 1984; Courtright 1974, 1980; Hazra 1948; Herbert; Rassat; Stevenson; Varadpande; Winternitz; Yoroi). Some have focused on the theological dimensions of Gaṇeśa's meaning to Hindus (V. S. Agrawala; Danielou; Heras; Navaratnam). Gadgil's impressive compilation of Gaṇeśa lore in Marathi stands out among contemporary works written in Indian languages; the rest are largely guidebooks to shrines and simplified summaries of myths and instructions for ritual performance.

Two Kinds of Origins

The one issue that has received a good deal of attention is the question of Gaṇeśa's historical origins. Gaṇeśa seems to make an abrupt and dramatic appearance into the mythology and iconography of Hinduism in the post-Epic or early Purāṇic period, around the fifth century A.D., bringing with him only a few faint traces of his possible prior whereabouts, and many scholars have staked out various claims as to his origins.

The search for traces of Gaṇeśa in the earliest literature has turned up a few items of significance, with much of their meanings in dispute. The *Ṛg Veda* contains an invocatory prayer addressed to a deity named Gaṇapati, "We call upon you, upon the hosts, the leader of the hosts (Gaṇapati) [*gaṇānāṃ tvā gaṇapatīm havāmahe*]" (ṚV 2.23.1). Devotees of Gaṇeśa point to this prayer as the source for their deity's existence in the most ancient, sacred, and authoritative of scriptures. Scholarly consensus, both Indian and Western, however, takes the view that this Vedic text refers not to Gaṇeśa but to Bṛhaspati, the divine priest, and that *gaṇa* refers to the assembly of the gods (e.g., see Bhandarkar, p. 149). In other Vedic texts the name Gaṇapati refers alternatively to Indra (ṚV 10.112.9) or Śiva (AB 1.21). A more promising lead is to be found in the *Maitrāyaṇī Saṃhitā* of the *Yajur Veda.* A brief prayer is addressed to "one having a trunk [*karaṭa*]" or the "one with the elephant head [*hastimukha*]" or to the "one having a tusk [*dantin*]" (TB 10.15). Louis Renou believes this reference confirms a Vedic origin for Gaṇeśa but also points out that "it is part of a litany, a *rudrajapa,* and comes precisely in the place in the *Yajur* text where there is an invocation to Rudra [*śatarudriya*]" (p. 273). It may be that these references to a being with elephantine characteristics pertain to Śiva as the slayer of the elephant demon, whose head and tusks he took as trophies of conquest, rather than to an elephant-headed deity. In either case it seems likely, on this evidence, that Gaṇeśa's origins are inextricably linked with Śiva so far as the Brāhmaṇic sources are concerned. A similar invocation in another Brāhmaṇic text addresses "the one with the twisted trunk [*vakratuṇḍa*]" (TĀ 10.1.5), also leaving it uncertain whether it is Gaṇeśa or Śiva who is being addressed. These Vedic and Brāhmaṇic references are slim evidence on which to establish the historical origins of the god. Nevertheless, they are vitally important to the later tradition of Gaṇeśa worship because they link Gaṇeśa with the Vedic corpus of literature and lend him the aura of its immeasurable authority.

Origins of another sort may be found in texts and iconography from about the second to fifth centuries A.D. Dharmasūtra texts mention a class of beings called Vināyakas who possess people and require ritual propitiation. None of these Vināyakas is described as elephant headed, but they are spoken of as creating obstacles. Iconographic sources from this period provide a few simply carved *yakṣas,* dwarfish guardian figures with elephant faces (Coomaraswamy 1928, p. 30, and 1928a, p. 7; Getty, p. 25, pl. 22). These sources offer a preliminary picture of Gaṇeśa's malevolent side and his connection with the *gaṇas.* They also suggest that Gaṇeśa's origins may well lie outside the Brāhmaṇic fold. Recent evidence from Indo-Greek coins uncovered by A. K. Narain suggest that an elephantine deity figure was worshipped as early as A.D. 50 in northwest India. This figure seems to represent strength and royal authority, both dimensions of the later Gaṇeśa, and is redolent of the elephant symbolism of South and Southeast Asia generally.

Many scholars have been inclined to read the myths of Gaṇeśa for clues to the history of his worship and the origins of his cult. The pitfalls of reading mythology as history written in cryptic form are well known, but the efforts in this direction, however misguided, give us some idea of the avenues pursued by scholars. Getty and others have seen the story of Gaṇeśa's confrontation with Śiva and his subsequent restoration and adoption as the lord of the *gaṇas* as a commentary on the process by which Gaṇeśa was elevated from obscurity into Brāhmaṇic recognition. Others have suggested that Gaṇeśa's origins are to be found among the aboriginal tribes whose totemic emblem was an elephant. Chattopadhyaya (p. 141) speculates that Gaṇeśa's adoption by Śiva is a "reflection of the process by which some tribe, originally bearing the banner of an elephant, eventually established its superiority as a victorious state." The Brāhmaṇic tradition eventually assimilated the worship of this outsider, as they had done with Śiva, but relegated him to the category of demon, that is, Vināyaka, the one who was defeated and then transformed into a devotee of Śiva. Gaṇeśa's powers are delegated to him by his conqueror. The same process is at work in the myth of Śiva's defeat of the elephant demon and Kṛṣṇa's defeat of the river serpent, Kāliya (see Hospital). Gaṇeśa's ambivalent character—both benevolent and malevolent, one who both makes and removes obstacles—may reflect, it is argued, a historical process in which he was originally regarded as an outsider and threatening figure but later was rehabilitated by his beheading and adoption into Śiva's inner circle. In this way he became acceptable to Brāhmaṇic sensibilities and therefore beneficent. This process of rehabilitation at the level of myth is seen to parallel a sociohistorical process in which tribal, South Indian, or lower caste groups were assimilated into the caste hierarchy as part of the Brāhmaṇic synthesis after the eclipse of Buddhism in India. It was during this period that the early Purāṇas and the temple architecture of the Gupta dynasty flourished.

In this search for a historical origin for Gaṇeśa, some have suggested precise locations outside the Brāhmaṇic tradition: South

Indian tribal traditions (Getty, p. 2), the Pilliyar caste of Tamilnadu—presently a cultivating community with strong Brāhmaṇic influences (Rassat, p. 24), the Mundas—a tribal people of central India (Risley, vol. 2, p. 113), the Gajas—a Naga tribe in the northeastern region of India (Heras, pp. 201–203), an animal cult (Crooke, vol. 1, p. 184), the Naga cult of western India (Kosambi, p. 24), or lower or outcaste sectarian groups that were gradually granted Brāhmaṇic acceptance (Ghurye, pp. 51–90). These historical locations are intriguing to be sure, but the fact remains they are all speculations, variations on the Dravadian hypothesis, which argues that anything not attested to in the Vedic and Indo-European sources must have come into Brāhmaṇic religion from the Dravidian or aboriginal populations of India as part of the process that produced Hinduism out of the interactions of Aryan and non-Aryan populations. There is no independent evidence for an elephant cult or a totem; nor is there any archaeological data pointing to a tradition prior to what we see already in place in the Purāṇic literature and the iconography of Gaṇeśa.

As long as speculations of Gaṇeśa's origins are being scattered about, I will add my own, for which there is no more compelling evidence, but neither is it any less plausible. It may be the case that Gaṇeśa emerged as a full-fledged figure, the son of Śiva and Pārvatī, the obstacle remover and doorway guardian, during the evolution from Brāhmaṇic traditions of sacrifice to Hindu patterns of temple worship, which saw the establishment of permanent shrines requiring constant maintenance of ritual purity and protection from malevolent forces. With the advent of these shrines after the turn of the millennium, imperial imagery replaced the more martial imagery of the earlier Brāhmaṇic tradition. Although Śiva himself may be an ascetic, the temple is his palace where he rules as the monarch of the universe. As his son, Gaṇeśa is the commander of his troops and, as it were, his heir apparent. The association of elephants with Gaṇeśa may reflect not a tribal totem but the ceremonial and military use of elephants by imperial dynasties of this and later periods of Indian history. Reading Gaṇeśa's mythology, one gets the impression that we are encountering an elaborate rationalization for an "invented" deity, rather like the old joke about the camel being a horse that was designed by a committee. It is unlikely that some assemblage of Brāhmaṇic mythographers invented Gaṇeśa in a self-conscious manner. It is not so implausible, however, that symbols of the elephant, obstacles, the need for progeny to domesticate a wild ascetic Śiva and his childless wife Pārvatī into a viable household, and the obligation to protect sacred temple enclosures from pollution and hostile forces may have coalesced into the figure of Gaṇeśa. This was in response to the new religious situation of early Purāṇic Hinduism in which the religious life of the tradition was increasingly orienting itself around large and complex ceremonial centers. It is impossible to say just how Gaṇeśa came into existence or whether there was a distinct Gaṇeśa before he appears in the modes he does in the Brāhmaṇic sources. Indeed, it may be that he was *always* a Brāhmaṇical deity. The point to be stressed is that we need not invoke a Dravidian or aboriginal hypothesis to create a theory about Gaṇeśa's origins; there may not be any compelling evidence for Gaṇeśa prior to his emergence into the Brāhmaṇic fold simply because he was never there.

The issue of Gaṇeśa's origins takes on a very different character when we look at the mythological tradition of Gaṇeśa in terms of its own assumptions and purposes. Here we are not concerned with origins in the historical sense. The mythological texts account for where Gaṇeśa came from by means of stories about his mother, Pārvatī—forming him by rubbing a substance on the surface of her body—or of his genesis from his father's laugh. The Purāṇas are concerned to determine Gaṇeśa's geneology, his pedigree. The texts are aware that there are variant and incompatible accounts of his birth, and they account for this inconsistency by placing different variants in different cycles of cosmic time. "Because of the distinction between eras," the *Śiva Purāṇa* insists, "the story of Gaṇeśa's birth is told in different ways. According to one account he is born from the great lord [Śiva]. When Śani looked at him his head was cut off and replaced with an elephant's head [BVP 3.11–12]. Now we tell the story of Gaṇeśa as it happened in the *śveta kalpa* when the merciful Śiva cut off his head (ŚP 2.4.13.5–6)." The Hindu cyclical structure of time allows the mythographers to maintain many variants by assigning each to a different era while maintaining the overall integrity of the story that is understood to be valid eternally.

The Purāṇic texts are concerned with determining Gaṇeśa's origins and establishing them within the framework of Śiva's cycle of myths, giving the elephant lord full recognition and authority under his father's umbrella. The texts stress that Gaṇeśa's capacity to remove and create obstacles comes from Śiva—through the adoption or initiation of Gaṇeśa as leader of Śiva's circle of *gaṇas*—and that Gaṇeśa's elephant head is the emblem of that authority, just as the elephant is the symbol of a king's authority in the world of human life.

This Purāṇic way of thinking about origins offers a helpful point of departure for our inquiry into Gaṇeśa's religious meanings, especially in view of the limited and ambiguous materials available about his origins in the historical sense. For our purposes it is sufficient for Gaṇeśa to make his appearance in the early Purāṇic period, the era that saw the rise of the Gupta empire and large permanent ceremonial centers for the worship and service of Hindu deities. There is no clear way of determining which of the many variants of his myths are prior to others. We shall simply treat them as a package. The same applies to the analysis of rituals associated with Gaṇeśa. Some ritual instructions are contained in the Purāṇas along with the myths, the latter sometimes being presented as etiological explanations for the former. For us it is more important to trace the thematic and metaphoric connections between the myths and rituals than to trace the historical development of ritual practices. Structural and thematic studies of this tradition are more promising areas of inquiry because they do not depend for their explanatory power on our ability to pinpoint precise historical settings. The limitation of this approach is that the myths and rituals appear to be in free fall, suspended somewhere in the historical process without clear and specific contexts, thus giving the interpreter more license to read contemporary interpretive concerns into the texts. The historical contexts are important in principle; it is simply the case that there is little to go on and that a more interesting conversation with the materials of the tradition is to be found in thematic, structural, and theological areas.

Gaṇeśa and the Study of Hinduism

I am attempting to locate my inquiry into Gaṇeśa in the context of the study of Hinduism as a religion. Such an effort requires at least a provisional definition of religion as a world of its own—a reality that endures through time and human community and is maintained and transformed by stories, attitudes, and beliefs that are acted out in rites, dramas, and festivals. It shapes and is shaped by the feelings, ideas, and behavior of those who practice it. It is essential for us to recognize the multifaceted character of the data and the complex interconnections among its various components. For example, myths about Gaṇeśa are frequently told on ritual occasions and presented as explanations for why rites are performed according to certain patterns. Rituals may commemorate episodes in the myths. When Hindus celebrate the annual festival on the fourth day of the month of Bhādrapada (August/September), they participate in the process of Gaṇeśa's coming into being as the Lord of Obstacles, just as in the festival of Divālī they recall the return of Rāma from his victory over the demon Rāvana and Sītā's release from her captivity. The rituals do not reenact the myths as though they were scripts; the connections between myth and ritual are less direct.

In the festival process in honor of Gaṇeśa, celebrants participate in a symbolic and social sequence of episodes that takes them through phases of relative destructuring—marked by public dancing, parading, and the relaxation of ordinary social hierarchical behavior—toward reintegration and the reassertion of normal social roles, with traces of feelings of euphoria at having passed through the festival process together. Gaṇeśa's annual festival complex—comprising domestic and temple worship [*pūjā*] followed by a public procession and celebration [*utsava*]—focuses on the shaping of a clay image of the god and bringing it to life ritually by the investiture of vital breath [*prāṇa*] in order to worship Gaṇeśa in the home for a period of several days, after which he is taken in procession to a river or other body of water to be immersed. From formless clay Gaṇeśa emerges into iconic form, his dispersed cosmic presence is condensed into recognizable objectification at the beginning of the festival. At the close of the public procession, marked as it is by merrymaking and occasions of ecstatic behavior by some participants, Gaṇeśa's form in the image is redistributed into its constituent elements as it dissolves in the water into which it has been so lovingly placed by his devotees. A similar process takes place in the myth when Pārvatī forms Gaṇeśa out of her bodily substance, her dirt, and brings him to life; there is the process of condensation of power and life into incarnate form. When Gaṇeśa confronts Śiva and, after his beheading, receives power and authority from Śiva as lord of the *gaṇas* and overcomer of obstacles, his power becomes again dispersed, but this time into universes of action, the beginnings over which he rules. Myth and ritual alike move through cycles, leading from chaos to condensation into order and then to distribution of that order back into the cosmos in ways that assure the deity's continuing presence. The cycle is repeated again in another time frame, whether it is a cosmic eon, as with the myths, or the annual festival that comes around predictably with the ritual calendar. There is not a one-to-one correlation between the myth and the ritual, rather they both move in similar directions, supporting each other within the larger framework of the universe of Hindu assumptions and practice.

A similar process of condensation and distribution appears to take place at the social level in the festival. In its Maharashtrian forms, various groups of celebrants, or *māṇḍaḷs,* move toward a heightened sense of generic bonding within the group and between groups as all converge on the worship of the deity as their common effort. This generic unity, what Victor Turner (1969) terms *communitas,* contributes to an enhanced sense of the coherence and bonding of all the participants, particularly during the long hours of procession that mark the concluding episode of the festival. The festival serves to codify, condense, and restate the paradigmatic process embodied in the myth and domestic ritual (*pūjā*) as it acts out the passage from chaos to order to the distribution of that order throughout the cosmos. The myths, the rituals performed in homes and shrines, and the public festivals in the towns and cities in Maharashtra are together the interlocking elements of a religious pattern of life having Gaṇeśa as its center.

It is not my purpose to develop a theoretical model of religion into which I then press my Gaṇeśa data to validate it, rather my theoretical concerns remain subordinate to the goal of rendering the myths, rites, and festival comprehensible in an interconnected way. Theories of religion are helpful in attempting to identify what is significant in a particular text or ritual, but it sometimes happens that the sources one studies will point to something significant that leads to abandoning or revising the theories. There is no magical protection that prevents an observer, or a participant for that matter, from interjecting his or her own more or less subjective reading or judgment. Hopefully, through the process of careful consideration of the sources (be they texts or fieldwork) and with the judicious guidance of various theoretical models that seem best to fit the sources, one can come up with a reading of the religious tradition that is fair and faithful to its own self-understanding and that contributes usefully to widening our understanding of the phenomenon of religion. Because this is done in the context of scholarly criticism and discourse, there is hope that others will see clearly what I have seen only partially and thus the process of understanding will move forward.

The following chapters will take up the principal myths, rites, and cultic traditions that set Gaṇeśa apart from the other deities of the Hindu pantheon. In examining each of these dimensions of the tradition, it is hoped that the relations between them will begin to display themselves and that the overall coherence of the tradition will become apparent.

2

The Mythology of Gaṇeśa

Sources and Methods

Whatever foreshadowings of Gaṇeśa appear in the Vedic and Brāhmaṇic sources, it is in the Purāṇas that the elephant-faced lord makes his unequivocal and dramatic debut. In these vast encyclopedic collections of stories of gods, ritual instructions, abstruse metaphysical and theological arguments, cosmogonic theories, and practical moral advice, we find many variations of myths about Gaṇeśa's birth, beheading, and restoration and his exploits among the gods, demons, and humans. We shall explore as many of these myths as possible, for there are not a great number and many either have never been translated before or only one variant among several significantly different versions of a particular myth is available. The purpose of this chapter is to tell Gaṇeśa's story as the texts themselves tell it.

A note about the chronology of these texts is in order. Only the roughest approximation of dates can be ventured. There are notoriously difficult problems involved in dating the Purāṇas. The texts represent compilations of shifting oral traditions that reflect various sectarian allegiances, with frequent interpolations of later materials into earlier strata of the texts. It is likely that some of the

Gaṇeśa myths are among these later interpolations, as are the myth of Gaṇeśa and Vyāsa and the writing of the *Mahābhārata* (as we shall see). Stories about Gaṇeśa appear in the early Purāṇas: the *Brahmāṇḍa, Matsya,* the Sṛṣṭikhaṇḍa of the *Padma,* and the *Harivaṃśa* (c. A.D. 300–500). In at least one case the same myth turns up in almost identical versions in two different texts from this period. More detailed accounts of Gaṇeśa's beheading are found in the middle and later Purāṇas: the *Devī, Liṅga, Śiva, Skanda, Vāmana,* and *Varāha* (c. A.D. 500–1300), with some sectarian elaborations and additional materials in the two Gāṇapatya Purāṇas, the *Gaṇeśa* and the *Mudgala* (c. A.D. 1300–1600). A number of Gaṇeśa myths are also contained in the Tamil Purāṇas, which probably were contemporaries of the later Sanskrit ones. Little more can be said with confidence about the historical location of these myths. Fortunately, our approach does not depend on determining which myths are prior to which others. We shall treat them all—including the non-Purāṇic myths drawn from folkloric sources from a more recent period—as constituting an ongoing tradition of story belonging to an evolving oral and textual tradition. Our approach depends on perceiving patterns within and among myths, their thematic elements, and finally, their meanings. It is reassuring to recall that the Purāṇas themselves are not particularly interested in locating their mythological materials in relation to historical events; the stories of the gods and the ritual and moral prescriptions are timeless and always valid in their application to particular situations.

When we turn aside from the twisted alleys of historical development to the more fruitful avenues of the thematic, structural, and interpretive dimensions in these myths, a number of questions of method or approach come to the fore. We begin our analysis of the Gaṇeśa cycle of myths confident that these myths have many meanings and that they reflect a protean form of narrative giving rise to multiple simultaneous interpretations. O'Flaherty (1973, p. 2) charts four levels of meaning possible in any given myth. First, there is the narrative level, the story itself in all its versions. Second, the metaphoric level in which the themes in the narrative level link one particular myth to others in the same or different cycles. In the case of Gaṇeśa, the themes of divine birth, beheading, sacrifice, thresholds, and elephants are metaphors that link his mythology to other stories in the Hindu tradition that also make use of these metaphorical possibilities. The metaphorical elements in the myth also tie it to the third level of meaning, that of cosmic law and metaphysics. At this third level exist implicitly the more abstract notions of *karma,* and power relations in the universe expressed, for example, in the tension between erotic desire and ascetic restraint. Fourth are the social and psychological dimensions of the myths, their meanings for human life and action. In the Gaṇeśa myths the subtle but powerful ambivalences within marital and family relations play an important part. To the four levels suggested by O'Flaherty, we shall add a fifth: the etiological level. Many of the Gaṇeśa myths link narrative with ritual practice and answer such questions as why Gaṇeśa is worshipped first before all other deities and why he got his broken tusk, his elephant head, and so on. The etiological level joins the narrative, metaphorical, and sociopsychological levels in the immediacy of the image and the ritual actions to be performed in response to it. It is important to note that these levels of meaning operate simultaneously. Any adequate treatment of the myths' possibilities for interpretation must take them all into account.

This approach to the mythology of Gaṇeśa is eclectic, but necessarily so to account for the multivocality of the myths themselves. For example, the story of Gaṇeśa's beheading is simultaneously: (1) an "explanation" of his elephant's head (etiological), (2) an account of the birth of a god (narrative), (3) a variation on the theme of sacrifice and expiation (metaphorical), (4) an expression of the mediation between the forces of saṁsāric attachment and the release of *mokṣa* (cosmological/metaphysical), and (5) an exploration of the ambivalence inevitable in the relations among fathers, mothers, and sons (sociopsychological). To ignore some or one of these interpretive possibilities in the pursuit of methodological or ideological purity is to reduce the myths to less than they are, depriving us of access to some facets of the richness of their meanings. No doubt there are many more meanings than the ones seen and presented here. Perhaps the reader will be led to discover some of them in response to the meanings that have been noted.

It is particularly difficult to know how to proceed from the point at which the various myths in their variant versions are assembled in the lush landscape of the Purāṇic texts (the narrative level) to an interpretation of these myths. We could start almost anywhere and work our way around, examining each theme and metaphor until all the myths are accounted for in a network or tapestry of meanings. My way out of this welter of possibilities is to seek the elements in the myths that are most common and recurrent or most striking in their uniqueness, to begin with these and thence be led to other myths that shed light on the first ones. The most striking, and obvious, recurrent element in the Gaṇeśa cycle of myths is the elephant head. Hence our analysis begins with an inquiry into elephant symbolism and mythology and its relation to the Gaṇeśa story. The elephant head in turn leads to the myths of Gaṇeśa's birth, beheading, and the receiving of his elephant head, which in turn leads to myths of his beheading. Beheading connects his mythology to the larger metaphorical universe of sacrifice, dismemberment, initiation, and theogony. Because it is Gaṇeśa's father, Śiva, who beheads him, the story is tied to the cycle of Śiva myths and to the issue of father-son relations. This opens up the possibilities of psychoanalytic interpretations, centering on the oedipal complex. The beheading also links Gaṇeśa's story to the tales of others beheaded by Śiva—the demons, for example—and therein lies another set of myths and thematic possibilities. Finally, Gaṇeśa is the Lord of Obstacles, a title and role given him by Śiva to compensate for his losing his original head and gaining the elephant head, which ties together a network of elephants, sons, demons, and obstacles. It is impossible to consider one element without, at least implicitly, including them all. Fortunately, not all the myths stress all the interpretive possibilities equally; some myths are more about family relations, others more about theology, and so on. The interpretation of the myths is not a linear movement from one element to the next, rather it is a network, a fabric, in which the pursuit of one thread of meaning doubles back onto others as it proceeds forward, knitting the whole cloth together as it goes along. It is easy to become confused and drop a stitch. But the myths carry their own fascination and, it is to be hoped, compensate for leaps or missing links in the fabric of my interpretation.

A remark regarding the form in which the more than seventy myths included here are presented is in order. It has been necessary in many cases to summarize a myth, rather than translate it in its entirety. Many of them in the original texts include long digressions into ritual instructions, theological elaboration, and hyperbolic descriptive detail, which would distract us from the locus of our inquiry. Where possible, I have retained much of the dialogue, to give the excerpts a richer flavor of the text. Where identical or closely similar variants appear in more than one textual source, I have so indicated in the citation. To facilitate further research, other related myths offering intriguing comparisons are also noted.

Elephant Symbolism in Indian Culture

Gaṇeśa's most striking characteristic is his elephant head. It makes him stand out from the crowd of other gods and serves as the occasion for many myths in the Purāṇic literature. The various stories disagree as to how Gaṇeśa came by his curious elephantine form: some myths say his parents, Śiva and Pārvatī, transformed themselves into elephants and made love "in the manner of elephants" and so brought him forth; others relate that Gaṇeśa's elephant head was a matter of circumstance, as when his father, Śiva, beheaded him and then to restore him to life sent servants to find the nearest available head, which happened to be that of an elephant. Other myths assign the elephant head to a specific elephant, such as the demon Gajāsura; in an earlier epoch Śiva had defeated and then danced his terrible doomsday *tāṇḍava* dance on Gajāsura's elephant head and wrapped himself in its bloody skin (see pl. 6). Still others tell us that Gaṇeśa's head once belonged to Indra's mount, Airāvata, who was defeated by Nandin, Śiva's bull vehicle, or that it was the head of Gajendra, the elephant-king saved by Viṣṇu from the clutches of the demon alligator (see pl. 7). The source of the head and the circumstances leading to its acquisition by Gaṇeśa are topics of great interest in the myths of Gaṇeśa's origins; we shall look at each of them in detail later. The important point, however, is whether the elephant head came from a specific elephantine creature or from no particular donor. Symbolically, Gaṇeśa and elephants are inextricably linked.

The elephant has enjoyed charismatic status in South Asia from the earliest times, and his representations in stone and painting are ubiquitous. The Indus Valley seals depict the elephant in graceful aspects standing over a manger, creating the impression that it was already a domesticated animal and of artistic and possibly religious importance (Zimmer 1955, vol. 2, pl. 2 b–c). The Vedic poets were impressed by the massive strength of the elephant, as when they sang of Indra, filled with *soma,* smashing the cities of his enemies "as a wild elephant rushes on this way and that, mad with heat" (ṚV 1.64.7). Huge and grey, the elephant also resembled the dark clouds of refreshing and violent rain that fed and replenished the parched land. Another name for Airāvata, Indra's elephant vehicle, was Abhramū or Abhramātaṅga, "who knits or binds the clouds" (Zimmer 1946, p. 106).

The association of elephants with rain and water finds expression in the myth of the annointing of the goddess Lakṣmī (Gajalakṣmī), wife of Viṣṇu and giver of well-being, at the time of the churning of the ocean of milk. As Lakṣmī rose out of the ocean seated on a lotus,

> Gaṅgā and the other sacred rivers stood there performing ablutions. And the elephants of the quarters of the sky took up their pure waters in golden vessels and poured them over the goddess, the queen of the universe. (VP 1.9.103; see pl. 3.)

The connection of elephants with water and rain is further emphasized in the mythology of Indra, who rides the elephant Airāvata when he defeats Vṛtra. This mighty elephant reaches down his trunk into the watery underworld, sucks up its water, and then sprays it into the clouds, which Indra then causes to rain forth cool water (MBh 5.97.7–8; MatsyaP 125.18–21), thereby linking the waters of the sky with those of the underworld. Although there appears to be no direct association in the classical texts between Lakṣmī and her elephant and Gaṇeśa, the connection has not been lost in contemporary Hinduism as indicated by a popular lithograph that depicts Gaṇeśa and Lakṣmī emanating out of the same lotus (see pl. 4). They are linked by the common figure of the elephant, but they share another important feature. Both are bringers of well-being, deities to whom Hindus turn in seeking the fulfillment of their wishes and goals.

The relationship of clouds and rain to elephants reflects more than the fact that elephants are round and grey and massive, like the grey monsoon clouds, and can spray water out of their trunks, like rain. The monsoon clouds bring both nourishing water and the possibility of destructive floods; the elephant symbol is equally ambivalent. This ambivalence springs from the opposition of wild and tame. The tame elephant, the paradigm of power domesticated, clears the wild jungles so that human habitations may be built. He carries the king in battle and ceremonial procession; he is, in short, the symbol of order. It is this order-creating and auspicious elephant, yoked to a golden chariot, that a king may offer ceremoniously to the gods as a great gift [*hemahasthimahādāna*] and so earn entry into the realm of Viṣṇu in the life to come (MatsyaP 282). The wild elephant, however, driven by heat of sexual desire or burning fever of disease, can create awesome destruction. This ambivalence of wild and tame in the behavior of elephants is reflected in a number of myths from both Hindu and Buddhist sources. The wild side comes out in one Buddhist story:

> Once when the Bodhisatta lived with a group of five hundred monks in the forest, one of them named Indasāmanagotta had a pet elephant. When the Bodhisatta instructed him to give up his pet, Indasāmanagotta said he would be unable to live without him. "You will live to regret it," the teacher said. Then one day when all the monks went into the forest to gather food and were gone for several days, the elephant fell into a frenzy when touched by a wind from the south. Then he tore up the hut, smashed the water jar and killed his master, Indasāmanagotta. When the Bodhisatta learned of all this from his disciples, he said, "We should not have any dealings with evil ones." (Indasāmanagotta J [no. 164])

Here the mad elephant represents attachment to desire. The disciple who could not give up his pet elephant was finally destroyed by him. Although the elephant in the story is the "evil one" with whom one should avoid contact, the blame shifts from the elephant to the south wind, the wind that comes from the inauspicious direction, the abode of demons. The conclusion of the story seems to be that a person's attachment to desire is like owning a wild elephant that will, in the inevitable course of things, turn on the one who holds it and devour him. The Bodhisatta's advice, to renounce the elephant, would have spared Indasāmanagotta his life.

In another Buddhist story we are presented with the other side of the elephant's character, that of virtue perfected, in an account of the Buddha in one of his previous lives as a white elephant:

> Once there lived a magnificent white elephant in the Himālayas who was surrounded by eighty thousand females and his mother who was blind. When he gave the other elephants food to take to his blind mother, they kept it for themselves, and neglected her. When he heard about their disregard for her, the white elephant took his mother to a cave in the mountains and stayed with her, taking care of her. Then once a man from Benares became lost in the forest. The elephant saw him and, lifting him onto his back, led him safely out of the forest. The king of Benares, whose royal elephant had just died, told all his subjects to report any suitable elephants they might see. The man then told the king about the splendid elephant who saved him when he was lost; and the king sent his trainers to bring the elephant to him at once. When the elephant had been brought to the king's palace, he refused to eat and began to wither away. But when the king learned of the elephant's longing for his mother and his worry over her well-being, he had a new city built for the elephant and his mother. Later, when the mother died, the elephant went away to live in a monastery. (Matiposaka J [no. 451])

In this story of asceticism and of devotion of son to mother, one theme we shall see playing an important part in Gaṇeśa's mythology: the virtuous white elephant does only good deeds. He cares for his mother, he leads the lost man from Benares to safety, he fasts until he can be reunited with his mother, and he lives a pure monastic life free from passion. Finally, this royal and virtuous creature, although surrounded with innumerable concubines saturated with erotic desires, remains chaste and dutiful to his mother and after her death lives the remainder of his life as a monk. The character of the blind mother living in the cave may suggest evocations of the goddess (Pārvatī) and link this tale with the mythology of Gaṇeśa. These two *Jātaka* stories present the extremes of the elephant symbol: the wild and murderous rejection of the master and the self-renouncing devotion to the mother. The *Jātakas,* although deeply Buddhist in their themes and organization of narrative materials, nonetheless draw heavily on Indian folktales and carry into them many contradictory views, including highly ambivalent attitudes toward the elephant.

Another way of expressing the ambivalence of wild/tame in the symbol of the elephant appears in a myth about the origin of elephants in a medieval text that details methods of care and training:

> Formerly elephants could go anywhere they pleased, and assume any shape; they roamed as they liked in the sky and on the earth. In the northern quarter of the Himālaya Mountain there is a banyan tree which has a length and breadth of two hundred leagues. On it the excellent elephants alighted (after flying through the air). They broke off a branch (which fell) upon a hermitage place where dwelt a hermit named Dīrghatapas. He was angered by this and straightaway cursed the elephants. Hence, you see, the elephants were deprived of their power of moving at will, and came to be vehicles even for mortal men. (ML 1.11–12)

In this story the elephants get their wings trimmed, just as Indra trims the wings of the horse (MBh 1.16.34–35) and cuts off the wings of the mountains (R 5.1), forcing them to remain stationary on the earth; however, in this myth it is the word of the ascetic rather than the sword of the king of the gods that succeeds in domesticating the elephant. The elephants lose their formlessness and ability to fly because they have inadvertantly disturbed the meditations of the ascetic, much as Kāma's wings—along with the rest of him—are burnt up by the fire of Śiva's third eye when Śiva's meditation is interrupted (BVP 4.39.40–52).

Another tale of the domestication of the elephant appears in the famous story of the Buddha's encounter with the mad elephant sent by his cousin Devadatta to destroy the enlightened one:

> He [Devadatta] let loose on the highway the lord of the royal elephants who rushed toward the Tathāgata with a noise like the thunder of black clouds at the doomsday and with the force of the wind on a moonless night. With murder in his heart the elephant rushed toward the Buddha, and the people cried out and threw up their arms. But without hesitating the Lord went on, collected and unmoved, and with no feeling of ill will. His benevolence made him compassionate toward all living beings and the gods followed devotedly close behind him. So even that great elephant had not the power to touch the Sage, who calmly went on his way. The monks who had followed the Buddha fled in terror while the elephant was still a long way off; and only Ānanda remained with the Buddha. But as the elephant came quite close, the Sage's spiritual

power [*prabhāva*] brought the beast to his senses and made him lower his body and place his head to the ground, like a mountain whose wings had been shattered by a thunderbolt. The Sage stroked the head of the lord of elephants as the sun touches a cloud with its rays. (*Buddhacarita* 18.40–53; Johnston 1937, pp. 36–40)

Rather than a warrior's sword or a sage's curse, it is the Buddha's "spiritual power" that tames the raging beast as his hand strokes the head in what may be a faint echo of a gesture of decapitation. The point of the myth is to draw attention to the magnificence of the Buddha, who with kindness can tame even the most fearsome of wild animals. The story continues: as a consequence of the elephant's domestication, its wildness is transfered to Devadatta, the instigator of this assassination attempt, and catapults him "to the regions below, hated by all equally, whether they be kings, citizens, Brahmins, or sages" (*Buddhacarita* 18.62). This account of the taming of the wild elephant alludes to the "thunder of black clouds at the doomsday" and likens the defeat of the wild elephant to the "mountain whose wings had been shattered." These associations echo the myths of Indra's domestication of the water demon Vṛtra and his cutting the wings off the mountains. The wildness of the storm, the serpent, and the elephant are connected through these myths and constitute a motif in the mythology of Gaṇeśa, who, like the elephant and the gods, must be tamed with offerings of food and propitiated with kind words (as we shall see).

His role as a guardian and protector is another important dimension of the symbol of the elephant; this is the tame side of his character. In Epic and Purāṇic cosmologies, elephants, having been brought forth out of the cosmic egg by Brahmā at the beginning of creation, stand as guardians of the four directions and the four intermediate directions. Airāvata, the guardian of the east, is their leader, just as Indra is the leader of the gods. These elephant guardians [*dikpālas* or *diggajas*], like the serpent guardians [*diṅnāgas*] and dwarfish protectors [*yakṣas*], hold the world of the gods on their backs and shoulders. They stand guard over the points of entry and prevent any evil or polluting forces from entering the world of the gods. This array of mythological guardians receives visual expression in the great temple complexes of both Buddhist and Hindu India. Rows of elephants, along with *nāgas* and *yakṣas,* can be seen carved in friezes along the lowest levels of these structures, and elephant statues frequently stand as guardians of the temple thresholds.

The duty of the guardian figure is to protect the purity of the inner shrine; he must keep out those who would seek to defile it. To the devotee seeking entry into the inner sanctum, the guardian of the threshold is the first obstacle to be overcome. If one approaches the shrine and pays homage to the guardian, indicating sincerity, and offers the appropriate gestures of supplication to the deities inside, then the guardian will grant entry. But if one is insincere or neglects the guardian in haste to reach the inner sacred world, then the guardian will place obstacles in the devotee's path and render worship fruitless. The guardians stand on the threshold between the profane world outside the shrine and the sacred territory inside. It is thus symbolically apposite that they are beings who themselves inhabit two worlds: the *yakṣas* live in the underworld as well as in the realm of the gods, the *nāgas* move both in the water and on land. The elephants, as we have seen, once inhabited the sky as well as the earth and, like Airāvata, their trunks reach into the netherworld of the demons in order to steal their water, which they then deliver to Indra. Through its symbolic associations, the elephant also straddles the boundaries between the wild and the tame, chaos and order.

In his role as Vighneśvara, the overcomer of obstacles, Gaṇeśa appropriates much of this guardian symbolism. In the sacred city of Kāśī (Benares), the presence of Gaṇeśa in this guardian capacity is fully expressed. The city is laid out as a model of the cosmos, in seven concentric circles. Each circle has a shrine to Gaṇeśa at the four directions and the four intermediate points, just as on the cosmic level, the *diggajas* (elephant guardians) stand watch over the regions of the sky:

> Gaṇeśa assumes a protective and guardian role as the "Lord of Obstacles," Vighneśa, who reigns at the threshold imposing and removing obstacles as he sees fit. There are fifty-six Gaṇeśa's in Kāśī, positioned schematically at the eight directional compass points in seven concentric circles, spreading out from the great Ḍhuṇḍrāja Gaṇeśa located at the center near Viśeśvara [Śiva] . . .

the pilgrim must pass through one chain of these threshold guardians after another as he approaches the center of the city. (Eck 1978, pp. 178–79)

As it is in the cosmos, and in the temple and the sacred city as earthly embodiments of the divine paradigm, so also does this pattern appear in the human world of the king and his subjects. The elephant is the vehicle of the king, who is the Indra among humans, just as the divine elephant Airāvata supports the Indra of the gods. The Vedic Indra rides a bull when he defeats the serpent Vṛtra, but in the Epic and Purāṇic periods Indra rides an elephant, perhaps partly because of its connotations as the royal conveyance. The elephant, moreover, not only resembles the serpent whom Indra has slain and thus domesticated, but in other mythic contexts the name Airāvata itself refers to the king of serpents (KP 1.40.10). Elephant trunk and serpent share certain undeniable characteristics and carry associations of force and power, both political and sexual.

On the most basic level the elephant is the quintessentially appropriate royal animal. The largest of beasts, it is as suitable for combat as a tank. Lavishly decorated, the elephant is a magnificent ceremonial vehicle for kings in processions. But the royal elephant also takes on symbolic meaning. The king's elephant is an expression of the people's welfare and the king's virtue. Kings denied nothing for the comfort and well-being of elephants in the royal stables. When the royal elephants were honored, the kingdom prospered, but woe to the king who foolishly gave away his elephant. Many stories tell of the drought and famine that befall the kingdom whose ruler fails to keep his elephants suitably (Kurudhamma J [no. 276]; Vessantara J. [no. 547]).

The association of elephants with royalty and auspicious events is reflected in the tale of the birth of the Buddha. Just after the Buddha's mother and father, Queen Māyā and King Suddhodana, had made love, the queen had a dream that "a white king elephant seemed to enter her body, but without causing any pain," and she conceived (*Buddhacarita* 1.3). When her time for delivery had come, the Buddha "came forth out of his mother's side, without causing her any pain or injury. His birth was a miracle, like those of Aurva from the thigh, Pṛthu from the hand, Māndhātṛ, the equal to Indra, from the head, and Kakṣīvat from the armpit" (*Buddhacarita* 1.10). These miraculous births recall that of Gaṇeśa, who was born when his mother rubbed her limbs with unguents and formed him from the residue.

Along with the ambivalence of wild/tame expressed in the stories of the mad and domesticated elephants, there is a sexual ambivalence in the symbol of the elephant. In the myths, elephants are male: the elephant guardians, the white royal elephant who is also the Bodhisatta, the elephant demon whom Śiva defeats, the elephant-king whom Viṣṇu saves, Airāvata, and, finally, Gaṇeśa himself. The male attributes of the elephant are so obvious as to need no comment. Not only the trunk but the tusk has phallic associations in some of the Gaṇeśa stories. The myth of the elephant guardians annointing Lakṣmī by spraying water over her seems the fullest expression of male fertility surrounding female fecundity. As O'Flaherty has shown, moreover, rain tends to be associated with male seed in the Indian tradition, whereas rivers appear as symbolic expressions of the feminine aspect of water (1980, pp. 20–21).

Despite these overwhelming associations of masculinity with the elephant, there are also distinctly feminine dimensions to the symbolic use of the elephant in the Indian context. According to the sexual taxonomy of Vātsyāyana's *Kāmasūtra,* women with large sexual organs are "elephants" to be paired with males with more than adequate members, termed "stallions" (*Kāmasūtra* 1.1–3). But such a pair is an unequal one, with the larger female expressing the "dangerous imbalance of power between a man and a woman and the necessity to control this imbalance" (O'Flaherty 1980, pp. 257–58). The Dharmaśāstra admonishes a man to "wed a woman free from defects of body, who has an agreeable name, and the gait of an elephant or a goose, moderate bodily hair, small limbs and teeth" (*Manu* 3.10). The poet Bhartṛhari made use of the erotic possibilities inherent in the elephant's form, comparing the thighs of a woman to an elephant's trunk and writing that her breasts "which swell like elephant's temples are a splendid resting place for pearls" (Miller, p. 87). The ichor, a thick saplike secretion oozing from the elephant's temples during the season of mating, is a pervasive symbol of the elixir of erotic desire that intoxicates the bees buzzing around it so that they foolishly cast aside and disregard all risks. As the Sanskrit poet Acala expresses it (SRK 115, Ingall's trans.):

Forgetful of the lotuses
and disregarding what the ear-stroke of the elephant will
do,
this honey-gatherer desires the pungent ichor.
Fie on craving
that costs the addict bee his life.

Closely related to these erotic images of the elephant are those involving wildness (as we have already seen). Sensual desire, the mortal enemy of ascetics, is a raging elephant in rut and must be brought under control as the mahout controls the elephant with his goad and hook. This symbolism comes through powerfully in another of Bhartṛhari's poems in which he tells of the wildness of the mind filled with desire (Miller, p. 93):

Though I search the triple world
through all its mundane passages
no man has met my vision's field
or come within my hearing's range
who could really bind
to a post of self-restraint
the raging elephant of his mind
with its drunken desire to court
the world of the sense.

We have seen that the elephant is a complex and highly inclusive figure. Associated with clouds and storms, like the horse and bull in the *Ṛg Veda;* standing at the threshold between the wildness of the jungle and the order of the kingdom; annointing goddesses; and bearing gods and kings on his back as they charge into battle, the elephant is a quintessential figure of fertility and order. He is also linked to the complex of erotic imagery because his movements are graceful like a woman's and his temples, like a woman's breasts, give forth a different but no less desirable fluid. His moods are unpredictable; when maddened in rut, he is the incarnation of destruction. From these aspects of his expansive character no single sexual role can be identified for the elephant, unlike the bull, stallion, cow, or mare. Depending on the context, he can be wild or tame, male or female. Throughout the history of Indian culture the tendency has been to see in the elephant the emblem of the cosmos itself, containing all dichotomies within his more than ample form. Gaṇeśa embodies many of these oppositional characteristics. The elephant-headed god is also a guardian of the threshold, at times under the control of others but sometimes beyond their reach, and he is unpredictable in his movements. He is the son of Śiva and Pārvatī; although clearly male, he moves toward the feminine pole with his tendency to identify closely with his mother. In his iconographic representations Gaṇeśa's masculine features are subordinated to his dwarfish, *yakṣa*like form, thereby leaving his gender less than precisely articulated.

Donors of Gaṇeśa's Head: Gajāsura, Gajendra, and Airāvata

The sources and circumstances behind Gaṇeśa's elephantine form have engendered much interest in Hindu mythology, and many explanations are given for how he came by his appearance. In some myths Gaṇeśa comes into the world already having his elephant form; in others—and they are the majority—he acquires his head from an elephant after losing his own in bloody conflict.

In one South Indian myth, Gaṇeśa asks his father Śiva how it is that he has the form of an elephant and his parents do not. Śiva explains:

> "I, in the company of Pārvatī, retired once to the forest on the slopes of the Himālayas to enjoy each other's company. We saw there a female elephant making herself happy with a male elephant. This excited our passions and we desired to enjoy ourselves in the form of elephants. I became a male elephant, and Pārvatī became a female one, and pleased ourselves, as a result of which you were born with the face of an elephant." (T. A. Gopinatha Rao 1/1, pp. 44–45; cf. Ziegenbalg, pp. 59, 61–62)

This story is one of the few in which Gaṇeśa is produced through the sexual union of Śiva and Pārvartī, but only after they have put on their elephant forms to "please themselves" as the elephants do. Here it is Śiva and Pārvatī rather than Gaṇeśa who undergo a change. This variant makes no reference to any beheading of Gaṇeśa as the prelude to his having the form of an elephant. He *always* was an elephant. In a related story, Gaṇeśa's elephantine origins are told with some intriguing variations:

> One day Śiva and his wife went to visit the audience hall of the gods. Two paintings in that hall attracted Umā's attention. They depicted two sacred syllables. She asked her husband what the

paintings meant, and Śiva said that one of them symbolized Brahmā, Viṣṇu, and Śiva, while the others represented their three *śaktis*. When Śiva had explained this to her, she desired to become a female elephant and for him to assume the form of a male elephant, just as such figures had been painted on the canvases. The husband and wife then took the forms of the male and female elephant, respectively. Their union produced an infant whose head had the form of an elephant. (Dessigane et al. 1964, pp. 15–16; see also, Zeigenbalg, p. 59)

This story requires some explanation. When Śiva and Pārvatī were in the celestial audience hall, the paintings they saw on the walls represented the two sacred syllables *a* and *u,* which together resembled two elephants in embrace forming the famous syllable *auṃ*. This syllable has special associations with Gaṇeśa, and devotees of the god point out that the syllable resembles the face of an elephant: with the *a* depicting the head and belly, the *u* resembling the trunk and the *anusvāra* (the *ṃ*) the plate of sweetmeats [*modaka*] offered to him. Hence this story of Gaṇeśa's origin is one of movement from abstract sound and calligraphic form to embodied existence, an Indian example of the word made flesh (M. Y. Joshi, pp. 28–31; see also Danielou 1964, p. 293).

In some myths Gaṇeśa is created in his elephantine form. In others he lacks a head for one reason or another, necessitating a search for a new head; the unfortunate elephant happens to be closest and so is called on to donate his own head to complete Gaṇeśa's creation. The first type of story is represented by the accounts of Gaṇeśa arising out of the sexual fluids of Śiva and Pārvatī after their bath, but outside Pārvatī's body (VāmP 28.64–66), or accounts of Pārvatī creating Gaṇeśa by rubbing the substances off the surface of her body:

Then she rubbed scented oil mixed with powder over her body and rubbed the dirt off into a human form which had the head of an elephant. Pārvatī playfully threw that son into the Ganges where he became so large that he extended himself as big as the world. (MatsyaP 154.502–4; PP Sṛṣṭikhaṇḍa 45.445–47)

Here the story is the dominant one of Gaṇeśa's origin from the rubbing of Pārvatī's limbs. When she throws him into the water, he immediately grows as great as the universe, recalling myths about Śiva's *liṅga* expanding to the heights and depths of the cosmos faster than Brahmā or Viṣṇu can catch up to its limits. Pārvatī's gesture of throwing her son into the river calls to mind the myth of the creation of Skanda (ŚP 2.41–42). In most other variants of Gaṇeśa's birth story, his creation by Pārvatī out of the rubbing of her bodily substances is followed by his beheading and restoration with the head of an elephant. In this version, however, we see the two stories collapsed together into a single creation narrative patterned after the creation of Skanda, with Pārvatī playing the male role by providing the engendering substance, the seed, and the river playing the female role by providing the womb out of which Gaṇeśa emerges fully formed with the head of an elephant.

One intriguing variation on the story of Gaṇeśa's elephantine beginnings appears in the *Skanda Purāṇa.* As Pārvatī rubs the substance off her body, she discovers to her dismay that she lacks enough rubbing material to complete her creation, the material necessary to make Gaṇeśa's head. Urgently she calls out to Skanda:

> "Quickly bring back some more rubbing material for a head so that this son of mine might become your brother, one who will be difficult for any enemy to conquer." In searching for the material as Pārvatī had asked, Skanda saw a superb elephant in rut, and he cut off his head and joined it to the body which had been made out of the rubbing material. "But, son, this head will be too large. Where did you find it?" Parvati said. But even as she cried out, "Don't, don't!" the head became joined to the body by the action of fate. (SkP 7.3.324–8)

After a frantic search Skanda comes to the rescue with the head of an elephant to complete the creation Pārvatī had undertaken, but she rejects this huge head from an animal in a rutted wild state as too large for the body she had made. However, fate seals the head to the body—as *karma* fashions bodies according to previous deeds in the transmigration process—to the astonishment of the mother. This myth appears to appreciate the unlikely combination of head and body, and it leaves responsibility for the merger to the inexorable and enigmatic movement of fate.

An unidentified elephant becomes the donor for Gaṇeśa's head in yet another account of his origins. Śiva seeks entry into Pārvatī's bath, only to be barred by her new son and guardian, Gaṇeśa. Śiva cuts off the youth's head in a fit of anger. Pārvatī, outraged at her husband's act, assembles her troops of *śaktis* and brings devastation to the gods. Seeing that he will be unable to conquer her, Śiva says to his *gaṇa* attendants:

> "Go in the northern direction and whatever person you meet first, cut off his head and fit it onto this body." (ŚP 2.4.17.47)

Although the particular elephant who is made to give up his head that Gaṇeśa might be revived is not named, the text does specify that he was found in the north, the auspicious direction of regeneration. Further, this elephant had only a single tusk, as though the head had already undergone mutilation in preparation for its transfer to Gaṇeśa. The single tusk is the subject of a number of myths in its own right and will be taken up later in the discussion about Gaṇeśa's beheading. Once the body is joined to the elephant head and sprinkled with appropriate water and holy speech, Gaṇeśa comes to life as though he had "awakened from a sleep," a process like that which takes place ritually in the installation of Gaṇeśa's images during his annual festival (ŚP 2.4.17.56).

Other myths are specific as to the identity of the elephant donor and thereby link Gaṇeśa's origin myth with other elephantine myths already current in the tradition. In one instance it is the demon elephant, Gajāsura, whose head Śiva takes to restore Gaṇeśa. Just after beheading Gaṇeśa at the doorway to Pārvatī's bath, Śiva fortuitously

> saw the elephant demon [Gajāsura] standing there. As soon as he saw him he struck off his head and took it, placing it on the child whom Pārvatī had created. In this way he caused him to arise. (SkP 3.2.12.20–21)

The presence of the demon elephant as the donor for Gaṇeśa'a head recalls the myth of Śiva's defeat of Gajāsura, the son of Mahiṣa:

> Gajāsura, the elephant lord of the Dānavas, remembered how his father, Mahiṣa, had been slain by Durgā. After performing asceticism [*tapas*] until its head scorched the heavens and sent all the gods running to Brahmā for refuge, Gajāsura received a boon from Brahmā that he would become invincible over the gods and

> could not be defeated by any man or woman overcome with lust. So he conquered all the gods and took up residence in the palace Viśvakarman had built for Indra. Arrogant in his power and neglectful of *dharma,* his mind was filled with evil thoughts. Finally, the elephant demon came to Kāśī where Śiva lived. Then the gods told Śiva about Gajāsura's evil deeds and the lord agreed to help them in destroying the demon. After a fierce battle in which Śiva defeated Gajāsura, the demon praised Śiva and begged him to wear his skin and be known as Kṛttivāsas, "the one wearing the skin." Śiva agreed, and praising his former rival, he transformed his body into a *liṅga* and established it on the spot where they fought, upon which the shrine called Kṛttivāseśvara now stands. (ŚP 2.5.57; cf. BrP 4.98–101; KP 1.30.15–22; see pl. 6)

This myth not only supplies the background for the demon elephant who gives his head to Gaṇeśa but also suggests a model for the Gaṇeśa story in other ways. In this myth the demon elephant, motivated by revenge for his father's dismemberment at the hands of Durgā, exchanges his ascetic achievement for a boon from Brahmā that protects him against all creatures who have desire. After threatening the gods and violating *dharma,* he and Śiva confront one another over the territory of Kāśī (Benares), the place Śiva loves even as he loves Pārvatī. When Śiva defeats the demon, he transforms him into a devotee and through the act of wrapping the animal's skin around himself and taking the form of the elephantskin-wrapped *liṅga,* Śiva insures his intimate union with his former rival. A different version of the story says Śiva received the elephant skin "with head attached and dripping with fat" as a wedding gift from Indra (PP. Sṛṣṭikhaṇḍa 45.423). A similar battle takes place between Śiva and Gaṇeśa. In this story, Śiva and Gaṇeśa quarrel over the territory of Pārvatī's private chamber, which like Kāśī is sacred to Śiva. Gaṇeśa is defeated and mutilated at Śiva's hands; then the lord restores Gaṇeśa, keeping him close by as the leader of his (Śiva's) *gaṇas* and giving him privileged access to all devotees' offerings as the one worshipped at the beginning of all undertakings. In both the Gajāsura and Gaṇeśa stories, the common theme is the taming of the adversary of the god Śiva through the process of dismemberment and restoration to divine intimacy. Each myth displays the power of Śiva as both the lord of destruction and creation.

Another variation on the battle between Śiva and the elephant adversary and on the source for Gaṇeśa's head draws on the categories of Sāṁkhya philosophy:

> Once there was a battle between Śiva and Gaṇeśa which had gone on for a long time without interruption. When the unconquerable Śiva, mounted on an elephant, saw that Gaṇeśa was made out of *prakṛti* [matter] and filled with *avidyā* [ignorance], he knocked him down along with the elephant on which he was riding. Then Pārvatī praised Śiva and asked him for a boon that he should restore her son whom he had just killed. So Śiva joined the head of the elephant to where Gaṇeśa's head had been and pulled out one of his tusks and gave it to him for his ascetic's staff. (SkP 1.1.10.29–38)

In this story Śiva's elephant vehicle gives up its head for his master, and the single-tusked form is accounted for by having Śiva remove one tusk and give it to Gaṇeśa for his ascetic's staff (*yogadaṇḍa*). The myth links Śiva's conquest of Gaṇeśa to Gaṇeśa's ascetic aspect, and the scene resembles an initiation into yogic discipleship. We shall return to this suggestive myth later, when we examine the theme of dismemberment and castration in the conflict between Śiva and Gaṇeśa, to compare it with other myths about the broken tusk. The initiatory symbolism of the ascetic's staff may also be seen in the rite of *upanayana,* the sacred thread initiation, in which the guru gives the young man a stick to symbolize his chaste mendicancy, which stick is also called a *yogadaṇḍa.*

According to another Purāṇic source, it is Indra's elephant vehicle, Airāvata, who unwillingly surrenders his head so that Gaṇeśa may be made whole. Śiva orders his companion, Nandin the bull, to go to the north and find a suitable head:

> Nandin wandered over the triple universe until he saw Airāvata lying down with his head facing north. As he started to cut off Airāvata's head the elephant gave out a loud roar, and Indra came there with the other gods. Then Indra and Nandin fought fiercely until Nandin defeated him and cut off Airāvata's head as the gods looked on bewildered. (BDP 2.60.50–52)

Like the account of the elephant-skin wedding gift, this myth variant clearly links the mythologies of Śiva and Indra in the circumstances surrounding Gaṇeśa and Airāvata, who play analogous roles as their lords' servants: Airāvata, the elephant-king vehicle, and Gaṇeśa, the lord of the *gaṇas*. As in many myths in the Purāṇas about the conflicts between Śiva and Indra, the ascetic Śiva easily overcomes the heroic but thick-headed Indra through his proxy Nandin. As the elephant head makes its transition from the body of Airāvata to that of Gaṇeśa, it loses one of its tusks, causing Gaṇeśa to be known as Ekadanta, the single-tusked one. In the severed head and the broken tusk we see that Gaṇeśa's new bodily parts get trimmed; the myth emphasizes that Gaṇeśa become a great yogi like his father (BDP 2.60.105). Indra is consoled by Śiva, who tells him to throw the headless body of Airāvata into the ocean of milk, from which he can churn another elephant mount, and the king of the gods receives an immortal bull from Śiva as compensation (BDP 2.60.93–94).

Another myth recalls the story of an unfortunate incident involving Indra and Airāvata and the irascible sage Durvāsas, an incarnation of Śiva in his destructive form as Bhairava:

> Long ago, Indra, intoxicated with wine and lust, made love with a beautiful nymph named Rambhā in the forest. Then Indra, whose mind remained filled with erotic passion, saw the sage Durvāsas who was on his way from Vaikuṇṭha [Viṣṇu's home] to Kailāsa [Śiva's home] filled with ascetic fire. Indra bowed to him and the sage gave the king of the gods a *pārijāta* flower. Indra then placed the flower onto the head of Airāvata, who was transformed into the form of Viṣṇu by the touch of the flower. Airāvata then abandoned Indra and ran into the forest. Durvāsas became enraged that Indra had dishonored the flower and cursed him to lose all his powers. (DBP 9.403–26; see also BVP 3.20.41–62 and Dessigane et al. 1960, pp. 9ff.)

This story also concerns the rivalry between Indra and Śiva, who here takes the form of Durvāsas. The powers of the sage make short work of Indra's wealth and sexual prowess. The *pārijāta* flower is an emblem of riches and erotic power, one of the flowers from the five coral trees that arose out of the churning of the ocean at the beginning of the cosmic cycle. In another story the goddess gave this flower to Durvāsas who in turn gave it to Dakṣa, who became so aroused by the scent of the flower that he made love to his daughter Satī "in the manner of a mere beast." This shameful action drove her to burn her body, that is, commit *satī*, and provoked Śiva to such a rage that he beheaded Dakṣa (DBP 7.30). In this myth Durvāsas curses Indra to lose his powers because Indra had failed to honor the gift of a sage. In a larger sense, however, the sage's curse represents the power of ascetic control over erotic pleasure. When the magic flower touches Airāvata, he becomes wild and disappears into the forest. In another variant, Airāvata makes a more dramatic exit, which in turn leads to an important connection with the story of Gaṇeśa's elephantine origins. Here the *pārijāta* flower is said to "remove all obstacles . . . whoever wears it shall be worshipped as the best among the gods" (BVP 3.20.53–54).

When Indra placed the flower Durvāsas had given him on Airāvata's head,

> that powerful elephant forcefully threw Indra down from his head and ran off into the dense jungle. There, being infatuated with desire, he forcibly made love with a female elephant. It is the nature of females to desire pleasure, and so the female elephant yielded to the male's passion. And there in the forest she gave birth to many young ones. Meanwhile, Viṣṇu cut off the head of the elephant dwelling there and put it on the shoulders of Gaṇeśa. (BVP 3.20.57–61)

Through this indirect route Gaṇeśa receives a head consecrated by the touch of the obstacle-removing flower, which originally came from Pārvatī's own hand. Airāvata's abandonment of Indra after the incident of the *pārijāta* flower is symbolic of the latter's more general loss of power. As a consequence of Durvāsas's curse, Indra must wander an anonymous beggar in the world, seeking finally a boon from Brahmā that leads to the churning of the ocean and the beginning of a new cosmic cycle.

As the donor of Gaṇeśa's new head, Airāvata contributes all the powers formerly belonging to Indra as the king of the gods. And all the associations of the elephant with royalty and power are transferred to Gaṇeśa as the new lord of the divine *gaṇas* attendant on Śiva. The story assumes that Gaṇeśa's power, like his physical form, could not have come from nowhere but had to be taken by force of arms, as with Nandin's beheading or by the power of the sage's curse, which caused Airāvata to become wild and subsequently to be beheaded by Viṣṇu. In the stories of the Airāvata cycle, it is Śiva, acting through his alter egos of Nandin and Durvāsas, who steals the power from Indra and makes it available to his newly adopted son Gaṇeśa.

According to another variant of the story of his origins, Gaṇeśa's elephant head appears through the courtesy of yet another divine elephant. In a text showing strong Vaiṣṇava influence, Viṣṇu is present at Gaṇeśa's beheading—this time performed by the sage Śani, or Saturn (the lord of suicides), standing in for Śiva—and sees Pārvatī's distress at the mutilation of her newly created son:

> When Hari [Viṣṇu] saw all of them in such distress, he rode Garuḍa and went in a northerly direction toward the Puṣpadhadra River. There he saw Gajendra, the king of the elephants, lying down in the midst of the forest. The elephant, surrounded by his calves here and there, lay faint from exhaustion from lovemaking, with his head turned toward the north. Immediately Viṣṇu cut off the beautiful head and laid the blood-smeared head on the back of Garuḍa. The dead body of the elephant fell onto his mate, who awoke and began to cry loud laments along with her children. Viṣṇu consoled the grieving elephant and cut off the head from another elephant and attached it to the first animal's body and brought him to life. Then he came to where Pārvatī was and, taking the child into his lap, he properly joined the head to the body. Kṛṣṇa caused life to come into him by shouting the *mantra* "*hūṃ*." (BVP 3.12.9–22; see pl. 7)

Gaṇeśa receives the head of Gajendra and so is made whole. But Gaṇeśa's restoration is the cause of Gajendra's mutilation; Pārvatī's joy is paid for with the grief of Gajendra's widow. Viṣṇu comforts the widow by restoring Gajendra with the head of another elephant, thus passing the action on down the chain of *karma,* as if stringing heads on a thread or flowers for a garland or beads for a rosary. This variant recalls the tale in which Viṣṇu beheads Airāvata after he had abandoned Indra. It links Gaṇeśa's head with that of Gajendra, the lord of the elephants. Gajendra appears to be a distinct character from Airāvata, although they nearly merge in this sequence of stories. The important myth of the *Gajendramokṣa,* the release of the elephant lord, is told in the *Bhāgavata Purāṇa:*

> Once, the king of the elephants, along with his wives and children, came to a splendid garden at the foot of the mountain that was surrounded by an ocean like the ocean of milk. With musk fluid oozing from his forehead, with bees swarming around it, the elephant plunged into the ocean to cool himself. He sprayed water

over the females and the females and young ones bathed and drank. Then a mighty alligator, who had become angry at this intrusion into the ocean, seized hold of the elephant's foot and held it fast in his jaws. When the wives of the elephant king saw that he was being dragged further and further into the ocean, they tried in vain to pull him back out. As the alligator and the elephant struggled with one another the elephant became increasingly weaker while the alligator grew stronger. When he saw that he could not free himself from the trap of the alligator's jaws, the elephant called out to Viṣṇu for refuge. When Viṣṇu saw the elephant's plight, he came there and pulled the elephant and the alligator out of the water. He transformed the alligator back into Hūhū, the celestial *gandharva* who had been cursed by the sage Devala [Nārada] because he had been sporting in the water with some women when Devala wanted to bathe. When Hūhū pulled on Devala's leg he was cursed to take the form of an alligator, only to be rescued from it by seizing hold of the leg of an elephant. (BhP 8.204)

In this myth of conflict between the alligator and the elephant, we see some similarities to the myths of Airāvata and Durvāsas. At the conclusion of the myth, we learn that the alligator is really a disguise of an erotic *gandharva,* who had been cursed by the ascetic Devala for touching him while he was bathing, much as the flying elephants had been cursed by the sage Dīrghatapas when they brushed against the tree under which he was sitting. By transforming the *gandharva* Hūhū into an alligator, the ascetic reverses their roles, for now the alligator is the one whose watery territory is invaded by the elephant. His biting the leg of the elephant echoes the theme of beheading, which we have seen at work in other myths. The conflict between the alligator and the elephant surrounded by his entourage of cows—like the conflicts between the sage and the *gandharva,* between Śiva and Gajāsura, and between Durvāsas and Indra—draws on the important theme in Hindu mythology of the tension between the powers of eroticism and asceticism. The tension between the alligator and the elephant cannot be resolved, and so they both edge their way to destruction. At this desperate moment the myth turns to the solution of *bhakti.* The intensity of the elephant's devotion to Viṣṇu frees *both* creatures from their animal incarnations, and Viṣṇu's grace gets the two animals past their impasse in spite of whatever previous karmic injustice put them there. The elephant-king's mutilation and near annihilation in the jaws of the alligator provides the setting for his liberation, just as Nandin admonishes Indra as he gets ready to cut off Airāvata's head, "Give up hope for Airāvata and go away, for one is better suited to give life's breath to the son of Śiva than your Airāvata" (BDP 2.60.56–57). This turn of events echoes another widespread theme, that of the curse of the god that provides liberation to his enemy; salvation by damnation. For the other elephantine characters who unwillingly give their heads to Siva for Gaṇeśa's resuscitation, the consequence of their dismemberment is restoration to a better situation in the inner chambers of the god's circle; the loser wins.

The elephant head is Gaṇeśa's most readily identifiable characteristic, his trademark, and the most frequent motif in the stories of his creation. It suggests all the symbolic associations of the elephant: wildness and domestication, phallic masculinity and feminine grace, and the protective guardian functions at the threshold. In addition, however, the mythology of Gaṇeśa makes use of particular elephant characters who serve in various contexts, both as supports for and as adversaries of the gods. In taking their heads, Gaṇeśa also takes their powers and aspects of their functions into his own composite identity. Like Gajāsura, Gaṇeśa continues to be an adversary of Śiva and the other gods in some myths—more often indirectly through clever deception than by force of arms. Like Airāvata, he remains loyal to his father and master. Like Gajendra, his near destruction through conflict with Śiva or as the consequence of a curse leads to the intervention of the deity—in Gaṇeśa's case that of Pārvatī—and to his liberation into full recognition and status in the world of the gods as the Lord of Obstacles and the guardian of the divine threshold. So Gaṇeśa has more in common with these elephant beings than simply a similarity of form. Each of them contributes something of himself along with his head; much as at the creation of the goddess Durgā, each of the gods contributes his power to help kindle the sacred fire out of which she is born (MP 82.8–11).

Gaṇeśa's Birth: Substance and Technique

Besides myths having to do with Gaṇeśa's elephant form, stories about his substance—what he was made out of and how he was made—have captivated the imaginations of the mythmakers. Some variants have Gaṇeśa come forth from his father's mind, identical to him in form, only to be cursed by a jealous Pārvatī to be ugly and have the head of an elephant. Most variants, however, place Gaṇeśa's origins within the substance of his mother's body, the dirt, unguents, and residue on their limbs. What is common to all the myths of Gaṇeśa's origins is that he is *never* born from the sexual union of his mother and father in their divine forms as Śiva and Pārvatī. Often one or the other of them creates him unilaterally. When they are both involved in this engendering, Gaṇeśa emerges out of their seed only after it has become leftover substance, mixed with the water of their bath, or when they have transformed themselves into elephants, as we have already seen.

This unnatural origin for Gaṇeśa is not in itself particularly strange, as many Hindu gods and goddesses are born in an unusual manner and sometimes unexpectedly: whether out of the cosmic ocean, sacrificial fire, spilling of seed, dropping of blood, the thought of the progenitor, or by some other means. Why is this type of birth story appropriate for Gaṇeśa? There are two mythic explanations for this. First, Pārvatī wants to fulfill her maternal longing for a child; second, she wants to have a son who will protect her from her husband's intrusions. Both accounts reflect excessive maternal feelings that seek to deny the father's role altogether.

According to the first type of myth, once when Pārvatī was feeling the desire for motherhood particularly strongly, she pleaded with Śiva to make love with her and conceive a son in her. But he replied:

> "Daughter of the mountain, I am not a householder, and I have no need for a son. This wicked group of gods gave you to me as a wife, but a wife is surely the greatest fetter for a man who is without passion. Besides, progeny are a noose and a stake. Householders need sons and wealth, and a wife is necessary to obtain a son, and sons are necessary for making offerings to the ancestors. But I do not die, goddess, and so why do I need a son? Where there is no disease, what is the need for medicine? Come, you are a woman and I am a man. Let us enjoy being the causes from which children arise and rejoice in the pleasures between men and women, without progeny." (BDP 2.60.10–14)

Śiva states the classic ascetic argument: sons are for those who are caught in the net of desire and rebirth. For the householder a son is a source of comfort and enjoyment to his father, and in death and thereafter a son will see that the father receives the appropriate *śrāddha* rituals and ancestral offerings to grant him safe passage into better rebirths. As Śiva has no death, he has no need of such rites nor of sons to perform them. The logic of his position takes him away from the involvement with worlds or sons; he is *puruṣa,* detached and free. But Pārvatī is the Mother of the world, and how can she be the mother without sons? She is *prakṛti* and must seek to fill the world with forms (SkP 1.1.10.27–36). Although he refuses to give Pārvatī his seed in order that she might conceive a son, he does eagerly desire for her erotic sport. For Śiva is not an ordinary ascetic misogynist; he values highly his erotic play but does not wish to transform it into instrumental activity by placing it under the goal of conceiving progeny. He wants to make love but retain his seed. Whatever sons there are to be between them will not come from their sexual union and Pārvatī's womb.

Another variant gives us a different reason for why Śiva and Pārvatī should not conceive a child. This story is set in the context of the conflict between Śiva and Indra, which, as we have already seen, is a theme in the background of many Gaṇeśa myths:

> When Rudra was engaged in sexual pleasure the worlds shook violently and the seven oceans became stirred up and the gods became filled with fear. Then the gods, together with Indra, went to Brahmā, saying, "The world is greatly disturbed, why is this?" Brahmā said to them. "Śiva is in the midst of lovemaking, I'm sure. When he becomes possessed by it these worlds become agitated." Then the gods said to Indra, "Come, let's go before it comes to an end. If their lovemaking is consummated, that child which shall be born as a result of their union will be imperishable. He will certainly deprive Indra of his position as king of the gods. (VāmP 28.31–35)

In this myth, as in many others in the Purāṇas, Indra attempts to shore up his deteriorating position as king of the gods by interrupting Śiva and Pārvatī, preventing them from conceiving a child who would displace him. It is a theme common to many myths of the births of gods and heroes; their appearance in the world threatens the comfortable order the established gods or kings enjoy. Any child born of such illustrious parents would be so exceptional as to cause all eyes to look at him, leaving Indra in the background. But beyond Indra's own self-interest, there is the larger threat to the gods, for the appearance of a child born naturally to Śiva and Pārvatī would combine their respective powers. Such concentrated power would bring the universe collapsing in upon them, giving Indra and the gods no place to stand. The gods' well-being lies in keeping the two divine movers neither too close together nor too far apart—difficult and delicate work at which they are not always successful. A similar theme appears in a slightly different context, a devotional rite to Śiva in Bengal, *Śiva-gājan.* Here the goddess (Pārvatī) arrives in the form of a water vessel but is not allowed near the image of Śiva even though all the celebrants recognize her to be his consort. The devotees explain that "the combination of the goddess with the main deity of the locality would be too much for mortals to bear; the combined force or power that flows from the union of Śiva and Durgā would destroy the people who want to share in this creative energy" (Östör, p. 120).

Although Indra is momentarily successful in interrupting the divine couple and in preventing Pārvatī from conceiving a child, later on the fluids from their lovemaking come to life on their own in the bath:

> Mālinī [Pārvatī's servant] began leaning and rubbing the goddess's golden limbs with her hands, using gentle and fragrant unguents, as Pārvatī reflected on the quality [*guṇa*] of her own sweat. When Mālinī left Pārvatī made an elephant-headed man out of her bodily dirt [*mala*], one who had the chest of a bull, four arms, and all auspicious marks. When she made him and stood him on the ground, she sat again on her throne. Then Śiva arrived and took his bath while seated on his throne. Below him sat the one born out of Pārvatī's bodily dirt. The sweat from Śiva and Pārvatī mixed together there on the wet ground, and out of that union came the one having the elephant's trunk, blowing air through it. Then the lord of the universe became content, recognizing him to be his own son. (VāmP 28.57–59, 64–66; cf. *Caturvargacintāmaṇi* 2.2.359)

Another variant of this story has Gaṇeśa born from a drop of blood shed at Śiva and Pārvatī's intercourse, thus accounting for

Gaṇeśa's characteristic red color (BhavP 2.4.31–33, cited in Gadgil, 1.48). As with other versions, Gaṇeśa arises out of the sexual fluids of Śiva and Pārvatī, but outside their bodies.

Two birth narratives appear to be collapsed together here: one tells of Pārvatī's forming Gaṇeśa out of her bodily residue; the other relates how the sweat (symbolizing sexual fluids or seed) from his parents' bodies is mixed together on the wet ground of the bath/throne room and spontaneously gives rise to Gaṇeśa. The latter version of the story suggests the context of the shrine, where the deity functions as a royal presence and is also bathed in the same location by the priests. In that holiest of holy places the residual substances of the deities, their *tīrtha* (bathwater), is of such potency that it can engender new beings outside the deities' bodies. The fecundating power of *tīrtha* is well known among devotees of shrines. So powerful is the engendering quality of Pārvatī's residue that (in a different version of the story) when a female demon drinks the unguents mixed with Pārvatī's body-rubbings, she becomes pregnant and so gives birth to Gaṇeśa (Getty, pp. 6–7). In this story, like the one in which Śiva and Pārvatī transform themselves into elephants in order to conceive an elephant-headed son, Gaṇeśa comes into being from the union of his two parents, but in this extracorporal manner.

Pārvatī's need for a son is as compelling as that of Śiva not to have one. Her childlessness is her greatest sorrow (BVP 3.2.24). On one occasion she pleads with Śiva to conceive a child with her, absolving him of any paternal obligations:

> "When you have conceived a child, you can return to your yoga, great lord. I will bring up the son and you can be a yogi. I yearn painfully for the kiss of a son's mouth; and since you took me for your wife you should give me a son. Your son will not desire marriage for himself, if you like, so you will not have a son, grandson, and descendents." (BDP 2.60.15–18)

Her argument rests on maternal desire. She willingly concedes all else to Śiva. He can return to his meditations without any further obligation, and his son can be as averse as his father to marriage and procreation. Yet, engendering a son by natural means would be contrary to Śiva's nature, and whatever sonship Gaṇeśa is to have to Śiva will be fraught with obstacles, which (as we shall see) the elephant-faced one is capable of overcoming to the astonishment and conversion of his father.

Another myth gives the opposite reason for Pārvatī's desire to have a son, not to join with Śiva but to keep him away:

> Once when Pārvatī was taking a bath, Śiva threatened Nandin, who was guarding the door, and went into the house. When that beautiful woman, the mother of the world, saw him arrive without warning, she stood up embarrassed. Then Pārvatī decided to follow the advice given earlier by a friend, thinking to herself, "I should have a servant of my own, a man of accomplishment who will be favorable to me and obey me and no other; one who will not wander even a hair's breadth from my side." As she was thinking in this way, she rubbed out of the dirt of her body a young man who possessed all good qualities: handsome, well-bodied, sturdy, well-adorned, and most valorous and strong. She gave him many garments, ornaments, and blessings. "You are my very own son. There is no one else here who belongs only to me," she said. (ŚP 2.4.13.15–32)

This myth reverses Pārvatī's relation to Śiva. Instead of wanting to seduce Śiva to conceive a son with him, she needs to keep Śiva away, to protect her autonomy. It is she who refuses his advances, whereas before he refused hers. In both cases the fundamental structure is the same: Śiva and Pārvatī are to have a son without *having* a son. Their child comes into being through unnatural means. This contradiction runs like a thread through the variations of Gaṇeá's birth stories. One or both of the parents will be surprised by his birth appearance, one will reject and deform him, and his restoration will be in the form of one who is both split and fused.

Like Father, Like Son

Most of the myths of Gaṇeśa's origins tell us that Pārvatī created him and Śiva beheaded him; one story, however, is important for the ways in which it inverts elements of the dominant myth:

> Formerly, all the gods and sages who were rich in asceticism undertook various actions and were successful in them. Then later, those who were on the wrong path were successful in their actions, while those on the right path achieved success only in the face of great obstacles. So the gods and the ancestors worried greatly and

talked together about how they might thwart the success of those who were on the wrong path. Talking together, those dwellers of the triple heaven decided to go to Rudra, the noble one. So they came to Rudra on Mt. Kailāsa and, bowing before him, said to him reverently, "O three-eyed lord who holds the trident, you should cause obstacles to arise for everyone without exception."

When the gods had spoken, Śiva was filled with the greatest joy and looked at Umā with an unblinking eye. As he was looking at her in the presence of the gods, he thought to himself, "Why is there no form of me in the sky? I have form in earth, air, fire, and water, but there is not one of me in space? As he was thinking this thought, he laughed, and a man took form out of the force [*śakti*] of his knowledge, as Brahmā had predicted. Amused at this, the lord said, "This one must have quarter parts of him made up of each of the elements." Then a creature took form, glorious, with a blazing face, a youth who emanated light in all directions. He looked exactly like Śiva, endowed with all the same qualities. As soon as he was born, this noble one captivated all the gods with his beauty, form, and radiance.

When Umā saw this exquisitely formed noble child, she looked at him with an unblinking eye. As Śiva saw her fickleness, which is the natural condition of women, he became angry, thinking this beautiful youth to be deluding to the eyes. So the lord cursed Gaṇeśa, saying, "Little boy, you shall have an elephant's head and a potbelly!" Then the lord, who had become filled with rage, rose up with his body shaking, and as he shook water spewed out from the pores of his hair and fell to the earth, springing up in various *vanāyakas* with elephant heads, black as *tamāla* trees and carrying weapons. Then the lord became confused, saying, "What is going on?" Then the gods said to him, "You have just performed a great and unparalleled miracle. Let this be the actions the gods asked from you. Let's gather around him [i.e., Gaṇeśa], but where did he come from?" While the gods were wondering about this, the *vināyakas* began to shake the earth violently. Then Brahmā, the four-faced one, jumped onto his unequalled vehicle and said, "You gods have been blessed by this three-eyed one who has such an auspicious [*śiva*] form. Śiva has favored your request by making an obstacle to your enemies." Then he said to Śiva, "Since this god arose out of your mouth, let him be the leader of the *vināyakas,* and they will be his followers. This one who was born from you and who has taken form in the four elements in the sky is the boon which you gave to the gods. (VarP 23.3–25)

The story opens with a familiar Purāṇic situation, the gods are losing out to the demons because their efforts are being thwarted by obstacles. They beg Śiva to redress the balance by creating a being who will set up obstacles uniformly for everyone, apparently in the confidence that given an even break the gods will prevail. Acceding to their request, Śiva looks at Pārvatī "with an unblinking eye," suggestive of erotic desire for her. He cannot take his eyes off her. Then he reflects that there is no part of him that is made up from the element of sky or space [*ākāśa, vyoman*]. According to the doctrines of Śaivism, all the elements of the world are manifestations of Śiva. To rectify the imbalance of powers between the gods and demons as well as the incompleteness of the cosmos owing to his absence in one of its elements, Śiva "laughed" forth a man made up from the power of his mind, a man who stood there before his eyes [*sākṣāt*] in person, indeed identical to his father. Here Gaṇeśa springs from the fourth element—sky/space rather than from earth, as he usually does in those variants in which he is identified as Pārvatī's child. On a different occasion Śiva created another lookalike, Vīrabhadra, out of his mouth in order to behead Dakṣa. He later threw this lookalike into the sacrificial fire and then restored him by giving him the head of a goat (VayuP 30.128–9). The notion that the child is brought into being from the father's laugh or breath, that is, proceeding forth from the mouth, has a precedent in the Upaniṣads, where it is said that the husband, in intercourse, breathes the power of procreative life into his seed (BĀU 6.4.11; cf. Tāṇḍya 16.14.5). This notion accords with the more general Vedic and Brāhmaṇic traditions in which the sacred speech chanted by its knowers in the context of the sacrifice brings the world of meaningful or real experience into being for the benefit of the ritual client and those whom he represents.

Once Gaṇeśa is created identical to his father, the difficulties begin. Śiva sees Pārvatī looking at this laugh-born clone of Śiva; she regards his new double with an "unblinking eye," just as Śiva had looked at her. The veiled hint of incest contained in the exchange of looks sends Śiva into a rage, and he curses Gaṇeśa to be ugly, with the form of an elephant with a potbelly. In his predictably excessive manner, Śiva generates more elephant-faced creatures, called *vināyakas,* out of his sweat, that fiery liquid that, like blood and seed, creates unilaterally—as when

Śiva creates demons out of his sweat and destroys Dakṣa's sacrifice (MBh 12.274.45; VāmP 44.41–43; cf. O'Flaherty 1980, pp. 33–40). These new beings created out of Śiva's rage are the answers to the gods prayers; Gaṇeśa receives lordship over this new army of elephant-headed *vanāyakas*, and the restoration of the cosmic imbalance is reassured, at least for the time being.

Gaṇeśa's creation from Śiva's mouth through his laugh is reminiscent of Brahmā's creation of the Vedas and *ṛṣis* out of his mouth and mind (MP 45.20–24). The same pattern occurs in the myth of Durgā's emergence from the collective energies [*tejas*] that the gods spewed forth from their mouths into the sacrificial fire like oblations (MP 82.8–11). As with the goddess (Pārvatī), the purpose of Gaṇeśa's creation is to save the universe from destruction by the demons who had greedily diverted the flow of sacrificial power and its benefits to themselves.

A number of the themes central to this story appear in inverted order in what we may take to be a variant. This tale appears in an early nineteenth-century English translation and is also attributed to the *Varāha Purāṇa*, although it does not appear in either of the Purāṇa's two published editions. Whether it is a translation of an authentic Sanskrit source or not, it does conform to the larger logic of the myth:

> Śiva looked at Pārvatī, and whilst thinking how he could effect the wishes of the gods, from the splendor of his countenance there sprang into existence a youth shedding radiance all around, endowed with the qualities of Śiva, and evidently another Rudra, and captivating by his beauty all the female inhabitants of heaven. Umā, seeing his beauty, was excited with jealousy, and in her anger pronounced this curse: "Thou shalt not offend my sight with the form of a beautiful youth; and therefore assume an elephant's head and a large belly, and thus shall all thy beauties vanish." (Kennedy, p. 353; cf. Dubois, p. 637)

In this story, as in the earlier one, Gaṇeśa emerges out of Śiva's "countenance"—in a manner not clearly specified—to help the gods. But Pārvatī sees that he is beautiful and that the other women in heaven also appreciate his lovely form and, out of jealousy, she curses him to be ugly. This is in contrast to the earlier myth in which Śiva curses him because he sees that Pārvatī finds him beautiful. The intensity of Pārvatī's anger might be interpreted as a reaction to her feelings of lust for Gaṇeśa, feelings that are both incestuous and adulterous. Common elements emerge in the two versions of this myth: Gaṇeśa is the creation of his father alone, in appearance indistinguishable from him; he causes conflict between Śiva and Pārvatī, which is only resolved at his own expense; and he receives a curse and changes his form so that he will be easily distinguishable from his father. Although there is no explicit beheading in this story, the curse is a sort of verbal beheading that results in Gaṇeśa's transformation into an elephant-headed figure. Elements in this myth recall the Brāhmaṇic tale in which Indra created Kutsa from his thigh, making him identical to himself. Kutsa then slept with Indra's wife, who could not tell him apart from Indra. Indra cut off Kutsa's hair, but Kutsa then disguised himself as Indra. Finally, Indra curses him to be a low-caste Malla (JB 3.199–200; cf. O'Flaherty 1976, pp. 334–35). A similar predicament arose according to a South Indian tale, when both Brahmā and Śiva had five heads, which Pārvatī resolved by cutting off one of Brahmā's heads so that she could distinguish him from her husband. (O'Flaherty 1973, p. 127)

In another story in which Śiva creates Gaṇeśa as a favor to the gods, the conflict between Śiva and Pārvatī is absent; but other notions about the father's role in the creation of children are at work. The gods, led by Bṛhaspati, bring their complaint to Śiva:

> Bṛhaspati said, "We have come here desiring a boon from you. You never put even a single obstacle before what the demons ask of you. Those who harm the gods simply pray to you and get their desires fulfilled. So you should bless us instead with an obstacle to those who harm us." When he heard this, Śiva, the lord who carries the *pināka* bow, took the form of Gaṇeśvara. Then all the *gaṇas* worshipped him, and Pārvatī welcomed the elephant-faced lord, and all the other dwellers in heaven rejoiced at what Śiva had done. Then this boy who had come out of the two of them, the embodiment of terror and auspiciousness, stood there dancing. This gentle son of Śiva and Pārvatī bowed to his father and mother. Śiva performed the rites appropriate for the birth of a son, holding him in his arms and kissing him on the head, saying, "You are my son, who has been born to destroy the demons and bring help to the gods and Brahmins who teach the Vedas. Stand there in the path which leads to heaven and create obstacles in the rites of anyone who has sacrifices performed but fails to pay the priests' fee [*dakṣiṇā*]. (LP 105.4–22; cf. SkP 6.214.47–66)

There appears to be some confusion in this story as to who created Gaṇeśa and how it was accomplished. First the story tells us that Śiva "took the form" of Gaṇeśvara (i.e., Gaṇeśa), yet later it says Gaṇeśa "had come out of the two of them." This may be less a matter of confusion that it would appear. The story reflects the ancient Indian view that a father reproduces himself in his son, thereby saving himself from death by passing a remainder of himself on to his offspring. The wife serves as the field in which the seed is planted and from which it is harvested. "After his wife conceives, the husband becomes an embryo and is born again from her" (*Manu* 9.8; see also AB 7.13; BVP 3.2.37; Shulman, pp. 223–67). It is said that Prajāpati saved himself from being devoured by Agni by making himself into another, which he then threw into the fire as a food offering, thus sparing himself from death (ŚB 2.2.4.9; O'Flaherty 1980, pp. 24–30). This notion of creation by splitting off a part of one's self complicates the relation between husband and wife, for she becomes the mother to the husband who is now her son. In the patriarchal traditions of Hindu society the son resembles the father in all socially and ritually significant ways. He takes his father's name, caste, privileges, obligations, and inheritance; at death the son gives new birth to the deceased father through the performance of funeral rites [*śrāddha*] that make the father's rebirth in a favorable direction possible. Śiva's creation of Gaṇeśa evokes the older Vedic tradition according to which the creative process resides with the father as the one who contributes the engendering power and the codes through which the son will be located in society and the cosmos.

The more pervasive versions of the myths relating to Gaṇeśa's birth, however, place Pārvatī in the spotlight as the source of his substantial body and form. These elaborate and fascinatingly subtle stories probably reflect the later full Purāṇic tradition in which the goddess figures more prominantly as an independent character.

Churning the Divine Body

In the cycle of myths in which Pārvatī makes Gaṇeśa out of the substance rubbed off the surface of her body, the conflict between the gods and the demons that caused Śiva to create Gaṇeśa is exchanged for a conflict between her and Śiva. Either Śiva is too far away, as when Pārvatī makes Gaṇeśa to relieve her loneliness during his long absence, or he is too close, as when she stations Gaṇeśa at her door to keep him away. These myths vary in important details, but they all draw on the older myth in which Skanda (Gaṇeśa's elder brother) is created out of Śiva's seed, which he spit into Agni's mouth when the gods interrupted his lovemaking with Pārvatī. Unable to contain the fiery seed of Śiva, Agni threw it into the Ganges, where it impregnated the six Pleades [*Kṛttikās*] who collectively gave birth to a boy with one body and six heads (MBh 3.213–19; ŚP 2.4.1–22; *Kumārasambhava* 9.11; cf. O'Flaherty 1973, pp. 261–77).

According to one myth, Śiva and Pārvatī had been making love on the Himālaya mountain for a long time with all comforts and diversions. Then Śiva left her to attend to his meditation on Mt. Mandara:

> Pārvatī remained with her father, feeling lonely. Then, after a long time had passed, she felt the desire to have a son. Along with the company of her friends, Pārvatī made a game with dolls [*kṛtimaputraka,* literally, "little sons that were fashioned"] by rubbing scented unquents mixed with powder over her body and rubbing out the dirt to form a man which had the head of an elephant. Pārvatī playfully threw that son into the Ganges where he became so large that he extended himself as big as the world. At that moment she called out to him, "son," and asked him to come to her. But the goddess Gaṅgā called him "son," and so he has come to be known by the name Gaṅgeya. (MatsyaP 154.500–505; PP Sṛṣṭikhaṇḍa 45.443–49)

When Śiva leaves Pārvatī to take up his ascetic life, she takes consolation in making a son by rubbing the dirt [*mala*] from her limbs and fashioning it into the elephant-headed shape of a son. Here she plays the male role. Her bodily substance is a substitute for seed, giving rise to Gaṇeśa in a manner similar to the way Skanda was made by Śiva casting his seed into the Ganges, where it is raised by the Kṛttikās. Pārvatī's male role is further suggested by her competition with Gaṅgā over which of them may call Gaṇeśa "son."

In another cosmic eon, Pārvatī and Gaṅgā were the daughters of Menā and sisters. Each wanted to be the mother of Śiva's son, and both practiced austerities to gain his attention (VāmP 25.5–

24; cf. Kramrisch 1981, pp. 342–43). This earlier competition lies in the background of the story told above; here Pārvatī first makes Gaṇeśa and then Gaṅgā receives the child made from her residue, just as the Kṛttikās received the seed of Śiva to create Skanda. The myth attempts to conceal the conflict between the two mothers, by giving the child two names, Gaṇeśa and Gaṅgeya. When Pārvatī throws Gaṇeśa into the Ganges, he imitates the action of his father's *liṅga,* which extended above and below the world faster than Brahmā and Viṣṇu could reach its limits (ŚP Dh 101–23; cf. O'Flaherty 1973, pp. 130–36). In this myth Pārvatī creates Gaṇeśa more in the manner of a man than a woman and functions as a father in Śiva's absence; indeed, when Śiva does return, he has to engage in a contest first with Gaṇeśa and then with Pārvatī before he will accept fatherhood. The symbolic maleness of Pārvatī's seed-dirt, her fecundating bodily residue, is further underscored in this story when Gaṇeśa emerges from the river "as big as the world." The river is the womb and Pārvatī acts as the giver of the seed. Here Gaṅgā is Pārvatī's alter ego, taking her place as mother just as Pārvatī takes Śiva's place as father. Gaṅgā is the mothering figure, the nourishing cow. She complements the androgynous creatrix Pārvatī, who takes Śiva's male function during his absences from the world. This method of creation echoes another ancient Indian notion involved in the myth of creation by the male, as when the sages churn Vena's thigh and bring forth the noble king Pṛthu (BrP 2.36.127–227) or when Prajāpati is said to have breasts and a womb—the full complement of androgynous characteristics and capabilities (O'Flaherty 1980, p. 28).

Some Purāṇic sources maintain that demons and humans have come from the divine rectum (BhP 2.6.8; LP 1.70.199; cf. O'Flaherty 1976, p. 140). One psychoanalytically oriented scholar claimed to have found a folktale in North India in which Gaṇeśa is produced from the excrement of his mother, although such a version has not been located in the Purāṇas (Berkeley-Hill, p. 330). Other folktales tell that the earth was formed from the feces of the god, which, when thrown into the water, immediately dried up to form the world (Elwin pp. 37, 44), a sequence recalling the birth of Skanda. Such "earth diver" tales of anal creation may give expression to unconscious male envy of the procreative powers of women, both human and divine (Dundes, pp. 1036–40). The stories of Pārvatī making Gaṇeśa by rubbing the residue off of her limbs involve a double reversal. Pārvatī imitates the mythical male creator, who by creating out of or off of his body imitates the female procreative powers. Here the woman masquerades as the man who masquerades as the woman. As we have seen, Śiva does not give Pārvatī his seed. She does not have the option of giving birth to Gaṇeśa in the normal manner that humans use—this is much the same predicament as the male creator—she must produce her offspring from her own substance alone by an alternative method outside the womb [*ayonijā*].

The scurf or residue out of which Pārvatī fashions Gaṇeśa is a clue to the deeper levels of his meaning. The texts use two words for this substance: *mala* and *lepa*. Each opens up a different range of semantic associations. *Mala* is dirt—specifically bodily dirt. Probably derived from the root *mla,* "decay, fade"; it makes its one and only Vedic appearance in the hymn to the Keśins, the long-haired ones. Describing their wild way of life, the poet says, "girdled by the wind, these sages clothe themselves with red dirt" (ṚV 10.136.2). The dirt mentioned here is the dirt naked ascetics rub on themselves, much like ashes. Following Grassman's gloss, O'Flaherty translates this stanza, "These ascetics, swathed in wind, put dirty red rags on" (1981, pp. 137–38). The "red rags" are suggestive of the saffron robes worn by various monastic and ascetic communities of later times. The redness of the dirt or clothing resembles the redness of Gaṇeśa's chthonic images found in shrines and at crossroads across India. *Mala* can also mean, depending on the context: dust, sweat, excrement, bodily defilements associated with childbirth, evil, darkness, and fertile manure (Diehl, pp. 103, 126). The term also appears in a philosophical context, signifying the dust covering the mirror. This, like the smoke hiding the fire and the membranes concealing the embryo, is a metaphor for desire and anger, which prevents us from seeing reality as it is (BhG 3.38). In the Paśupata school of Śaivite philosophy, *mala* means primordial darkness, "the evil which resides in the soul" (Hara, p. 10). It particularly means false knowledge [*mithājñāna*], synonymous with the Advaita Vedānta notion of *avidyā* (ignorance). In its fullest meaning, *mala* has a wide range of associations that link bodily existence, darkness, evil, and ignorance—all tied to the cosmological principle of *prakṛti,* and so connected in turn to Pārvatī. *Mala* is the "carnal residue of her existence," the auspicious dirt that is both part of her and apart from her (Kramrisch 1981, p. 320). It is auspicious dirt—polluting, yet fertile—dirt as Mary Douglas describes it in *Purity and Danger*. This *mala* is the material drawn from the boundary of the goddess's body, a fit substance for the one who himself resides at the threshold.

The second term used to refer to Gaṇeśa's bodily substance is *lepa*, meaning dirt or residue. The word also has a more specific and perhaps more primal meaning. Derived from the root *lip*, "smear," the noun *lepa* indicates that which is smeared or wiped off. In the context of Brāhmaṇic ritual, *lepa* refers to the "particles or remnants wiped off the hands after oblations to the three ancestors" (Monier-Williams, p. 902).

In the rite of *sapiṇḍīkaraṇa*, performed for the deceased ancestors of the immediate three generations past, the descendant ritualist makes "bodies" out of balls of cooked rice called *piṇḍa*. The ancestors of the fourth through seventh generations removed are not given full measure of *piṇḍa* offerings because they are already so close to heaven they need only a small amount of *piṇḍa* to sustain them successfully in the higher realms. They are given the wiping [*lepa*], what is left over from the *piṇḍas* offered to the more immediate ancestors; hence they are called *lepabhāgins*, "eaters of the left-over offerings" (Knipe, pp. 111–24). Over a period of ten days the priest builds a symbolic embryo for the deceased out of the rice ball offerings, or *piṇḍas*. On the first day the head is created, followed in successive days by the neck and shoulders, torso, limbs, genitals, and concluding with the digestive powers and thirst, enabling the ancestors to receive the food offerings from their living descendants. The similarities between Gaṇeśa's birth story and this process of piling up a symbolic body, much as the sacrificial bricks are piled up to make the body of the cosmic person [*puruṣa*], gives the story strong Vedic and Brāhmaṇic resonances.

This association of Gaṇeśa's birth and *lepa* with rites to the ancestors takes on additional significance when compared with the Vedic myth of Mārtāṇḍa, the eighth son of Aditi:

> When you gods took your places in the water with your hands joined together, a thick cloud of mist arose like dust from dancers. When you gods, like magicians, caused the worlds to swell, you

> drew forth the sun that was hidden in the ocean. Eight sons there are of Aditi, who were born from her body. With seven she went forth among the gods, but she threw Mārtāṇḍa, the sun, aside. With seven sons, Aditi went forth into the earliest age. But she bore Mārtāṇḍa so that he would in turn beget offspring and then soon die. (ṚV 10.72.6–9; O'Flaherty trans. in O'Flaherty 1981, p. 39)

The name Mārtāṇḍa means "dead in the egg" and is an epithet for the firebird of Indo-European mythology. It also refers to the sun that is born and dies in its periodic risings and settings. In this hymn, Aditi either throws Mārtāṇḍa aside when he is born or miscarries him (O'Flaherty 1981, p. 40). In one commentary on this hymn the following story is told:

> Now Aditi had eight sons; seven of them were fine but the eighth, Mārtāṇḍa, she brought forth unformed. It was only a lump of matter mixed together, as wide as it was high, the measure of a man, they said. Then the gods, the sons of Aditi said, "That which has been born after us must not be lost. Come, let's make a shape for it. So they shaped it the way a man is shaped. The flesh which they cut away and threw down became an elephant. (ŚB 3.1.3.3–5; cf. MP 102–8)

In another related myth of Mārtāṇḍa, it is said that Aditi made offerings of rice balls [*piṇḍa*] to the gods in order to obtain sons. From her first set of offerings she received three sets of twins, but, impatient for more sons, she ate the offerings before the gods could receive them. Then she had another set of twins, one of whom was Mārtāṇḍa, the one born from the egg destined for death (MS 1.6.2). In her desperate desire for sons, Aditi stole the offerings for the gods, offerings that would have been essential for the gods to lend their auspicious powers to make the creation of those sons possible. The connection between rice food for offerings and seed is implied in one Upaniṣad, which advises the husband and wife, if they wish to have a son, to eat cooked rice along with milk products (BĀU 6.4.14–16). Rice food serves as a substitute for male seed (ŚB 13.1.1.1–4). Eating it is said to increase both the production of semen in men and the likelihood of engendering male offspring (Carstairs, p. 160; Inden and Nicholas, pp. 54–55; O'Flaherty 1980, pp. 28, 257). In stealing the rice food offerings to the gods, Aditi abrogated their earlier roles in the creative process by, in effect, stealing their seed. By reversing the flow of offerings, taking rather than giving, she turned the auspicious movement to an inauspicious conclusion. In addition to performing a ritual error, she denied the gods participation in the creation of her sons. Hence, Mārtāṇḍa was made out of what came from the mother alone, the flesh; the bones, which according to the ancient Indian view are provided by the father, were missing (O'Flaherty 1980, p. 30) This left Mārtāṇḍa in the shape of a lump, "as wide as it was high." Furthermore, because the gods did not receive the rice offerings, they lacked the food from which they could make the seed that would provide Mārtāṇḍa with immortality.

As we have already seen in the myths in which Śiva creates Gaṇeśa, the assumption is that the father, through his seed, establishes the link with mortality by making the son, who is the part of himself that will be carried into the future through his descendants. In her eagerness to have a son, Aditi eats the rice offerings, an action reminiscent of the prenatal Brāhmaṇic rite of *viṣṇubali* in which the pregnant woman eats offerings of rice in the eighth month of her pregnancy to assure the birth of sons (Kane 2/2, pp. 226–27). She does what the male gods do, she eats the food, both giving and receiving. In this respect her actions resemble that of Pārvatī when she creates Gaṇeśa, taking the role of the male. Pārvatī forms this creature Gaṇeśa like a lump of matter, and his elephantine appearance recalls that of the elephant made up of pieces left over from the creation of Mārtāṇḍa.

The story of Mārtāṇḍa and the elephant-shaped leftover and that of the birth of Gaṇeśa are connected on a deeper level by the theme of the aggression of the mother against the son. Aditi condemns Mārtāṇḍa to mortality and formlessness by cheating the gods out of their rice offerings. As a consequence of this, she brings forth a son without male participation—the gods are left out and there is no seed to make Mārtāṇḍa's bones and give him immortality through descendants, both of which are carried by males. The theme of maternal aggression in the myths of Gaṇeśa is more veiled; but it is there—as we have seen in the myth where Pārvatī curses Gaṇeśa to be ugly and as we shall see in the myth where she places him at the doorway to be cut down to size by Śiva and left over in a formless pile or when she insists that the cursed sage Śani look upon Gaṇeśa even though she knows his glance will mutilate anything it strikes. The story of Aditi and

Mārtāṇḍa is the quintessential myth of maternal aggression and mutilation in the Vedic corpus, and it is also connected to the Gaṇeśa birth stories through the motifs of the creation material that is both seed and *piṇḍa* (rice offering) and the elephant that is created from the formless leftover parts of Mārtāṇḍa. Both Mārtāṇḍa and Gaṇeśa are made up out of the remainder, the leftover, which is both dangerous because of its associations with death and fertile because of its connection with the egg and birth. They emobdy the principle contained in the notion of *vāstu* or *ucchiṣṭa,* the remainder. As Shulman observes, "The remainder contains the germ of a new birth. Like leavings generally in Hinduism, the remnant of the sacrifice is impure and polluting; at the same time it is a fertilizing, life-giving substance" (pp. 90–91). Mircea Eliade makes the following observation about the more general ontological implications of such creations out of leftovers, "Creation springs forth from abundance. The gods create out of an excess of power, an overflow of energy. Creation is accomplished by a surplus of ontological substance" (p. 97). Both Śiva and Pārvatī are capable of creating Gaṇeśa without the participation of the other. As deities, each has this "surplus of ontological substance" from which to fashion additional divine beings. This metaphysical abundance overrides any gender-specific considerations so far as the intent of the myths is concerned.

These notions of sacred residue may also include that of *prāśita,* the leftover portion of food that is taken out first and eaten by the Brahmins after the gods have been fed (ĀŚS 3.1.1). When Prajāpati was committing incest with his daughter in order to create the universe, Rudra/Śiva shot him with an arrow. The gods were eager that no part of the god be lost, just as the sons of Aditi were anxious that the body of the eighth son not disappear, and so they made it the first part of the offering (GB 2.1.2). This "danger-laden morsel," as Kramrisch describes it, was so potent that it burned out the eyes of Bhaga and caused Pūṣan's teeth to fall out (ŚB 1.7.4.5–8; Kramrisch 1981, p. 326). The primacy of place given to this portion of the sacrificial offering and to Prajāpati's body suggests a connection with Gaṇeśa as the one who is worshipped first for the success of endeavors to follow. If his worship is forgotten or neglected, he also becomes "danger-laden" and withdraws his obstacle-removing powers, leaving the worshipper at the mercy of his or her own evil *karma.*

The substance out of which Gaṇeśa is made is dirt, impure and dangerous. Yet, it is powerfully auspicious, like the dung and urine of the cow, the bathwater [*tīrtha*] of deities and sages, the leftovers from the sacrifice [*ucchiṣṭa*], the remaining food offerings to the deity returned as *prasāda* to the devotees, all of which are transformed into life-giving substances by contact with deities and sacred persons. Gaṇeśa's bodily form and matter come from the residue of his mother, and this places him in a relationship of hierarchical inferiority to and dependence on her, a dependence expressed mythologically in his unwillingness to marry because no woman could be as beautiful as his mother is. Pārvatī is the only person whom he does not confront. He comes into conflict with the full array of gods—especially his father—humans, and demons, but he never crosses his mother. There are occasions in which she inflicts aggression on him, but he never initiates any toward her.

Another version of Gaṇeśa's origins is told in connection with the founding of a shrine, in a myth that combines many of the elements we have been examining:

> Gaṇeśa is the son of Śiva and Pārvatī, or rather the latter for he was produced from the unguents with which the goddess had anointed herself. With the water of her bath they were conveyed to the mouth of the Ganges and were there imbibed by Mālinī, a goddess with the head of an elephant. She gave birth to a boy who had four arms and five heads of an elephant. Gaṅgā chose him for her son, but Śiva declared him to be the son of Pārvatī. He reduced his five heads to one and enthroned him on Añjanagiri as the "remover of obstacles." (Jacobi, pp. 807–8, citing Jāyadratha's *Haracaritacintāmaṇi* 18; cf. Getty, pp. 6–7)

An elephant-headed goddess, or (possibly) a demon [*rākṣasī*], or one of the mothers attending Skanda, drinks Pārvatī's bathwater, that residue made sacred and potent by contact with her body, much as Aditi ate the rice offered to the gods to become pregnant with Mārtāṇḍa. Unfortunately for Pārvatī, the child Mālinī produces does not resemble her. As Gaṅgā and Pārvatī quarrel about who is the true mother of the child, Śiva interrupts their dispute and reduces the five heads of the child to one, as he did when he cut off Brahmā's fifth head when the latter looked lustfully at Pārvatī. Śiva then installs Gaṇeśa as the Lord over

Obstacles in the particular shrine associated with this variant of the myth.

The seed-substitute provided by Pārvatī was so potent that it produced a child who had five elephant heads to Mālinī's one; Śiva makes Pārvatī the true mother by trimming Gaṇeśa's extra heads and declaring him to belong to her. Mālinī may be seen as Pārvatī's "other" self, her female aspect, because she had taken on the role of the male in giving the seed. These two "mothers" together make up a singly androgynous parent. Śiva's part is more that of an initiator, the *ācārya,* who gives the child his social identity and instructs him in the sacred teachings and powers related to making and removing obstacles.

Gaṇeśa's birth from the dirt-seed of his mother—her impersonation of male generativity—underscores Pārvatī's fundamental androgyny. This may be why the Purāṇic tradition contains myths in which either Śiva or Pārvatī creates Gaṇeśa; each of them can operate androgynously, although the more frequently attested variants place the creative role with Pārvatī. This may be an index of the relatively late period historically in which Gaṇeśa's mythology found its way into the Purāṇic corpus—at a time when the *Śākta* notions of creative power as fundamentally feminine prevailed.

An altogether different method of creation is evident in the story of Pārvatī and the *aśoka* tree, a tale related to the Gaṇeśa birth narratives. Just after she had created Gaṇeśa, Pārvatī raised up a shoot of an *aśoka* tree with water she had herself carried from the river. Summoning the seven sages, she performed all appropriate auspicious rites. But the sages said to her, "What will be the fruit given by this tree-son which you have made?" She replied, "If a wise man digs a well in a village where there is no water, when the water appears he rejoices in heaven. But a pond is worth ten wells, a lake worth ten ponds, a daughter worth ten lakes, a sacrifice worth ten daughters, a son worth ten sacrifices, and a sacred tree [*druma*] worth ten sons (SkP 1.2.27.17–23; see also: MatsyaP 154.506–12; PP Sṛṣṭikhaṇḍa 45.449–58).

In this story the birth of Gaṇeśa apparently does not satisfy Pārvatī's longing for motherhood, perhaps because Śiva had not participated in his engendering, although he was the object of her desire. She compensates by making a son out of an *aśoka* tree, whose name means "without sorrow." When the sages mock her by asking what fruit such a tree-son will bring, she tells them that the tree has greater value even than a son. The material out of which Gaṇeśa emerges—dirt [*mala; lepa*] and wood—are those materials the makers of images use in creating the images for worship. It may be that Pārvatī cannot make a son the way humans make sons, but she does make sons the way humans make gods, forming them out of the materials of the earth and endowing them with breath and life to be fit containers for their divine presence (BDP 2.60.27–29; SkP 3.2.12.11–13). Thus though her sons are made of dirt, they have the power to give lifelike seed.

Another interpretation of this episode in the myth comes to light when examined in relation to the rituals of marriage [*vivāha-saṃskāra*]. On the first day of the marriage sequence the groom is bathed and his body rubbed with a mixture of turmeric and oil [*gātra-haridrā*]. A portion of this mixture is then sent to the bride and, after bathing, she is anointed with this substance. This action "seals out undesirable substances from their bodies and begins the process of transforming their two bodies into one by operating on the surfaces of their bodies." (Inden and Nicholas, p. 41) The *lepa* that Pārvatī uses in engendering Gaṇeśa may include this golden-colored seedlike substance that is both purifying and potent. Seen in this way, then, Gaṇeśa is actually made out of Śiva's substance mediated by Pārvatī's creative activity, just as the child is made from the father's seed mediated by the mother's womb.

The means used in Gaṇeśa's creation are as important as the substance from which his body is made. In most versions of the story, Pārvatī rubs Gaṇeśa out of the substance on the surface of her limbs. This rubbing recalls the widespread Indian tradition of creation accomplished through stirring the *soma*, and rubbing the fire sticks in Vedic sacrifice, and churning the ocean of milk in Purāṇic cosmogonies. In rubbing her limbs Pārvatī creates like a man, as when the sages churned the thigh of the wicked king Vena to create his son, the righteous king Pṛthu (O'Flaherty 1976, pp. 321–48). The association of the thigh with the phallus in the Indian tradition dates from the *Ṛg Veda* (RV 8.4.1). It may be significant that Pārvatī does *not* create Gaṇeśa by rubbing her breasts or form out of her breast milk. Indeed, in most myths Pārvatī cannot nurse children because her breast milk will poison them; although in one variant myth she does bring Gaṇeśa to life by giving him her breast after Śiva had created him in jest out of piece of her garment (BDP 2.60.27–28). Even here, however, the child she holds to her breast is doomed soon to lose his head and require Airāvata's in its place.

Another aspect of Pārvatī's creative technique also deserves attention. In several versions, Pārvatī is said to form Gaṇeśa into the shape of a man or son as though she were making a *piṇḍa* body for an ancestor or a clay image of the deity for worship, like those used by Gaṇeśa's devotees in domestic and public devotion (MatsyaP 154.501–3; SkP 3.2.12.11–12; GP 214.4 ff.). In their use of metaphors of rubbing and churning, the myths presuppose a cosmogonic and ritual setting. For both the substance and techniques involved in creating Gaṇeśa, his mythology reaches deeply into the classical Hindu imagery of creation, with its great themes of generation by stirring and churning, as well as into the patterns of ancestral worship of the Brāhmaṇic tradition, with its notions of propagative and androgynous substances. By these means the mythology of Gaṇeśa becomes woven into the larger fabric of Hindu mythology and blended into its grand design.

The Severed Head and Broken Tusk

Gaṇeśa is the elephant-headed god, made from Śiva and Pārvatī's divine substance, but he is also the beheaded god. Accounts of his decapitation or mutilation appear in nearly all the variants of his creation myths. Even where he does not literally lose his head, the loss is implied in Śiva's curse that he become ugly and have the head of an elephant because Pārvatī looks at him too lustfully (VarP 23.17–18). As with the myths of his elephantine head and the substances and methods of his creation, the stories of his beheading show variations that contain clues to Gaṇeśa's religious meaning and further display the narrative agility of the mythographers who lent their imaginations to his creation.

The Head

In many versions of the story, Pārvatī created Gaṇeśa to keep Śiva and all other potential intruders away from her bath, to protect the privacy and sanctity of her inner chamber. To that end she placed Gaṇeśa as the doorkeeper and guardian, instructing him to prohibit anyone from entering:

> Then at that time the great lord arrived and desired to enter the house. Gaṇeśa, who was standing in the doorway, did not let him in. Then the lord became angry and the two of them started to fight with each other. Gaṇeśa struck the great lord with his axe; but the great lord, raising his trident, struck off Gaṇeśa's head, which fell to the ground. When Pārvatī saw that her son had fallen to the ground in this way, she began to cry loudly. And when Gaṇeśa collapsed on the ground there arose a great lamentation throughout the whole world. When Śiva saw that Pārvatī was so bereaved, he thought to himself, "What have I done wrong?" (SkP 3.2.12.15–20; see also DP 111–16; MBhP 35)

Pārvatī makes no exceptions to Gaṇeśa's instructions to guard the door, he is to keep out *all* would-be intruders. When Śiva arrives at the door, just returning from his long period of fierce asceticism, he presents himself as more than eager to enjoy the goddess's company in the setting of her private chamber. After he and Gaṇeśa do battle, and Gaṇeśa is decapitated, Śiva pleads his own innocence when Pārvatī comes and rages at him for destroying her son. The story masks the implications of the father killing his own son by making Śiva and Gaṇeśa necessarily ignorant of one another's identity. Even when Śiva reveals to Gaṇeśa his identity as Pārvatī's husband, it does not matter because Gaṇeśa's task is to prohibit any intrusion; but Gaṇeśa does not tell Śiva that he is Pārvatī's son. It is essential that the perpetrator of the crime should not know the implication of his action. This theme of father/son aggression is one to which we shall return.

The battle between Śiva and Gaṇeśa is not only one between father and son, it also represents an extension of the tension between Śiva and Pārvatī—for Gaṇeśa acts as an extension of Pārvatī's power, just as Gaṇeśa's physical form is an extension of her form. The conflict between the two "parents" takes a richer and more detailed form in the version of the story from the *Śiva Purāṇa*. After Pārvatī made Gaṇeśa from her bodily residue [*mala*], she said to him, "You are my son, my very own. No one else belongs to me. No one else is to enter my quarters without my permission" (ŚP 2.5.3.26–28):

> When she had placed him at her doorway in this way, she went inside to take her bath. Then Śiva, who indulges in every form of play and is expert in all, arrived at her door. Gaṇādhipa [Gaṇeśa], not knowing he was the lord Śiva, said, "You cannot enter without my mother's permission. She is taking her bath. Where are you going? You must leave." And after he said this he picked up his staff and pushed Śiva back. Then Śiva, seeing all this, said, "You are a fool! Don't you know who I am? I am none other than Śiva!" But then Gaṇeśa beat him with his staff, and Śiva, who is skilled in all forms of play, became enraged and said, "You fool! Don't you even know that I am Śiva, the husband of Pārvatī? Little boy, I am going into my house, why do you block my way?" (ŚP 2.5.13.31–35)

The story continues that Śiva called together his *gaṇas* to go and ask Gaṇeśa why he had refused the husband of Pārvatī entry into her bath. They argue with him that they, not Gaṇeśa, are the real doorkeepers. Śiva orders them to remove Gaṇeśa from the doorway and a battle follows after much shouting and taunting. One of Pārvatī's servant women overhears the argument and tells Pārvatī:

> When this man who belongs to us [i.e., Gaṇeśa] is taunted, it is though we are being taunted. So, gentle lady, don't give up. Śiva always squeezes you like a crab, O Satī. What will he do now? His arrogance will turn in our favor. (ŚP 2.5.13.38–39)

Pārvatī's servant returns to Gaṇeśa and admonishes him to remain firm in his resolve to protect his mother's doorway at all costs. Śiva hardens his resolve also and he exhorts his own troops:

> "It is wrong to fight over this, for you are my own *gaṇas* and he belongs to Gaurī [Pārvatī]. But, if I back away from this fight, people will say, Śiva is always cowed by his wife. It is a serious matter to know what to do. That *gaṇa* of hers is only a child; what power could he have? Besides, you are experts in battle and you belong to me. Why should you avoid this fight and therefore be of no use to me? How can this woman be so obstinate! Especially to her husband! She is the one who has brought this on. Pārvatī will indeed reap the results of her action." (ŚP 2.5.14.57–61)

The battle resumes, with each side hardened in its determination to prevail over the other. Unable to dislodge the mighty staff-wielding Gaṇeśa, Śiva's *gaṇas,* led by Nandin and Bhṛngin, are repulsed. Śiva realizes that Gaṇeśa can be destroyed only by some act of deception. At that moment the other gods arrive and Śiva sends Brahmā to propitiate Gaṇeśa, but he too is violently rebuffed. After repeated attacks by both Śiva and Viṣṇu, Gaṇeśa begins to weaken. Then in a final moment just as Gaṇeśa knocks Viṣṇu down, Śiva sneaks around behind and standing to the north of Gaṇeśa cuts off his head with his trident. At that moment Pārvatī, seeing what stroke of ill fortune has befallen her son, flies into a rage. Determined to destroy all the gods and other creatures in retaliation, she calls together her army of *śaktis*. Only after the most strenuous efforts at propitiation and the promise that he will restore Gaṇeśa's severed head and appoint him as the chief over his *gaṇas* does Śiva manage to cool Pārvatī's wrath and save the gods from fiery destruction. Śiva orders his *gaṇas* to go to the north and return with the head of whatever one they find there (which happens to be an elephant) and to fit it onto the lifeless shoulders of the fallen Gaṇeśa. Śiva revives Gaṇeśa by giving him his own energy [*tejas*] and recites Vedic *mantras* to bring him back to life. When Pārvatī sees that her son has been restored, she promises that Gaṇeśa shall receive the worship of all and remove all obstacles (ŚP 2.4.15–18).

In this more elaborate account of Gaṇeśa's battle at the threshold of Pārvatī's bath and his beheading and restoration, the conflict between Śiva and Pārvatī serves as the context for Gaṇeśa's creation, destruction, and resuscitation. Pārvatī wants to protect the access to her inner chambers. Her bath symbolizes the locus of power associated with her sexuality, her *śakti;* were Śiva to enter and take possession of it, the distinction between them—the distinction essential to maintaining the world—would be lost. Her bath also has associations with the inner sanctum of her shrine, that place where, in the form of her image, she resides on her throne and receives the purifying and satisfying baths from her priests. It is understandable that she would seek to protect the boundaries of this center of power from defilement by outsiders. But in making Gaṇeśa—the one born of her own auspicious impurity—her guardian, she puts him in jeopardy and makes him vulnerable to Śiva's inevitable conquest. As the doorkeeper [*dvārapāla*], Gaṇeśa represents the dangerous transition from the profane world to the inner sacred enclosure. Although Pārvatī contributes to Gaṇeśa's mutilation by placing him at the liminal threshold where he must battle the mighty Śiva, she also sets the stage for his ultimate elevation to the rank of lord over Śiva's army of *gaṇas,* empowered to place and remove obstacles and receive the first offerings from devotees in worship.

The figure of the doorkeeper is prominent in the mythology of Śiva. Doorkeepers appear as Śiva's sons, like Vīraka, Gaṇeśa, and Nandin, although they may work for him or against him. They often protect Śiva or Śiva and Pārvatī together, but they also attack them, as we have seen in the episode at Pārvatī's door. From the point of view of the devotee who wishes to enter into the presence of the deity in the shrine, the doorkeeper is a potential threat as the one who may prevent intrusion into the sublime world of the deity's private territory. The doorkeeper's task is to prevent the deity and devotee from coming into contact, to protect the former from interruption, and to keep the devotee out. But the deity cannot remain aloof from the devotee; there must be an intrusion. The doorkeeper is caught in the middle. He is destined to be mutilated and defeated. But the fate of the doorkeeper is double. He may suffer separation of head from body, but he also experiences union with god. Gaṇeśa is beheaded, but he is restored to a better position than he had when he was created. O'Flaherty describes the double role of the doorkeeper this way:

> Ultimately, therefore, the doorkeeper symbolizes danger to the worshipper about to enter the temple . . . as well as the assurance that he will ultimately reach his god. Though the doorkeeper or interloper is often mutilated, he is restored. . . . It is, in any case, the head of the doorkeeper who survives despite his mutilation—indeed who becomes immortal because of it, remaining at his post to warn the would-be interloper of the dangers and rewards in what he is about to undertake. (Berkson, p. 30)

This encounter between Śiva and Gaṇeśa at the threshold recalls another tale of Śiva and Pārvatī's quarrels in which Vīraka, Śiva's doorkeeper and Pārvatī's stepson, plays a role:

> Once in jest Śiva called Pārvatī "Blackie" [*Kālī*] because her skin looked black like a serpent. She was offended by his remark, and so went away to practice asceticism to obtain a golden skin. Vīraka, Śiva's doorkeeper, begged her to take him with her, because he feared that Śiva might vent on him his rage at Pārvatī's

leaving. But she told him to stay at Śiva's door and guard it so that no other woman could enter, for Śiva is a notorious womanizer. Vīraka remained at Śiva's door, obeying his mother Pārvatī. As she was leaving, another goddess, Kusumāmodinī, appeared before her, and Pārvatī instructed her to tell her if any other woman went to Śiva's door.

Then the demon Āḍi saw that Pārvatī had left, and remembering the hatred between his father, Andhaka, and Śiva, he practiced asceticism until he received a boon from Brahmā that he would remain immortal so long as he never changed his form. Then the demon went to where Śiva was, and seeing Vīraka at the door, he took the form of a serpent and slipped past the guard unnoticed. Then he took the form of Pārvatī and placed teeth like thunderbolts in his vagina and went to seduce Śiva. But Śiva became suspicious and realized that it was a demon in disguise. So, laughing to himself, he placed a weapon on his phallus and satisfied the demon's lust as he screamed in terrible pain and died.

In the meantime, Kusamāmodinī, not knowing that the woman with Śiva was the demon Āḍi in disguise, went and told Pārvatī that Śiva was committing adultery. Enraged that Vīraka had failed to keep watch at the gate, Pārvatī said to him, "Since you have abandoned me I will turn you into a stone marked with the syllable [*mantra*] of Gaṇeśa [i.e., *Oṃ*]." Her anger was so great that a fierce lion appeared from her forehead, which attracted Brahmā's attention. When she told him that Śiva had called her "Black," Brahmā gave her the boon of a golden skin and transformed the lion into her vehicle. Then she became filled with remorse for abandoning her husband, and returned to Śiva. When Vīraka saw her coming he did not recognize her in her new golden form, and kept her from entering Śiva's palace. He said, "A demon in the form of a goddess has entered here unnoticed in order to stay with the god, but Śiva destroyed him. He reprimanded me that I should not let any woman get past me. Only my mother can come in." Then Pārvatī was overcome with grief when she realized she had cursed Vīraka unjustly, but she was unable to take back her curse. However, she did tell Vīraka that he would be reborn as Nandin and become the guardian of Śiva's door. (SkP 1.2.27–29; cf. MatsyaP 154.542–78. See also Kramrisch 1981, pp. 364–65; O'Flaherty 1975, pp. 252–61)

In the story of Vīraka, most of the elements present in the Gaṇeśa myth are reversed. Whereas Pārvatī creates Gaṇeśa to protect her from Śiva's intrusions, here she orders Vīraka to spy on Śiva to see if he is letting other women into his private chambers. The demon Āḍi sneaks past Vīraka, disguised as a serpent, and then masquerades as Pārvatī, who wrongly concludes that Śiva is behaving adulterously and that Vīraka has switched allegiance from her and conspired to protect Śiva. She feels doubly abandoned, both by husband and son. In her sorrow and rage she curses Vīraka to be abandoned as she turns him into a stone, a stone nevertheless bearing the auspicious mark of Gaṇeśa. Brahmā appears and explains to her that she has cursed Vīraka unjustly. It is too late to undo the damage, but Pārvatī does manage to modify the curse and turns Vīraka into Nandin, thereby enabling him to remain close to his lord as his chief *gaṇa* and beloved disciple. In this myth it is Pārvatī rather than Śiva who stands outside the threshold seeking entry, and Vīraka fails to recognize her, just as Gaṇeśa does not recognize Śiva in other myths. She transforms Vīraka into Nandin, recreating him in the form of an animal, partly to remove the force of the curse, and thus she repairs the separation between her and Vīraka by keeping him in the doorway. Śiva does similar things with Gaṇeśa in other tales when he puts him back together with the head of an elephant. The body is separated from its head by Śiva, a loss that is not fully restored. But Gaṇeśa remains visible in his new and modified form as the elephant-headed doorkeeper.

The story of the beheading and restoration of Gaṇeśa receives a different emphasis in two related myths. His role as Pārvatī's infant son is the point of departure in both stories. According to one version, Śiva created Gaṇeśa out of a piece of Pārvatī's garment as a mock-child when she had pleaded with him to conceive a child with her. But she held the child to her breast and he was brought to life through the touch of her breast milk. Astonished that her magic was as impressive as his own, Śiva said to Pārvatī:

> "Goddess, I gave you that son who was made out of cloth as a joke, but through your good fortune he became a real son. What is this miracle? Give him to me and let me look at him. He is a real son indeed, even though he is made from cloth. But how did life enter into it?" As he said this, Śambhu [Śiva], lord of the mountain, took his son in his hands and laid him down, examining him carefully and thoroughly checking all his limbs. Then, remembering the flaw from his birth, Śaṅkara [Śiva] said to the goddess, "This son of yours was born with an injury brought about by Śani,

the planet of suicides. He will not live long, but an auspicious death will come to him quickly. The death of a virtuous one causes great sorrow."

As Śambhu, the maker of the child, said this, the boy's head, which was pointing to the north, fell from his hand. When the little boy's head had fallen to the ground from her husband's hand, Pārvatī was overwhelmed with grief. She picked up the body whose head had been cut off and cried, "My baby, my little baby!" Astonished at this, Śiva took his son's head in his hand and said sweetly to the goddess, "Do not cry, lovely Pārvatī, though you grieve for your son. No grief is greater than that for a son, but nothing so withers the soul. Stop your sorrowing. I will bring him back to life. Goddess, join his head onto his shoulders." And so Pārvatī joined that head on as he had told her to do, but it did not join properly. Then Śiva thought about this, and at that instant a voice from the sky said, "Śambhu, this head of your son has been injured by a harmful glance; therefore your little boy will not live with this head. Put the head of someone else on his shoulders and revive him. Since you held the boy in your hand with his head facing north, fetch the head of someone who is facing north and join it to him." When Śaṅkara heard this voice from the sky, he consoled the goddess and called Nandin and sent him out to find the suitable head. (BDP 2.60.35–50)

In this story, the son whom Pārvatī had wanted to fulfill her maternal longings and whom Śiva had created as a joke, himself becomes the victim of an even crueler joke. When Pārvatī brings him to life and hands him to Śiva, who inspects him for auspicious marks, he tells her of the curse of Śani, who, according to Hindu astrology, is the bringer of misfortune if he appears on one's astrological chart. The myth attempts to shift the blame from Śiva onto the fate inherent in the constellation of forces apparent at Gaṇeśa's birth. Among Tamil-speaking Hindus of Sri Lanka, it is believed that only Śiva has the power to counter the destructive influence of Śani (Pfaffenberger, p. 261). Hence in both these myths Śani acts as Śiva's destructive "other" self. Śani does the beheading and Śiva can appear in his own form as the one who restores Gaṇeśa to life. Although the myth tries to blame Śani for Gaṇeśa's beheading, it is Śiva's fateful touch that causes the head to sever. When all efforts at repair fail, a mysterious voice from the sky announces that Gaṇeśa is fated to have the head of another, one whose head, like Gaṇeśa's at the moment of its fall from Śiva's hand, is pointing to the north, the auspicious direction. Śiva then dispatches Nandin to find the appropriate head, which as we have seen, turns out to be that of Airāvata, Indra's elephant vehicle.

This story wrestles with a contradiction. Gaṇeśa cannot keep his original form; it simply will not hold together. The head and the body, once severed, cannot be reunited; but the story is reluctant to blame Śiva for the beheading and transfers the problem to Śani and a fate ordained for Gaṇeśa before his birth. But Gaṇeśa's fate to be beheaded still lies in Śiva's hands, for it is his touch that precipitates the decapitation. In the earlier myth Śiva beheaded Gaṇeśa because of the doorkeeper's refusal to let him inside Pārvatī's bath, but here Śani, the personification of astrological or karmic fate, takes Śiva's role. The fact that it is Śiva who orders Nandin to return with a suitable head gives away his complicity in the beheading even though the myth is unwilling to acknowledge it directly and tries to conceal Śiva's aggressive action by invoking the preexisting fate decreeing that Gaṇeśa must lose his original head and get a new one. The new elephant head is his "real" head, the one he is ordained in the story to receive. It is the head displayed in his iconography. The elephant head is the one that expresses his true nature. Indeed, the myth might be read as the story of how he became completed by receiving his true and appropriate head. Viewed this way, then his first head, the one that gets cut off, is the mask that has to be removed through beheading to enable him to reveal his real head. Thus Gaṇeśa's dismemberment becomes the violently auspicious prelude to the completion of the god's form through which he graciously appears to his devotees. The pursuit of the "real" head recalls the Vedic myth of Dadhyañc, the priest who knew the secret of how to bring the sacrifice to successful completion. Indra threatened Dadhyañc that if he ever told this secret to anyone, he would cut off Dadhyañc's head. The Aśvins, the horse-headed twins, overheard Indra's remark and came to Dadhyañc asking to be initiated as his pupils in order to learn the secret of the sacrifice. Dadhyañc told them of Indra's threat, but they replied that they would cut off Dadhyañc's head and hide it from Indra, replacing this secret-knowing head with that of a horse. Dadhyañc agreed and told them the secret. Then, when Indra returned and beheaded Dadhyañc's horse head, the Aśvin's replaced the horse head with Dadhyañc's original head (ŚB 14.1.1.18–24). In this way Dadhyañc's "real" head, the one knowing the secret of the sacrifice's power, was actually the head that replaced the head decapitated by Indra. This ancient myth of Dadhyañc's beheading and restoration by Indra provides the narrative architecture that later on was possibly the pattern for the various myths of Gaṇeśa's beheading and restoration.

Śani's role in Gaṇeśa's dismemberment comes into focus more clearly in the second myth. Like the story we have just examined, this variant portrays Gaṇeśa as the passive infant who is the victim of a terrible deed. In this heavily Vaiṣṇava rendering of the story, in which Gaṇeśa is actually an incarnation of Kṛṣṇa, the beheading episode opens with Pārvatī and Gaṇeśa assembled with the other deities, presumably for the rite of *nāmakaraṇa saṃskāra*—the life-cycle rite in which the child is given his name:

> Then the great ascetic Śani, the son of Sūrya, arrived there. He came to pay homage to the new son of Pārvatī, and said to Viśālākṣa, the doorkeeper, "Servant of Śiva, I have come here at the command and invitation of Viṣṇu and the other deities to look upon the child of Pārvatī and pay homage to her. When I have seen the child in her presence I shall return home." Viśālākṣa obtained Pārvatī's permission for him [Śani] to enter, and Śani came in to where the goddess and child were, but he kept his eyes cast down. Pārvatī said, "Why, O lord of the planets, do you keep your head down, why won't you look at me or my son?"
>
> Śani explained to her that he had been a devotee of Kṛṣṇa for his whole life, always keeping him in the forefront of his mind. His father arranged for him to marry the daughter of Citraratha, but he and his wife both remained celibate and performed asceticism. "But once," Śani said, "this enchantress of the minds of sages [i.e., his wife] adorned herself richly in jewels and came to me when she had finished her bath. When she saw that I was engaged in meditation at the feet of Viṣṇu, she smiled and rolled her eyes flirtatiously, desiring to make love with me. But when she saw that I was absorbed in my asceticism and not aware of anything else, she realized that her fertile time would pass unfulfilled, and so she cursed me, saying, 'You don't even look at me out of concern for my time of fertility. Therefore anything you look upon will become destroyed.' When I completed my asceticism I did make love with her but she was unable to take back the curse although she

wanted to. Since then, because of fear of harming living things, I keep my head hung down, not looking at anyone."

Pārvatī and her attendants laughed mockingly at Śani and she demanded that he look upon her child. And so, with great fear, and only out of the corner of his eye, Śani gave a quick glance at the child's face. But instantly his glance severed the child's head and that headless body lay in Pārvatī's lap covered with blood, and then the head went up to Goloka and united with Kṛṣṇa. (BVP 3.11.10–3.12.7)

In this version of the story the onus of Gaṇeśa's beheading undeniably rests on Śani, but here too there are complications in blaming him. His decapitating glance resulted from his wife's curse when he had attended more to his asceticism than to his conjugal duties and enjoyments. His predicament parallels that of Śiva, who had likewise refused his wife's entreaties to become a father. The destructive force wielded by Śani's glance is reminiscent of Śiva's capacity to mutilate his opponents when he does not want to be disturbed from his meditations by erotic distractions, an awesome power that he unleashes on Kāma and other interlopers. Here Śani carries the blame for Gaṇeśa's beheading; other versions reluctantly admit it was really Śiva.

As the story continues, there is an attempt to compensate Śani for his destructive role and also to express concern for the elephant whose head was taken to provide Gaṇeśa with a replacement. After Viṣṇu beheaded Gajendra and took his head for Gaṇeśa, the elephant-king cried out in grief. Moved by compassion for her loss, Viṣṇu, "separating the body from the head of another elephant, joined it onto this elephant [Gajendra] and brought him back to life with his brahma-knowledge" (BVP 3.12.15–16). Just as the myth shifts the blame for Gaṇeśa's decapitation from Śiva onto his surrogate Śani and then to his wife, it tries to resolve the moral dilemma of sacrificing an innocent elephant to replace the head that replaced Gaṇeśa's original head. It invokes the principle of the chain of *karma,* raising the possibility that past deeds lie behind that unfortunate elephant's beheading. Therein, potentially at least, lies another tale. One's gain is another's loss. Although Śiva remains in the background in this version of the story, the conflict between Śani and his wife parallels that of Śiva and Pārvatī, thus the structure of the story remains constant, although the names are changed to protect the guilty.

The motif of displacing the blame for Gaṇeśa's beheading is continued in this myth. After Gaṇeśa is restored with his new elephant head, Pārvatī curses Śani to be lame:

> But Yama and the other gods objected to her, saying that Śani was under a curse and she insisted that he look on her child. Therefore Śani had committed no sin and Pārvatī was wrong to curse him. Yama threatened even to curse Pārvatī in return, but Brahmā insisted that Pārvatī's curse was done out of female fickleness and anger. Pārvatī then realized that Śani was innocent but she could not take back the curse, and so Śani remained lame. (BVP 3.12.40–58)

Yama, the lord of the dead, led the others in coming to Śani's defense. Yama had himself been cursed to be lame by the shadow form of his mother when he had protested that she neglected him in favor of the other children (MP 105.1–30; cf. O'Flaherty 1980, pp. 180–85). His story is the reverse of Śani's, who is cursed because he neglected his wife. Yama and the other gods remind Pārvatī that it was she who compelled Śani to look on Gaṇeśa even though he had warned her about the curse. She contributed to Gaṇeśa's mutilation, just as she did when she placed him in the doorway to confront Śiva. But the myth is not content to leave the blame with the mother goddess. Brahmā steps in to shift the onus onto "nature" and "female fickleness and anger"—the misogynist solution: blame the woman! Even when Pārvatī does recognize that she was wrong to be angry toward Śani, she is unable to rescind the curse; the word once spoken, like the seed once planted, cannot be taken back, fate must have its day. She is like the wife of Śani who was unable to undo her curse even after he had met his marital obligations as she demanded. In one way or another everyone in the story stands under a curse—it is a situation that unites all the characters.

The story draws on the larger theme of mutilation by the female/mother figure—dismemberments, symbolic castrations—such as we saw at work in the case of Aditi/Mārtāṇḍa. The mutilations occur in response to some kind of abandonment: wife by husband, son by mother. Gaṇeśa and Śani, not to mention Gajendra, are victims of female erotic desire. Śani had failed to satisfy his wife's erotic desires, just as Śiva had failed Pārvatī when they were interrupted by the gods disguised as mendicants; in both cases the forces of ascetic restraint won out over erotic desire, but at a cost. Only Gajendra is the true victim, for he had satisfied his wife but was beheaded anyway at the moment just after he had fulfilled his conjugal role. He is the true sacrificial victim, the one whose dismemberment enables the reintegration of a being of greater significance in the scheme of things. Gajendra receives full restoration when Viṣṇu replaces his head with one identical to his original one. Gaṇeśa's elephant head is a permanent reminder of his beheading, thus only a partial restoration. Śani's lameness is mollified but never fully healed, and so he is left to limp like Yama for the rest of his days.

In these variations of the myth of Gaṇeśa, the forces of maternal desire for procreation come into conflict with those of ascetic withdrawal. Once Gaṇeśa comes into the story and his birth is accomplished, he finds himself in the middle, in the liminal territory of the doorway. Whether his father Śiva, the surrogate ascetic Śani, or the movements of fate cause his decapitation, it is inevitable that the marks he must carry as the visible emblem of that conflict be applied.

The Tusk

Gaṇeśa's mutilation takes a different form in the myth in which he loses his tusk in battle with Paraśurāma, the son of Jamadagni, as he stands at the threshold guarding *both* his parents, who are inside making love. As in the other stories, Gaṇeśa falls victim to excessive and intrusive power, and as elsewhere Śiva's hand can be seen at work in the background. The episode begins with Paraśurāma returning from defeating the sons of Kārtavīrya and their demon army, whom he had slain with the aid of an axe Śiva had given him with the boon that it would never be used in vain:

> There Paraśurāma saw Śiva's palace, surrounded by all the universes, and at the eastern gate he saw Skanda standing on the left and Vināyaka [Gaṇeśa] on the right, adorned with jewels and sitting on seats studded with precious gems. He bowed to those two, whose valor was like that of Śiva himself, and the two guardians gathered around him. As Paraśurāma was about the enter the palace Gaṇeśa said to him, "Wait, the Lord is in there sleeping with Umā; I will ask their permission and then take you in there

with me. Wait a moment, brother." When Paraśurāma heard this, being in a hurry, he said, "As soon as I have gone inside and paid homage to these two parents of the universe, I will return immediately to my own palace. It was because of Śiva's power that I have been able to slay the many armies of demons which were strong in their powers of delusion." Then Gaṇeśa replied, "You will have your audience, but today the Lord is in there with the goddess. You see, when a man and a woman are having intercourse, whoever disturbs their pleasure will surely go to hell—especially when it is one's parents, or guru, king, or twice-born, when they are making love in private. Anyone who sees someone else's lovemaking will certainly lose his own wife for seven births. And whoever sees the buttocks, breasts, or face of someone else's wife, mother, sister, or daughter is the worst kind of person."

Paraśurāma replied, "Don't you think I know that? Have you lost your senses, are you just trying to make some kind of joke, or did those words just slip out of your mouth? This injunction from the Śāstras is meant for those who are unstable and filled with lust; but there is no sin for a child or one who is without desire. So, I will go into their bedroom, and you, little boy, can stay here! I will do the proper thing. You say it is *your* parents who are in there, but Śiva and Pārvatī are the father and mother of the whole world." When he had said this, Paraśurāma prepared to go in, but Gaṇeśa immediately jumped up and blocked his way.

Then a battle of words arose between them and they began to push and shove each other with their hands. Skanda saw them fighting and tried to push them apart. But Paraśurāma, the destroyer of the prowess of his foes, became very angry at Gaṇeśa. He picked up his axe and got ready to throw it. When Gaṇeśa saw this he quickly lifted him up with his trunk, lowering him down through the seven regions of the world and finally down to the ocean at the innermost part of the earth, until Paraśurāma became so frightened he wanted to die. Then Gaṇeśa returned him to where they were standing, but because he had been whirled around in this way he was convinced he had been defeated. Then, when Paraśurāma saw that Gaṇeśa was still standing there looking unruffled, he flew into a rage and threw his axe at him. When Gaṇeśa saw the axe coming toward him and saw it to be the very same axe which his father had given to Paraśurāma, he did not want its throwing to be in vain, so he took the blow of the axe on his left tusk.

When the tusk fell to the ground all the worlds shattered and trembled with fear. There arose a great commotion as the gods in

> heaven stood by and watched. Skanda and the others cried out in distress. Then Śiva and Pārvatī, who heard the noise from the falling of the tusk, came there also. Pārvatī asked what had happened. Skanda explained it to her as Paraśurāma listened. Then Pārvatī became angry and turned to Śiva, saying, "This Paraśurāma, your disciple, is more like a son to you. You gave him this axe by which he conquered the whole world. Now that he has completed it, he has even given you Gaṇeśa's tusk as a payment [*dakṣiṇā*]. So now your work is completed, there is no doubt. Then you take care of him, this Paraśurāma, your worthiest disciple, for you are his great guru and he will do your housework. I won't stay here a moment longer. I will take my two sons and go to my father's house. Virtuous people take better care of their slaves than you do of me. You have not said even one thing in defense of your own son." When Pārvatī had finished speaking in this way, Śiva remained silent. (BrP 2.3.41.30–2.3.43.42; cf. BVP 3.41–45)

This myth rearranges a number of elements we have seen at work in other stories of Gaṇeśa's beheading. In the other myths Gaṇeśa stands at the threshold of the bath to keep Śiva and Pārvatī separated, but here his job is to keep them together, to prevent any interruption of their union. This time the intruder is Paraśurāma who has come to honor Śiva for lending the saving power of the weapon that enabled him to defeat the demon enemies, much as a devotee might come to a shrine to thank Śiva for the power enabling him to flourish in the world and stave off evil influences. Although it is Paraśurāma who finally cuts off Gaṇeśa's tusk—an act that rattles the cosmos and that succeeds finally in interrupting his parents, just as Gaṇeśa's beheading by Śiva had brought Pārvatī out of her private quarters—he does so with Śiva's axe. In this way Paraśurāma and Śiva, explicitly or implicitly, deny Gaṇeśa's status as Śiva's son. Paraśurāma argues at the doorway that Śiva and Pārvatī are the parents of all the world and therefore Gaṇeśa has no privileged claim as their son; Pārvatī castigates Śiva for not coming to Gaṇeśa's aid, commenting with bitter sarcasm that Paraśurāma is the real son because he wields the emblem of his father's masculine power, his mighty staff. Each of these events: the gate-crashing interruption of Śiva and Pārvatī's erotic play, Śiva's denial of Gaṇeśa, and Pārvatī's departure serve to undermine the cozy, familial atmosphere in which the myth opened.

In having Paraśurāma come to Śiva's door to pay him homage for the gift of the magic axe, this myth reverses a pattern we have seen elsewhere when the gods interrupt Śiva and Pārvatī's lovemaking. Here Paraśurāma arrives at the end of the cycle of chaos and the rule of demons, and the celebration of the axe represents the affirmation of order, whereas in the previous myths the gods seek to prevent the onset of chaos that would result either from Śiva and Pārvatī's prolonged lovemaking or from the birth of the child who could combine the full force of their respective powers. Paraśurāma's conflict with Gaṇeśa at the doorway consists of a series of denials. He denies that Gaṇeśa has legitimate authority to prevent him from gaining access to Śiva and Pārvatī, which is parallel to Śiva's failure to recognize Gaṇeśa when he encountered him at the threshold of Pārvatī's bath. Paraśurāma denies Gaṇeśa's sonship by claiming that all beings are Śiva and Pārvatī's children. When Gaṇeśa invokes the rules of the Śāstras regarding the consequences of voyeurism on one's own family, especially one's mother while engaged in sexual intercourse, Paraśurāma mockingly claims that he is both their child and one who is free from lust and therefore exempt from such restraints. These denials reverse the argument Śiva makes to Gaṇeśa in other versions of the story in which he shouts at him, "Don't you know who I am?" Thus claiming himself to be an exception to Pārvatī's order that Gaṇeśa prohibit all intruders from entry.

In this myth the breaking of the tusk replaces the beheading scene. The story either assumes that the beheading and restoration has already happened or that Gaṇeśa was created with his elephant-headed form already in place. As with his beheading in the other myth variants we have examined, Gaṇeśa accepts his dismemberment as a divine necessity. He accepts his own mutilation in the conviction that Śiva's axe must never miss its mark; as in the other beheading stories, he places obedience to Pārvatī's command above his own safety.

The issue of Śiva's fatherhood arises in a number of ways in this myth. Pārvatī chastises Śiva for failing to come to Gaṇeśa's defense, preferring his devotee Paraśurāma to his own son. She ironically calls Gaṇeśa's broken and bloody tusk Paraśurāma's *dakṣiṇā,* the gift or payment the disciple offers his guru. The tusk serves as Paraśurāma's trophy from his conquest at the threshold-turned-battlefield, which he offers up to Śiva as an emblem of his devotion and in gratitude for giving him the weapon with which he could seize such a prize. Pārvatī interprets Śiva's preference for Paraśurāma to mean that he prefers this relationship of discipleship—forged in the ascetic world and symbolized in the axe/staff given to Paraśurāma as the guru gives a staff to his disciple on initiating him into the stage of studenthood during the ritual of the investiture of the sacred thread [*upanayana*]—to the father/son relationship within the world of the householder. This apparent demonstration that Śiva's ascetic orientation is stronger than his family ties, together with his abandonment of Gaṇeśa, provokes Pārvatī to leave Śiva and, taking her children with her, return to her father's house where the loyalties of kinship will not be undervalued. So the myth comes around full circle. Attempting to protect Śiva and Pārvatī's private world, the doorkeeper Gaṇeśa loses the battle to the intruder, who mutilates him and provokes the dissolution of the divine household. As a result of the battle at the threshold and Gaṇeśa's mutilation, Śiva and Paraśurāma move to one side and Pārvatī and Gaṇeśa to the other. But the myth appears to be uncomfortable with this conclusion and seeks to give it a happy ending. Later in the story Kṛṣṇa arrives with Rādhā, and they both give off such lustrous energy [*tejas*] that Śiva and Paraśurāma are drawn to it. Kṛṣṇa persuades Pārvatī to forgive Paraśurāma, much as the gods attempted to convince her to take back her curse on Śani in the earlier myth. The tension dissolves in an elaborate dance in which sons and disciples move from one parent's lap to another to the accompaniment of metaphysical music:

> When she heard Kṛṣṇa's words, Pārvatī was astonished. Then Rādhā said, "Matter [*prakṛti*] and spirit [*puruṣa*] are entangled in one another, although in the world they appear as separate. Between you and me there is not the slightest distinction. You are Viṣṇu and I am Śiva, who have become split apart. Viṣṇu has taken your form and dwells in Viṣṇu's heart. Paraśurāma was born from Viṣṇu [i.e., become his *āvatāra*] but is a devotee of Śiva. Gaṇeśa, who is Śiva incarnate, has become a devotee of Viṣṇu. There is no distinction to be found between our husbands." When she had said this, Rādhā lifted Gaṇeśa onto her lap, and smelling his head and touching his wounded cheek she healed him immediately. Happy and put at ease by Rādhā, Pārvatī picked up Paraśurāma, who had fallen contritely at her feet. When Kṛṣṇa saw how those two

> women embraced Gaṇeśa and Paraśurāma, lovingly he picked up Skanda and placed him on his own lap. Then Śiva, who was delighted by all this, honored Kṛṣṇa and took him into his lap. (BrP 2.3.42.46–56)

This version of the reconciliation between Śiva and Pārvatī after Gaṇeśa's mutilation appears to parallel those in which Śiva finally recognizes Gaṇeśa as his son and adopts him to be the leader of his *gaṇas*. Although the wound can be healed, the tusk, like the first head, cannot be replaced. It has become forever separated. Repair and reconciliation mark the end of the story, but the traces of the breach in the form of something that is missing—the tusk—or something brought in from somewhere else—the elephant head—remain as an essential reminder that in the midst of wholeness and tranquility there is an inevitable and necessary breach.

The two forms of mutilation, beheading and detusking, come together in another myth about a battle between Śiva and Gaṇeśa:

> Once there was a battle between Śiva and Gaṇeśa which had continued for a long time without interruption. When Śiva, who was mounted on an elephant and unconquerable, saw that Gaṇeśa was made out of matter [*prakṛti*] and filled with ignorance, he knocked him down along with the elephant he was riding. Then Pārvatī praised Śiva, the conqueror of enemies, and asked him for a boon. "This one whom you have killed is indeed my son, there is no doubt. But he did not recognize you because he was made of matter. So bring him back to life in order to please me." Then the great Rudra smiled at her and brought life back into Pārvatī's son. He joined the head of an elephant to where his head had been cut off, and so it was that Gajānana (Gaṇeśa) came into being through the grace of Śiva. Although he was the son of Māyā (Pārvatī) he became one who was without illusion [*nirmāyā*]. In order to have an ascetic's staff he pulled out one of his own large tusks. Then Śiva made him the leader of his *gaṇas*, all obstacles and other powers. (SkP 1.1.10.29–38)

Set within the framework of Sāṁkhya philosophical categories, this myth combines elements from others we have already examined. This time the battle between Śiva and Gaṇeśa is reminiscent of the conflict between Śiva and the elephant demon Gajāsura. The story does not say when the battle was taking place, simply that it had been going on for a long time, like the battle between the gods and demons, a conflict inherent in the universe itself. The beheading and restoration with the elephant head follows the patterns by now familiar, although here the quest for the new head drops out of the story. The issue of blame for Gaṇeśa's mutilation is resolved differently here when we are told that Gaṇeśa failed to recognize Śiva because he was made of matter [*prakṛti*], presumably the matter of his mother's bodily dirt. His eyes were filled with darkness [*tamas*], making him unable to recognize his father. Pārvatī carefully disguises her outrage at Gaṇeśa's dismemberment behind her gesture of praise to Śiva for his victory, and it only comes out in the form of a request for a boon for her devotion: she tells Śiva to restore Gaṇeśa to life. This variant of the beheading tale introduces the act of self-mutilation by which Gaṇeśa tears out his own tusk and holds it like a yogin's staff, like his father holds his trident. The gesture is reminiscent of the time his father broke off his own phallus when he saw it was no longer of use except to create progeny (KP 2.37; O'Flaherty 1975, pp. 137–41). This act of self mutilation makes Gaṇeśa more like his father.

As a weapon of conquest, analogous to the axe that Paraśurāma received from Śiva to cut off Gaṇeśa's tusk, the tusk is prominent in two myths involving implicit beheadings in which Gaṇeśa comes out the winner. The first is a South Indian myth about Gaṇeśa's battle with Gajāsura, the elephant demon:

> Gajāsura had obtained the privilege of not being killed by a beast, a man, a god, or a demon. Pulliar [Gaṇeśa] not being one of these, as he was half god, half elephant, was the only one who could deal with him victoriously. The giant broke off the god's right tusk, but Pulliar, using it as a javelin, transfixed Gajamukha [Gajāsura], who transformed himself into a rat and became the vehicle of the god. (Jouveau-Dubreuil, pp. 41–42; cf. Getty, p. 15; GP 2.134)

In this myth, which is itself a transformation of the myth of Gaṇeśa's beheading by Śiva and recalls Śiva's murder and restoration to discipleship of the demon Āḍi, Gaṇeśa uses his tusk to transform the elephant-demon adversary into a rat vehicle, to trim him down to size. The story is interesting when looked at in relation to the Śiva-Gajāsura-Gaṇeśa cycle of myths. Śiva defeated Gajāsura, whose head was taken to replace Gaṇeśa's original one. Gajāsura now appears in the above myth as Gaṇeśa's enemy and is transformed through mutilation into his vehicle. Gaṇeśa's rat vehicle is thus really the elephant demon whose head belongs to Gaṇeśa. By the chain of transpositions forming this garland of heads, these three characters are indissolubly linked together as transformations one of another.

The second myth of the tusk acting as a weapon places the conflict between Gaṇeśa and the moon, when the moon saw him in a compromising situation:

> Once Gaṇeśa received innumerable sweets [*modaka*] from his devotees which he ate until his belly became large and distended. Then, mounting his rat he proceeded home. Suddenly a serpent crossed the road in front of the rat. Drawing back in fright, the rat knocked Gaṇeśa down, causing his belly to split open and all the sweets to roll out on the ground in all directions. Gaṇeśa gathered up all the sweets and killed the serpent, taking its body and tying up his belly with it. The moon, who had been watching all this, laughed out loud uproariously, which made Gaṇeśa furious. So he pulled out one of his tusks and threw it at the moon, which caused darkness all over the earth. The gods became distressed at this and pleaded with Gaṇeśa to restore the moon and take back his tusk. But Gaṇeśa agreed to do so only on the condition that the moon gain and lose its light by waxing and waning each month. (Getty, p. 20; cf. T. A. Gopinatha Rao, vol. 1/1, p. 51; Russell and Lal, vol. 4, pp. 39–40)

This myth rearranges many of the elements we have seen in other variants. The myth opens with Gaṇeśa already fused in his elephant-headed form and suffering from too much of a good thing: he had filled his belly to overflowing and has satiated his legendary appetite for oral gratification. This situation roughly parallels the pursuit of genital gratification between Śiva and Pārvatī that forms the background for the story of Gaṇeśa's birth. Gaṇeśa's gluttonous excesses cause him to fall from his rat and split open his belly, as his parents amorous play shook the universe. The moon happened to witness all this, although Gaṇeśa clearly regarded it as voyeurism on the moon's part. The moon's mocking laugh provoked Gaṇeśa to tear out his tusk and throw it like a trident to sever the moon in two, to undergo waxing and waning, just as Śiva had split him apart in their battle. Although

Gaṇeśa restores the moon at the end of the story, as his father restored him, the traces of the conflict nevertheless remain in the cycles the moon moves through and thus gives testimony to the wounding and healing process.

The link between Gaṇeśa and the moon becomes more firmly established in the myths of Rāhu and Kīrtimukha. When Viṣṇu, disguised himself as the goddess Mohinī and distributed the ambrosia to the gods at the time of the churning of the ocean, the demon Rāhu tried to steal it:

> Disguising himself as a god, the demon Rāhu took a seat in the row of gods and began to drink the ambrosia [*amṛta*]. But the Sun and Moon discovered him and pointed him out. Just as he was drinking the elixir Viṣṇu cut off his head with his discus so that his headless body, which had not yet received the nectar, fell down dead. His head had obtained immortality because of the nectar and Brahmā made him a planet; but because of his hatred of the Sun and the Moon, he chases them on the new and full moon days. (BP 8.9.24–26; cf. MBh 1.17.4–9; MatsyaP 251.8–16)

In this myth of disguise, theft, and mutilation, Rāhu attempts to steal the ambrosia stirred out of the ocean of milk at the potent time of creation; ambrosia, like its Vedic antecedent *soma,* confers immortality on anyone who drinks it. When the Sun and Moon expose Rāhu's theft, he loses his body, but his head survives because it had been transformed by contact with the auspicious drink. In recognition of his immortal head, Brahmā gives Rāhu quasi-divine status as a planet. But Rāhu transfers the force of his own beheading and his rage at losing his body to the Sun and Moon; hence they too periodically lose their bodies in the form of eclipses. The Rāhu story takes a different turn in another myth about Rāhu's battle with Śiva, a myth that has affinities with those of Śiva and Gaṇeśa:

> When the demon king Jalandhara had defeated the gods and conquered the triple universe, he sent his messenger Rāhu to Śiva to persuade him to give up his beautiful wife, Pārvatī. Rāhu went to Śiva at Mt. Kailāsa and told him that since he was an ascetic and lived in a cremation ground he was not properly providing for his wife. Because Jalandhara had taken all the gods' possessions from them, only he could give Pārvatī the luxury she deserved. Therefore Śiva should please the king by surrendering his wife to the messenger, Rāhu.

When Śiva heard this message he became angry and a man with the face of a lion appeared between his eyebrows. The man had hair standing on end and flames pouring out of his eyes, and he leaped out at Rāhu, trying to devour him. Terrified by this creature, Rāhu called out to Śiva for refuge, and the lord called off this *gaṇa*. Then this lion-faced *gaṇa* said to Śiva, "Why have you taken him from me? I am tormented by hunger. What can I eat, O lord?" Then Śiva said to him, "If you need food so badly and if hunger torments you, then eat the flesh of your own hands and feet." So the man ate the flesh of his own limbs until only his head was left. Then Śiva, pleased by his obedience, said, "You shall hereafter be known as Kīrtimukha, the face of glory, and you shall be my doorkeeper and one of my great *gaṇas,* heroic and fearsome to all evil ones. Whoever fails to honor you cannot please me. From that time on, Kīrtimukha stood at the entrance to the lord of the gods, and those who do not worship him at the outset will find their worship in vain. (ŚP 2.5.19.30–51)

The myths of Rāhu, Kīrtimukha, and Gaṇeśa overlap in many ways. In each of them hunger and overeating set the stage for the action to follow. Gaṇeśa has eaten too much and his belly splits open, calling down the mocking laughter of the moon. Rāhu is greedy for the ambrosia but loses his body when the gods discover him. Rāhu carries Jalandhara's hunger for Pārvatī, and the contest with Śiva calls forth from the god's forehead the hungry *gaṇa* who, when denied Rāhu for a meal, has to dine on his own body until, like Rāhu, only his head is left over. But this head, the leftover part, proves to be the *gaṇa*'s auspicious remainder. Śiva rewards him for his suffering, just as he rewards Gaṇeśa, by placing him at his doorway and giving him the power to place and remove obstacles. This latter myth may also be linked to the story of Śiva's defeat of Gajāsura, who, when Śiva takes his skin, calls him Kṛttivāsas, "the one clad in a skin." The theme that holds all these myths together is beheading, or splitting, and the power released by that action. When Gaṇeśa splits open his belly, he transfers the power of that action to the moon through his tusk; Rāhu redirects the force of his beheading to the Sun and Moon in the form of eclipses and Kīrtimukha turns his ravenous hunger onto himself and devours his own body. Each of them finds himself left in some sort of halfway condition: half elephant, eclipsed planet, or headless body at the doorway.

The myths of Gaṇeśa and Kīrtimukha share other elements as well. Gaṇeśa either must prevent Śiva from gaining access to Pārvatī or contend with Paraśurāma to keep him from interrupting Śiva and Pārvatī in their private quarters. As Jalandhara's alter ego, Rāhu attempts to take Pārvatī away from Śiva, leading to the creation of Kīrtimukha, who must eat himself when Rāhu's timely supplication to Śiva saves him from being devoured. In both myths the point at issue is where Pārvatī belongs, her location, and in both myths the victim of Śiva's wrath obtains compensation by remaining close to Pārvatī at the threshold. The link between the myths of Gaṇeśa and Kīrtimukha as guardians of the doorway emerges fully in the iconography of an eighteenth-century Javanese carving of Gaṇeśa with the face of Kīrtimukha on the back (Zimmer 1946, pp. 179–84). Like Gaṇeśa, Kīrtimukha's image is placed at the doorway in Śiva's temple. Heinrich Zimmer comments on the double-sided symbolism of this figure:

> Kīrtimukha serves primarily as an apotropaic demon-mask, a gruesome, awe-inspiring guardian of the threshold. The votary, however—the orthodox devotee—greets the "Face" with confidence and faith, for he knows that Kīrtimukha is an active portion of the substance of the divinity himself, a sign and agent of his protective fiend-destroying power. (Zimmer 1946, p. 182)

The mythology of Gaṇeśa's beheading draws on the earlier stories of Indra and his exploits in defeating various opponents. Along with his horde of *maruts,* the precursors to Śiva's *gaṇas,* Indra destroys and dismembers Vṛtra, Triśiras, the three-headed demon, and many others. One of the myths of beheading that most closely resembles the stories of Gaṇeśa's mutilation is found in the tale of Indra cutting up the sons of Diti in her womb. Diti was the mother of the demons and Indra's stepmother:

> Diti grieved because all her sons had been slain [at the time of the churning of the ocean]. She practiced asceticism for a long time in order to have a son who would one day slay Indra. Then, disguised as a servant, Indra came to where she was and served her virtuously, bringing her fire, food, and water, and massaged her limbs when she became tired. Diti became pleased with this servant and promised that he would share with her sons in the conquest of Indra. But Diti once lay down to sleep

> with her head where her feet should have been. Seeing that she was sleeping in this impure position, Indra rejoiced and entered her womb and cut her embryo into seven pieces. When she awoke Indra explained to her that he had slain her embryo and cut it into seven pieces because she had slept in an impure position. Diti pleaded with Indra that the seven pieces of her embryo become the guardians of the regions of the seven winds; one to wander in the world of Brahmā, another in Indra's world, a third in heaven, and the remaining four to become deities and wander in all the four directions. (R 1.45–46; cf. O'Flaherty 1975, pp. 91–94)

In this myth Diti practices asceticism to create a child who would compensate her for the children she had lost and protect her from Indra's destructive power, much as Pārvatī created Gaṇeśa in order to enjoy the pleasures of motherhood and keep Śiva away. Indra appears in disguise as a servant, tending to Diti's needs, just as Gaṇeśa served Pārvatī's, and when Diti commits the ritual error of inverting her head and feet, turning things upside down, Indra seizes on this circumstance of reversal to abandon his supportive relationship with Diti and abort her child. As she lies asleep with her head pointing to the north, Indra enters her womb, crossing its threshold from the south. The south is the location of danger. In his battle with Śiva, Gaṇeśa faces the south; then when the gods need to find him a new head, they look to the north. After Indra has slain Diti's son, he grants her request that the seven pieces, like the seven sons of Aditi in the myth of Mārtāṇḍa, may become the lords of the winds and directions [*dikpālas*]. After beheading Pārvatī's son, Śiva grants him dominion over the threshold, which according to some versions of the story faces south. Through it must pass all devotees and adversaries. One Bengali variant of the Gaṇeśa story has it that Śiva sought a replacement head from a cow elephant who had the misfortune of sleeping with her head pointing to the north (Gupte 1919, pp. 42–43). Hence Gaṇeśa's theriomorphic androgyny is made explicit; he has a female animal head and a male torso.

The connections between the myths of Diti and Indra and Gaṇeśa are more evident in a curious variant to the story of Gaṇeśa's beheading found in Raja Radhakant Deb's nineteenth-century Sanskrit encyclopedia, the *Śabdakalpadruma,* which attributes the story to the *Skanda Purāṇa*. Śiva narrates the story to Skanda:

> Once Gaṇeśa, in the form of a headless child, was talking with a sage. The sage said, "If you have taken this incarnation in order to reveal righteousness, then quickly reveal to all the head which destroys sorrow; and bring joy to the hearts of all the gods." This son of Pārvatī, who had no head, replied to the sage, "Once before when King Maheśa bowed at your feet you gave him a blessing. You said to him, 'Your liberation will come through birth in the womb of an elephant, accomplished by Śiva's hand.' All this has now come to pass and this one in the womb has a lovely head, honored by Śiva. And he is the one whose head will complete my incarnation." The sage's heart was filled with this miracle and he said to the child, "Lord, you possess all forms and times, you are the lord of all, you know what I said to the king, I cannot comprehend your form as the lord." Then Nārada, who had been listening to all this, said, "How did you become incarnate without a head in the first place? Did someone cut off your head when you were in the form of a child? Remove my confusion, merciful and supreme lord." Drinking in Nārada's words, the child said, "A certain demon named Sindūra took the form of a breeze, and in the eighth month he entered the womb and cut off my head. Now I will kill him [i.e., Maheśa] because he has the elephant's head." When Nārada heard this he said to the lord who had taken the form of the child, "We gods know nothing about how that head was joined to you. You must have joined it yourself, according to your own nature." And just as the sage said this, the son of Umā appeared to all, complete in all his limbs as the elephant-headed one. (*Śabdakalpadruma,* vol. 2, p. 291)

In this fascinating, although tangled, story it appears that King Maheśa (also a name for Śiva) either committed some sin or was cursed to be born as an elephant or was the incarnation of the demon Sindūra. The king came to the sage for absolution and received it in the form of a prophecy that he would be reborn as an elephant that Śiva would slay, thus making of him a sacrificial offering and giving him salvation. So the king was reborn in the form of an elephant, with the head fated to be given to Gaṇeśa. When Gaṇeśa was in the eighth month in Pārvatī's womb, a demon named Sindūra took the form of a breeze and cut off his head, as Indra cut up Diti's embryo in her womb. Thus Gaṇeśa was born headless; after a conversation with the sage, Gaṇeśa vows to kill the king who possesses the beautiful elephant head. Nārada confesses his astonishment that Gaṇeśa could join the elephant head to his own body, but instantly he appears before all the sages and gods in his recognizable form with its elephant head.

In addition to the similarities of this story to the myth of Indra slaying Diti's embryo, it shares important resonances with the ancient Vedic myth of Dadhyañc, the priest who knew the secret of how to make the sacrifice effective in achieving its results. When Indra threatened to behead Dadhyañc if he ever revealed this secret, the Aśvin twins apprenticed themselves to Dadhyañc in order to learn it, agreeing to remove Dadhyañc's original head and replace it with the head of a horse. When Indra discovered the secret had been told, he beheaded Dadhyañc's horse-head, and the Aśvins restored him by replacing his original head. Just as Dadhyañc's original head, the one that contains the secret knowledge of the sacrifice's power, must be hidden from Indra, so in this story Gaṇeśa's elephant head must be rescued from King Maheśa (i.e., Śiva) to make Gaṇeśa physically complete and thus release his obstacle-removing powers. In both stories the fulfillment comes from getting the right head in place complete with sacrificial knowledge and the power to bring success in undertakings and bestow salvation.

Like so many myths of beheadings, this story equivocates on the identity of the beheader. First we are told that the king will be born as an elephant so that Śiva can slay him and give him salvation, much as he had done with Gajāsura when he slew him and wrapped himself in the elephant-demon's skin—thus allowing his perpetual intimate proximity with his lord—or when he beheaded Gaṇeśa and then gave him the reward of lordship over his troop of *gaṇas*. But here the story also maintains that Gaṇeśa's head was taken while still in Pārvatī's womb by the demon Sindūra in the form of a breeze, thus allowing Gaṇeśa in turn to behead King Maheśa in the form of an elephant and take his head. By attributing the original beheading to the demon Sindúra, this myth (like others we have seen) attempts to shift the blame for Gaṇeśa's mutilation. Even when the beheading myths do not hesitate to point the finger at Śiva as the aggressor, they go out of their way to show that Śiva was provoked into it by Gaṇeśa's intransigence at the doorway. It is clear from these variants of the beheading story that the myths are uncomfortable in placing the blame for Gaṇeśa's mutilation on his father, although in fact they do so, albeit in clever and indirect ways. In the following chapter we shall explore some interpretations of this disguised father/son aggression as it finds expression in familial and ritual relationships in the Hindu context.

One final beheading myth from ancient Sri Lanka is worth noting for the ways in which it combines and rearranges elements in the story:

> At that time Basmasurā [*sic*] was a servant of the god Iswara [Śiva]. The goddess Umayanganā [Pārvatī] was married to Iswara. While Basmasurā was employed under Umayanganā she went alone to the river to bathe . . . and pulled up a small quantity of Singarael (a plant) and created from it a prince, and instructed him to remain and protect her. She then entered the water. A tale-bearer went and falsely told Iswara that Basmasurā had gone to watch the goddess bathe. Then Iswara mounted his elephant, and taking his sword, proceeded to the spot. He cut off the prince's head, which fell into the water. The goddess thereupon came out of the water and said to Iswara, "Why did you behead the prince whom I have created?" Iswara replied, "I thought he was Basmasurā; if you can create another prince, do so." Then the goddess said, "If you will cause the prince whom I have created to come to life again I will create seven more." Iswara agreed to this. But he was unable to find the head, and he therefore created a white lotus plant. He then cut off the head of his elephant and fixed it on the neck of the beheaded prince and named him Gaṇa Deviyā [Gaṇeśa]. (Parker, p. 156; cf. O'Flaherty 1980, pp. 321–22)

This myth opens with the familiar setting of Pārvatī's bath. Pārvatī takes Śiva's servant Basmāsura to guard her while she bathes. In the river she pulls a plant from the mud and fashions it into a son, much as she had made Gaṇeśa from the "mud" on the surface of her limbs in other versions of the story. Śiva is falsely told that his servant is a voyeur and has seen Pārvatī in her nakedness. In his outrage he mistakenly beheads the son Pārvatī has created. Pārvatī promises to make seven more sons out of the river if Śiva will restore the one she has created. Later in the myth we learn that six of the seven merge together to form Skanda, whereas the seventh, reminiscent of Mārtāṇḍa, escapes. When Śiva tries to find the original head, it has disappeared; he must therefore make a head from a lotus plant accompanied by the head of his elephant vehicle, like the fateful *pārijāta* flower resting on Airāvata's head. Again too, the blame for Gaṇeśa's beheading points to Śiva, but then shifts to the tale-bearer who deceived Śiva with the lie that Basmāsura was lusting after Pārvatī as she bathed in the river. This false accusation against Basmāsura parallels the tale told against Vīraka who was tricked by the demon Āḍi when he entered the doorway disguised as a serpent and then changed into Pārvatī's double.

The myths of Gaṇeśa's beheading display a number of variations and draw on many of the motifs that are prominent in the mythologies of Indra, Vīraka, Rāhu, and others. In and through these variant myths run several common threads. First, Gaṇeśa's beheading is inevitable and necessary, for only when he receives his new head can his full identity and power emerge. As with Dadhyañc with the horse's head, it seems that Gaṇeśa's head must be removed to make way for the "real" head, the one he is destined to have in order that he may be made complete. This point finds support in the version in which he is born without any head at all and Pārvatī sends Skanda to bring his first and only head, that of an elephant. Second, the beheading takes place in some threshold location: the womb, doorway, or riverbanks. These places are, in Victor Turner's (1969) phrase, "betwixt and between" two orders of reality. There are all marginal regions where dangers and possibilities dwell together more intensely. Gaṇeśa's ambiguous territory tends to be tied in with the conflict between his mother and father. He is caught in the middle, made from her substance but mutilated and restored by his action. Third, the source of Gaṇeśa's decapitation lies with his father. Even in those myths in which Gaṇeśa loses his head by the actions of fate, a curse, a sage, or Paraśurāma, Śiva is always present in the background while these other forces and persons stand in for him. But the myths attempt to conceal this fact in various ways, as though they must admit it, but not openly. Finally, Gaṇeśa is both the victim and victor in these myths. He loses his head, frequently being caught from behind or otherwise deceived into his own mutilation, but he gains a new head and more important status by virtue of his humiliation. His new power and authority over the *gaṇas,* obstacles, and beginnings come from his being at once broken and whole. This paradox is echoed in a number of other important oppositions: inside/outside—symbolized by the threshold, placing/removing obstacles, animal/deity, wild/tame, and so forth. Implicit in these myths are two pervasive and significant themes in Indian religion: sacrifice and initiation. Because the myths are about familial relations fraught with violence and restoration, they raise questions of interpretation usefully pursued, but not limited to, the approach of psychoanalytic theory. These themes and interpretations, along with others, will be taken up in the next chapter.

3 ◘

Ritual, Psychological, and Religious Themes in the Mythology of Gaṇeśa

Now that we have explored many of the varieties of Gaṇeśa's myths and their parallels in other stories that make up the vast corpus of Hindu mythology, it is appropriate to turn our attention to some of the interpretive questions we might bring to these stories. How are we to read these myths? What is their significance to Hindu and Western readers or listeners? So much of the process of reading or hearing and interpreting any story is related to the assumptions, beliefs, and tastes of the reader or listener. There is no single "true" meaning of the myths. Instead there are various readings to which we might subject the myths. Some of the readings may be closer to the assumptions and life experience of a Hindu audience, others may seem farfetched to a traditional Hindu but will make sense to a Western reader. In this situation, as we stand before the myths in search of ways to interpret them within the context of their own culture and beyond it, an approach that takes methodological eclecticism seriously makes the most sense.

In this chapter we shall first look thematically at the major episodes in the Gaṇeśa story—birth, beheading, restoration, thresholds, obstacles, and so forth—to see where related themes find clear articulation in Hindu culture. We begin here because it is out of this tradition that the myths and rituals originate. Once this indigenous context has been explored, we shall move our inquiry in ways that can take advantage of other interpretive methods, such as psychoanalysis. None of the approaches we shall explore are definitive; all are suggestive. Our purpose is not to fight the battle of methodological verification or falsification but to continue moving through the myths in various ways, gaining an insight here and there that makes them come alive and move us to an understanding of the worlds from which they come and the worlds from which we come.

Sacrifice and Initiation: Breaking Up and Making Whole

The beheading of Gaṇeśa fits into a larger pattern of beheadings, mutilations, and dismemberments in Hindu mythology, especially in the cycles of myths associated with Indra and Śiva. In the Vedic texts Indra beheads and otherwise mutilates a host of opponents. He splits open Vṛtra to release the waters and restore the balance of the cosmos that had been withheld in the serpent's body (ṚV 1.32.1–15). He cuts off Dadhyañc's head as punishment for revealing to the Aśvins the secret of releasing the power of the sacrifice (ŚB 14.1.1.18–24). And Indra lops off the three heads of Triśiras when he is masquerading as a priest of the gods in order to subvert them (*Bṛhaddevatā* 6.149–53; MBh 5.9.1–43). Viṣṇu's head is inadvertently severed by the string of his own bow, and is then replaced with the head of a horse (ŚB 14.1.1.1–15). Indra beheads Namuci, whose head pursues Indra shouting in protest (ŚB 5.4.1.9–10; cf. MBh 9.42.28–37). Śiva destroys Brahmā's fifth head with his thumbnail (ŚP 3.8.36–60; cf. O'Flaherty 1973, pp. 123–30). He attacks Dakṣa's sacrifice, beheading him and turning his head into the sacrificial offering, thus completing the rite that he had originally set out to destroy (KP 1.14). Durgā takes the head of the demon Mahiṣa to punish him for trying to seduce and destroy her (MP 80.21–44). We have already looked at the dismemberment of Diti's embryo and the inverted beheadings of Rāhu and Kīrtimukha, the former when he tried to steal the ambrosia at the churning of the ocean and the latter when Śiva cursed him to devour his own body. These are but a few of the legions of heads of gods, demons, and humans lying about on the sacrificial battlefields of Hindu mythology that are strung together, like flowers into garlands, to adorn Śiva and the goddess.

Beheadings take place as punishments and as a way of inducing humility or of transforming the opponent into a devotee, as we saw in the myth of Gajāsura's defeat by Śiva and in some of the Gaṇeśa beheading stories. Death by beheading has the advantage of drama and decisiveness. The violence calls attention to the awesome power released when the head is severed from the body and the blood flows, distributing its life-containing substance (Brubaker 1979).

In a number of myths beheadings take place in pairs, which allows a number of possibilities for exchange of heads and bodies, with some unexpected but auspicious results. The sage Jamadagni falsely accused his chaste wife, Reṇukā, of adultery and ordered his son Paraśurāma to cut off her head as punishment. But the son's sword cut too wide a swath and also took off the head of an untouchable woman who was standing near Reṇukā. As a boon from his father for his obedience Paraśurāma restored his mother, but with the body of the untouchable woman. In this way the restored goddess Reṇukā combines the head of a high-caste deity with the body of an untouchable. At the level of village religion, this myth enables the goddess to appeal to a broad combination devotees from many castes and provides the village with the religious unity to support its social divisions (Brubaker 1977). A similar predicament results from the exchange of head and body in the delightful tale (on which Thomas Mann based his novella *The Transposed Heads*) from the *Kathāsaritsāgara:*

> Once a young washerman named Dhavala went to the pond to bathe. There he saw a beautiful girl, Madanasundarī, of the same caste. Immediately he fell passionately in love with her and began to waste away from the pain of separation from her. Eager to make him happy, his parents arranged for the two to be married as soon as possible. A while after their marriage Madanasundarī's brother came to visit and the three of them together went on a pilgrimage to the shrine of the goddess [Durgā]. Struck by the beauty of the temple, Dhavala urged his wife and brother-in-law to go inside, but they refused, saying they had no suitable offering to give the goddess. So he went inside the temple alone. There, in a

> moment of intense devotion, he cut off his own head and offered it to the goddess. After a while, when he did not return, his brother-in-law went into the temple to look for him. Seeing Dhavala lying there beheaded he was overcome with grief and cut off his own head as well. Finally, when neither of them returned, Madanasundarī also went into the temple. Seeing her husband and brother dead on the floor, she prayed to the goddess that she might be reborn again to the same husband and brother, and then she tied a creeper vine around her neck as a noose. But the voice of the goddess said she was pleased with the offerings they had made and told her to rejoin the heads and bodies of her husband and brother. Overjoyed at the goddess's grace, in a moment of confusion, she attached her husband's head to her brother's body and her brother's head to her husband's body. Immediately they came to life. When she realized what she had done, she became perplexed. (KSS 6.80)

Madanasundarī's perplexity of mind is understandable. Which of these hybrid men is now her husband and which is her brother? To put it more boldly, to which of these men is she to be unfaithful and with whom is she to commit incest? (Brubaker 1979). The tale resolves this dilemma by saying that it is the head that counts; it is the highest point on the body, the source of speech, and, according to yogic traditions, the repository ultimately of seed (see O'Flaherty 1980, pp. 17–61).

In the case of Gaṇeśa, the original head cannot rejoin the body once it has been severed, whether because it keeps sliding off, as when Pārvatī tries to stick it back on, or because it disappeared into the heavens upon becoming separated from the body. So Śiva must find a new head, as he did with Dakṣa, giving him a goat's head after he had taken Dakṣa's original head (ŚP 2.2.42.13–43.26). Once the elephant head is placed on Gaṇeśa's shoulders, it sticks on as if it had always belonged there, bringing him back to life with enhanced power and authority. One variant of the story appears to recognize the awkwardness of putting such a large head on so small a child and takes the opportunity to have Śiva supply an etymology for Gaṇeśa's name, Vināyaka. Śiva says to Pārvatī:

> "Since, daughter of the mountain, the head is the leader [*nāyaka*] standing on the body, and you told me the head was too large when Skanda joined it to the body, and by its preeminence it is the

leader [*vināyaka*] of the body on which it stands, we shall name him Mahāvināyaka." (SkP 7.3.32.15–17)

The head has preeminence for yet another reason in addition to the fact that it rests on top of the body; in every variant in which a beheading occurs, the head is Śiva's contribution to Gaṇeśa's creation. In cutting off his original head, Śiva removed that premier part of his son made completely from Pārvatī's substance. Śiva's creative activity follows on his destructive cycle here as elsewhere. He must first de-create Gaṇeśa before he can re-create him, at least partially, in his own image. The elephant trunk, which perpetually hangs limp, and the broken tusk are reminiscent of Śiva's own phallic character, but as these phallic analogs are either excessive or in the wrong place, they pose no threat to Śiva's power and his erotic claims on Pārvatī.

Once Gaṇeśa receives his new head he not only carries on as before as Pārvatī's son—as if the beheading were only a flesh wound—but he improves his stature by becoming Śiva's adopted son and lord of his attendants, and he enjoys the privilege of being worshipped before all other gods and of having the power to remove obstacles.

As a major motif in Gaṇeśa's story, the severed and transposed head draws much of its power from the larger Indian theme of sacrifice. That quintessential Vedic-Brāhmaṇic arena in which the ritual specialist—the "knower"—assembled his own universe out of the parts of fire, speech, offerings, knowledge, and sacrifice was the paradigmatic and abstract universe out of which the world of human and divine experience, power, and immortality was understood to come. In the form of the cosmic person, Puruṣa/Prajāpati was dismembered in the sacrifice and his pieces made up the universe (ṚV 10.90). This world of the sacrifice was, as Jan Heesterman describes it:

> A cosmos which is violently broken up to be put back together again. This is in accordance with the cyclical conception of the universe underlying the ritual literature: the constantly alternating movement between the poles of disintegration and reintegration, death and birth, nether world and upper world; an idea which found its clearest systematic expression in the building of the fire altar conceived of as the restoration of the disintegrated cosmic man. The pivotal point, however, is that actual death and disinte-

> gration have been eliminated. Abstraction enabled the ritualists—and this is the rationale and achievement of the ritual system—to do away with the actuality of death. Death has been rationalized away. (p. 24)

At the center of the sacrificial ground, buried beneath the altar of bricks is the head, taken from an opponent in agonistic struggle. The violence of the beheading belongs to the world of myth; it is the task of ritual to unite what has already been rent asunder. The head is the container of the priceless treasure, the mysterious essence of Agni, the location of seed and *soma,* the place of speech. The Brahmins themselves—the knowers and chanters of the sacrifice—have been made from Puruṣa-Prajāpati's head. In the Vedic tradition the head did not belong to the gods; they had to discover it or steal it from others—in a competition between them and the demons—binding the two groups together in a struggle for the head that completed the sacrifice when it was severed and gave forth its life-bestowing substance (Heesterman, p. 27; cf. Danielou 1964, pp. 280–81). In this context the hosts invited the guests to the sacrifice to subvert them and take their precious heads as offerings to the gods. In his destruction of Dakṣa's sacrifice, Śiva inverts this pattern; Dakṣa fails to invite Śiva, who then takes Dakṣa's head for the offering in an act that both destroys and completes the sacrifice. Although the ritual moves toward the pole of restoration between the pairs of forces—death/immortality, demons/gods—the myth retains the traces of the violence that preceded the sacrifice, and indeed made it both necessary and possible. In the ritual the head was that of an animal: a horse, bull, ram, or goat (ŚB 6.2.1.1–2,15). In later stages, no doubt under the influence of the ascetic tradition with its emphasis on noninjury [*ahiṁsā*], the ritual reduced its emphasis on the bloody dimensions of the sacrifice and focused on the clay *ukhā* pot in which the fire was transported and the *soma* offerings kept (ĀŚS 16.27.7). The *ukhā* pot, like the *soma* it contains, had to be fetched, just as in the more ancient tradition of the horse sacrifice, the animal had to be followed for a year before it could be captured.

The ritual emerges as the model of restoration and integration, with the sacrificer incorporating the universe into himself as he is reborn in the sacrifice. The difficulty with this model is that the ritual paradigm of order and balance, abstraction and encoded sacred speech, and gestures and pure substances does not accord with everyday reality. Into this impasse myth enters:

> The contradiction between system and reality is obvious if we consider that the abstract ritual means have to be explained by a mythology which stresses violence. The violence excluded from the ritual is relegated to mythology. The ritual can only picture restoration; its counterpart, destruction, can only be expressed mythologically. (Heesterman, p. 30)

The ritual builds on the violence that has taken place in myth, a violence conducted offstage; it cleans up and repairs the dirty but necessary work done by the myth.

When we consider the myths of Gaṇeśa's creation, beheading, and restoration in the light of this sacrificial paradigm, additional nuances appear. Pārvatī creates Gaṇeśa out of the dirt of her body, in a process analogous to the making of the *ukhā* pots. She brings him to life by standing him up and breathing life into him or telling him to come to life, movements reminiscent of those of the priests bringing the *ukhā* pots to life by sprinkling them with *mantras.* In the later tradition of image worship [*pūjā*], Gaṇeśa's image is fashioned out of clay and brought to life by the invoking of vital breath [*prāṇa*] into the image by the worshipper. In the myth, Śiva and Pārvatī come into conflict over Gaṇeśa's head. Śiva wins by taking the original head. But, having performed the destruction of Pārvatī's creation, he must restore it with a second and permanent head, one that completes Gaṇeśa and restores him to his mother. With the second head comes order and harmony. Another way of reading the myth is to see Śiva and Pārvatī contending over which of them will keep Gaṇeśa's original head. Pārvatī remains offstage during this part of the contest, acting through the alter egos of her *śaktis,* who contend with Śiva and his *gaṇas* at the doorway. When Śiva restores Gaṇeśa with the elephant head—thus completing the sacrifice by destroying the offering—he contributes the elephant head with the flaccid trunk, a caricature of his *liṅga,* as the remainder that makes the restoration possible and brings Gaṇeśa to life. Gaṇeśa thus becomes the embodiment of restoration, an unlikely but nonetheless vital and powerful reality whom all gods and powers must acknowledge if their undertakings are to be successful. The violence inherent in the myth of Gaṇeśa's creation is deflected onto

Gaṇeśa himself and from him passed on to others as he wields his power as the obstacle maker and remover. In this context it is interesting to note that iconographically as well as ritually Gaṇeśa always appears in his restored form. There are neither images representing Gaṇeśa before he had his elephant head nor any sculptural or other visual representations of the primal act of beheading. The Gaṇeśa we see, his image [*mūrti*], is the restored one, the beneficiary of the process of sacrificial dismemberment and resuscitation. The primary imagery and logic of the Gaṇeśa birth story is sacrificial; the Indian paradigm of sacrifice provides the myth with its basic rules and moves.

The myth of Gaṇeśa—his formation, mutilation, and restoration—expresses another fundamental paradigm in the Hindu tradition, that of initiation. Gaṇeśa undergoes a difficult passage beginning with, in Van Gennep's terms, a "separation" from his mother, followed by a "liminal" period at the threshold in which he suffers wounding and loss of identity, and concluding with a "reaggregation" or restoration, with a new head and adoption by Śiva as his son and as lord of the *gaṇas* (pp. 65–115). It is as though the myth charts Gaṇeśa's initiation into divinity; many elements of his myth reflect the imagery of Hindu initiation rites. There are two major initiatory models in the Brāhmaṇic tradition from which Gaṇeśa's myth appears to draw: the first is the *dīkṣā,* the rite of consecration when the sacrificer [*yajamāna*] undergoes a symbolic rebirth into the sacrifice in the manner reminiscent of the self-sacrifice of Puruṣa; the second is the *upanayana,* the ceremony that confers twice-born status on a young high-caste male, in which he begins his period of study and apprenticeship [*brahmacārya*] to a teacher [*ācārya*], receives his sacred thread, vows to remain chaste, and learns the quintessence of all sacred Vedic speech, the *gāyatrī mantra.* A more detailed look at these two ceremonies, especially the latter, will underscore the complexity and richness of Gaṇeśa's story.

When the *soma* sacrifice is about to begin, after the barber has shaved off his body hair and pared his fingernails, the priests sprinkle the sacrificer [*yajamāna*] with water, identified as seed, and purify him by smearing fresh butter on him and rubbing him with twenty-one handfuls of *darbha* grass (AB 1.3.1; ŚB 3.1.2.1–12). In doing this, the priests make the sacrificer "into an embryo again" (AB 1.3.1). Then they conduct him to a "womb-hut [*dīkṣitavimita*]" where he sits doubled up in a fetal position. They cover him with a cloth garment (identified as a caul—the membrane covering the fetus) tied with a strand of *muñja* grass as well as with a black antelope skin representing the placenta. The sacrificer closes his fingers into fists and thereby "holds tightly in his hands the sacrifice and all the gods" (*ibid.*). This doubling up symbolically returns the sacrificer to that primal creative moment when he takes the gods and the cosmos into himself, when there "is no misfortune for him" (*ibid.*). While in the womb-hut and in renouncing food, he makes himself into a food offering, an oblation, to the gods (ŚB 3.3.4.21; 11.1.8.4). He refrains from contact with others and must only speak in an inaudible or babbling fashion, like that of an infant. In the womb-hut, surrounded by embryonic symbolism on all sides, the sacrificer undergoes a death and rebirth process: death back into the womb, ridding himself of his previous contamination, and being reborn from the womb as the offering to the gods and beneficiary of the welfare they bestow in return (see Kaelber, pp. 57–58).

The passage of the sacrificer in this initiation ritual and that of Gaṇeśa's creation and the events that follow run along parallel lines. The sacrificer begins his passage into the world of the sacrifice as an embryo. He then becomes purified and prepared as a food offering to the gods, a sacrifice in his own right. Similarly Pārvatī makes Gaṇeśa and places him in the doorway, an intermediate space analogous to the womb-hut of the *dīkṣā*. Gaṇeśa's sacrifice to Śiva follows; Śiva takes the role played by the gods in the sacrifice, which culminates in his beheading Gaṇeśa and receiving that head as a kind of offering. Śiva, albeit reluctantly, restores Gaṇeśa as a reward for his self-sacrifice, much as the gods reward the sacrificer with wealth, sons, and long life for his offering of himself and his *soma*. Śiva gives Gaṇeśa a new head and a new lease on life, just as the gods give the sacrificer immortality and well-being. The similarities between the myth and ritual are suggestive. Although we need not suppose that the myth was self-consciously patterned on the *dīkṣā* rite, we see the pervasiveness of this initiatory pattern in the imaginations of the mythmakers and the possibilities it offered for thinking about the origins of this deity.

There is more striking similarity between the story of Gaṇeśa and the initiatory rite of *upanayana,* the investiture of the sacred thread. The *upanayana* ritual appears to draw some of its symbolism and structure from the *dīkṣā* rite, and it parallels more closely the processes experienced by Gaṇeśa in the myth.

From the Upaniṣadic period, the *upanayana* ceremony has been the premier rite of passage for high-caste, particularly Brahmin, males. Although there are many versions in both texts and practices, the basic structure of the rite follows. On the day before the rite is to be performed—after Gaṇeśa, Śrī (Lakṣmī), and other deities are propitiated—the young man is smeared with turmeric and required to spend the night in absolute silence. As Pandey, in his major study of Hindu rites of passage, comments, "the yellowish powder gave a show of embryonic atmosphere and absolute silence made the boy a speechless child anew" (p. 128). The following morning the boy and his mother share a final meal together, for after his initiation he will eat with the other males of the household separately from the women and children. Then the boy's father and mother conduct him to the canopy under which the Vedic sacrificial fire has been kindled. After a purifying bath and shaving of body hair and tonsure [*cūḍākaraṇa*], the body is given a garment [*kaupīna*], originally made of a deer skin, like that worn by ascetics. The priests then give the boy a staff [*daṇḍa*]. The boy announces to his new teacher that he intends to become a *brahmacārin,* a student and disciple; the teacher [*ācārya*] signals his acceptance of the boy in apprenticeship by tying around the boy a girdle made of three strands of *muñja* grass, signifying the three Vedas that will be the core of his studies. Then the *ācārya* invests the boy with his sacred thread, three strands representing the three *guṇas* and tied together by a *brahmagranthi* knot symbolic of the presence of Brahmā, Viṣṇu, and Śiva. The *ācārya* also gives him an *ajina* (or upper garment made from an antelope skin), which like the *kaupīna* garment carries strong associations with the practices of ascetics and may also be reminiscent of the antelope skin used as an embryonic cover for the initiant in the Vedic *dīkṣā*.

The investiture of the thread marks the major transformation in the rite, the point at which the boy moves into category of *brahmacārin* and must remain obedient to its obligations. Once this investiture of the thread has taken place, the *ācārya* gives the *brahmacārin* a staff [*daṇḍa*]. He takes it saying, "My staff which fell down to the ground in the open air, that I take up again for the sake of long life, holy lustre, and holiness" (PGS 2.2.14).

As with the *dīkṣā* rite, the *upanayana* encompasses the processes of separation, liminal ambiguity, and reaggregation. On the day prior to the rite, the boy passes backward into his first human birth. He is smeared with the embryonic substance and kept apart, silent, and bound to his mother for his source of food. As the rite begins, he is separated from her and his human birth through the ritual acts of bathing, shaving, and receiving his ascetic garments—garments that in the *dīkṣā* rite were explicitly identified as the caul and placenta appropriate to his new birth into the sacrifice, the world of the gods. Early sources for the *upanayana* state that when the *ācārya* receives the student as his apprentice he "places him like a foetus and carries him for three days in his belly" (AV 42.215) or becomes pregnant with him (ŚB 11.5.4.16; cf. Kaelber, p. 56). In becoming "pregnant" with the *brahmacārin,* the male *ācārya* gives birth to him androgynously into a spiritual lineage and a new life, a life explicitly identified with the sacrifice into which the sacrificer is born through the *dīkṣā.* Once the student has been reborn into his new life, he receives garments, girdle, and thread, each of which has associations with the embryo, caul, placenta, umbilical cord, and with renunciation as well—the path that leads through death to rebirth. While in this new embryonic state born of the *ācārya,* the student inhabits a liminal location in which his whole identity depends on his teacher. The *ācārya* teaches him how to behave, how to observe the complex rules and obligations appropriate to his new life, how to perform the fire sacrifice, how to utter divine speech, and so on. When the student receives his staff, it is the staff he says that "fell to the ground." From a psychoanalytic perspective, this ritual move may be read as a symbolic castration, in that his ascetic/guardian staff protects him while he remains celibate. Once the *ācārya* has made the *brahmacārin* into a man—that is, has given him his second birth as a *dvija,* a twice-born Hindu—he is fit to return to the world of his family, no longer as their son but as a begging ascetic from a new and spiritual lineage. The *brahmacārin* ritually begs food from the assembled family. He begs as one coming from a new and spiritual lineage. His return for alms constitutes his reaggregation into the human world, a world that now knows him and responds to him in his new and elevated status.

The ritual passage of the *brahmacārin,* like that of the sacrificer in the *dīkṣā* rite, bears some striking resemblance to Gaṇeśa's experience in the myth. When Pārvatī makes Gaṇeśa out of the substance of her body, her role is similar to that of the boy's mother who smears him with turmeric. Indeed, according to one variant of the Gaṇeśa birth story, Pārvatī uses turmeric [*haridrā*] as the unguent with which she rubs her limbs to bring Gaṇeśa into being (MBhP 35). The yellow color of the turmeric is suggestive of seed, gestation, and power. It features prominently in the embryonic symbolism of the Vedic *dīkṣā* rite and is a common feature of many rituals to the goddess (Pārvatī) (cf. Ayyar, pp. 74–75; Hiltebeitel 1982, pp. 80–81). In placing Gaṇeśa in the doorway—the liminal location—and giving him the staff of the guardian, Pārvatī separates him from herself. Gaṇeśa's defeat and resuscitation by Śiva parallels the initiatory process carried out on the *brahmacārin* by the *ācārya.* Gaṇeśa's beheading is like the cutting of the student's hair, particularly the tonsure. Śiva's adoption of Gaṇeśa as his son and his giving him his name and lordship over his retinue corresponds to the *ācārya* giving birth androgynously to the *brahmacārin* and instructing him in his duties as a student and twice-born male. Like Gaṇeśa, the *brahmacārin* remains celibate, an apprentice to his adoptive father. The return of the *brahmacārin* to the family as an ascetic beggar recalls the scenes in the Gaṇeśa myth in which he is presented to the assembled deities for the first time as the Lord of Obstacles whom they must now recognize as having a new and elevated status.

These structural parallels between the passage of Gaṇeśa and that of the *brahmacārin* helps to explain why Gaṇeśa is such an appealing figure to humans in spite of his obvious physical differences from them. His passage is like the passage of all twice-born Hindu males, like them he has experienced the process of maternal separation, initiation through symbolic mutilation by a new "father" (the *ācārya*), and the arduous reaggregative socialization and acculturation necessary to make him a recognizable entity in the social world. Gaṇeśa knows their passage because it is also his own, and this commonality of experience renders him accessible in ways the other gods are not. Gaṇeśa is their ally and advocate in the court of divine beings and powers. As human initiates ascend to the realms of the gods through the ritual of the *upanayana,* Gaṇeśa descends to the world of humans through myth. They meet in the middle—on the threshold—whence they emerge as new beings broken and made whole and filled with potential knowledge and power.

Father, Mother, Son, and Brother

The myth of Gaṇeśa parallels aspects of human experience beyond the restricted world of ritual initiation. It is a tale of family relations and reflects the unconscious ambivalences of early forgotten childhood experience. One need not be an ideological Freudian to see the fruitfulness of raising psychoanalytic questions about a myth that involves such a violent and complex account of father/son relations. The extent to which the myth of Gaṇeśa explores these relations and the sensibilities that attend them, it reaches beyond its Indian context and takes on universal meaning and appeal.

The story begins even before Gaṇeśa arrives, with the tension between the mother and father over whether to have a child at all. The mother fervently desires a son; the father resists. The extended "family" of gods impedes the couple's opportunities for intimacy—they continually interrupt Śiva and Pārvatī just at the point in their lovemaking when the natural engendering of a child might occur. After Gaṇeśa's arrival, the myth evokes the playful intimacy and warmth between the mother and her newly created son, an intimacy enjoyed while the father remains at a distance. Eventually the mother must let the son go; the son must confront the father and compete with him for access to the mother. In this conflict the son does not stand a chance against the father's overwhelming strength. The son positions himself between the mother and father, calling forth the mother's protective instincts. The son submits and sacrifices his own claims on the mother to gain acceptance from the father on the father's terms. The father, however, does not demand total submission: he wounds rather than kills. Whether out of guilt or grace, the father makes the son into his own image and gives him a place to stand—near but beneath him in stature. In this Indian setting the oedipal theme finds a different resolution. The confrontation between father and son for the mother ends with the defeat of the son, followed by his restoration to the proximity of his mother, but not to intimacy with her (cf. Ramanujan).

As a story about the inner experience of individual psychosexual development and family relations, the myth of Gaṇeśa deals with the brute facts of human connections at the most intimate of associations. Such truths are not comfortably admitted at the conscious level of family and social life; but they are projected onto the gods. At the distance by which the divine and human worlds are separated, the repressed and forgotten feelings of the maturation process can be encountered without intolerable psychic shock. As a story of family conflict and reconciliation and the process of individuation, the myth invites the methodological insights of psychoanalysis. Like dreams, myths are maps of unconscious feelings and repressed regions of early childhood experience. The story of Gaṇeśa gives us insight into the Indian experience of being a son; the disguised ambivalences of life in the network of familial relations. As the Indian psychoanalyst Sudhir Kakar points out:

> The enormous popularity of Gaṇeśa throughout India, a phenomenon of considerable puzzlement to Indologists, can thus be partially explained if we recognize Gaṇeśa as the god for all psychic seasons, who embodies certain "typical" resolutions of developmental conflicts in traditional Hindu society. . . . In effect, the boy expresses the conviction that the only way to propitiate the mother's demands and once again make her nurturing and protective is to repudiate the cause of the disturbance in their mutuality: his maleness. (pp. 101–2)

To explore the ways in which Gaṇeśa's myth is a guide to the " 'typical' resolutions of developmental conflicts" in traditional Hindu family contexts, we shall look at the several pairs of relations that operate in the myth: father/mother, mother/son, father/son, and brother/brother. It might be objected that the "typical" traditional family does not conform to the nuclear model of father, mother, and son(s) but rather consists of the extended kinship unit encompassing three and four generations, with cousins and in-laws dwelling together in close proximity, and that authority and conflict are thus diffused among a number of parent surrogates. This is certainly the case at the level of social life; in the myth, however, there is only what anthropologist Brenda E. F. Beck calls the "kin nucleus," the fundamental relations that carry the heaviest emotional burden of ambivalence. What we wish to explore is not the empirical familial relations that exist on the level of day-to-day social life but the "concepts and feelings about kinsmen that are expressed less directly in mediums such as folklore and ritual prescription." (1974, p. 2). With the Gaṇeśa myth we see the kin nucleus boldly articulated.

Father/Mother

Gaṇeśa's origins, like those of every human son and daughter, are found in the context of the relationship of his parents. As we have already seen, Śiva and Pārvatī quarrel over the question of children. Pārvatī longs to have a son, to "feel the kiss of a son's face," as she tells Śiva pleadingly (BDP 2.60.21). Her intense desire reflects the longing of Indian women to have children. In traditional Hindu culture, giving birth to a son is the most fulfilling contribution a woman can make to the well-being of the family. Not only does she bring forth a child who will give her the emotional satisfaction and intimacy she seeks but also she has offered the supreme gift to her husband and his kinsmen—a male heir, one who will carry out the *śrāddha* ritual by which his father will be conducted safely into the world of the ancestors after his death. Giving birth to a son confers enormous status on the mother; it is proof of her procreative power and capacity to provide for the welfare of the entire family. Indeed, it is confirmation of her divinity. Pārvatī's childlessness is her greatest sorrow. Her wish for a son is so overpowering that in Śiva's absence she creates a son of her own out of the abundance of her potentiality—a feat of generative alchemy that every childless wife might wish to emulate.

Śiva, the father, does not see parenthood as such an unmitigated blessing. For the lord of asceticism, whose pursuit of the renunciatory path has freed him from the clutches of *saṃsāra* (the curse of death and rebirth), a son is but a fetter and a nuisance. The son's ritual role, although crucial in the world of humans, is irrelevant to the deity. Furthermore, a child will be a distraction to the mother, turning her attention away from erotic interest in him. He prefers that they remain lovers, unfettered by the interruptions and annoyances that accompany the pattering of little feet. Śiva expresses his resistance to procreation, which is so characteristic of the renunciatory perspective and reflects the fear of loss of autonomous power that comes with the loss of semen (cf. Carstairs, pp. 83–87; O'Flaherty 1980, pp. 43–53). The son may provide assurance to the father that his passing into the next world will not go unrecognized and dishonored; however, in that very assurance lies the reminder that fatherhood itself is a state of bondage to *saṃsāra.* Withdrawl from attachment is the straighter path, the road to renunciation and freedom. Śiva is not the only one threatened by Pārvatī's desire for children. The gods know that a child of this union would displace them; compared to him their powers would pale to insignificance. Hence they must interrupt the divine lovers before any consummation and conception might take place. Frequently they disguise themselves as wandering mendicants, renouncers, to remind Śiva where his loyalties ought to belong. Similarly, although the parents of an Indian married couple insist on the urgency of having sons, "every effort is made to hinder the development of intimacy within a couple that might exclude other members of the family, especially the parents" (cf. Kakar, p. 74).

In those variants of the myth in which Śiva does participate in Gaṇeśa's engendering, he does so reluctantly or unwittingly, his seed inadvertently falling on the ground and mixing with Pārvatī's in the bath, as it did with Skanda's birth. His motives are ambivalent. He agrees to a son as a boon to the gods, his devotees—not because of his own desire. The gods need a son to protect them from the demons, just as the family needs sons to protect them from the demons of hunger, neglected ancestors, loss of status, and even extinction of the lineage. The husband is reminded that to engender a son is a sacred duty, part of his obligations to those who are themselves the authors of his own existence and support. His act of engendering is like an oblation into the sacred fire of the wife's womb [*yoni*]. In the human realm, children—even sons—are a mixed blessing. They advance the family's fortunes within the realm of *saṃsāra,* but they deny them the option of release [*mokṣa*]; they bring the mother fulfillment and intimacy, but they preoccupy her to the exclusion of the father. This ambivalence would be destructive to the cohesion of the family if admitted openly; its expression is left to the narrative world of myth where it can be done indirectly. It is comforting to know that even the gods, whose intimacies are an open secret, also face such dilemmas.

Mother/Son

Pārvatī longed for a son. Her longing was made all the more poignant by Śiva's interminable absences and resistance. Her desire generates enough power to turn bodily dirt mixed with unguents into seed and engender a baby without Śiva. Astonished by her own creative power, she fondles the child, enjoying him like a young girl with her doll. She tells Gaṇeśa that he belongs only to her, he is the flesh of her flesh, there is no difference in essence between them. The descriptions of Pārvatī's doting enjoyment of her son evoke the delight with which Indian women indulge their young children. As Carstairs notes:

> Hindu children, almost without exception, begin life with a wonderfully rewarding experience. During their first year they are never separated from their mothers for more than a short time, and they are given the breast generously, whenever they feel hungry or upset. . . . In the Hindu family, because he experiences so little frustration, the child develops an assurance that the support and succor will never be denied him—hence his constant (and even unrealistic) optimism in later life. (p. 157; cf. Kakar, pp. 80–81, 126–33)

The relationship between the mother and son is an especially tender one, creating in the son a lifelong bond of loyalty and affection. The son regards his mother with the reverence owing the goddess, the eternal giver of all benevolences. Women saints and chief female devotees of male gurus are frequently called "Mother" by their disciples.

In the myth Pārvatī has other reasons for creating Gaṇeśa than the enjoyment of mothering a son—she seeks protection from the intrusions of her husband with his insatiable erotic expectations. So she stations Gaṇeśa at the door to her private chambers, her bath—symbolic of her sexuality. There at the doorway he stands between his mother and father. As the story proceeds, he must face his father alone, abandoned by his mother, for she remains out of sight, and she is drawn out only after the damage is done. But in one related myth about doorways she does not leave him behind; her alienation from Śiva strengthens her maternal bond with Gaṇeśa. After Śiva has insulted Pārvatī by calling her "Blackie [*Kālī*]," she vows to leave him and return to her father's home, and she then stations her other son, Vīraka—the one whom Śiva had made—at the doorway to spy on her husband's extramarital amorous exploits. Fearing his father's unpredictable manner, Gaṇeśa pleads with Pārvatī to take him along with her. She agrees, saying, "He will laugh at you, my son, because you have an elephant's face, just as he laughs at me. Therefore, come with me; go where I go" (SkP 1.2.29; cf. O'Flaherty 1975, p. 255). Pārvatī and her strange looking son have a common bond in suffering the ridicule of Śiva, and they shelter one another from his unique sense of humor.

Gaṇeśa first encounters his father in a violent confrontation, which the myth attempts to palliate by saying that son and father do not recognize each other. He experiences a jolting transition from the warm inner regions of his mother's world to painful subordination to his father's cutting authority, literally. His passage is thorough: he is cut in half, given a "second birth" as his father's son according to the father's terms, which even the mother must accept.

The myth evokes a process similar to the developmental one that Hindu males experience around the age of four to five years. They are taken quite abruptly from the easy and undemanding world of their mothers, a world in which the father has become largely absent or peripheral, and they are placed under the strict and emotionally distant authority of their fathers. The son longs for the tender, undifferentiated, less demanding world of intimacy with his mother, a longing that may lead him to idealize his mother in his adult memory. Kakar comments on the interplay between the abruptness of this transition and its tendency to increase the son's bonding and identification with his mother. This traumatic "second birth" separation from the mother tends to foster in the son's inner world a

> regression to an earlier "happier" era and a tendency to consolidate one's identification with the mother in order to compensate for her loss. . . . In spite of the emotional "riches" that a long and intense loving reciprocity with the mother may store up in the individual's inner world, this same intense exclusivity tends to hinder the growth of the son's autonomy, thereby leaving the psychic structure relatively undifferentiated, and the boundaries of the self vague. (p. 130; cf. Carstairs, p. 159; Dube, p. 149)

This abrupt separation not only tends to deepen the attachment to the mother, encouraging in the son an unconscious desire to remain eternally the child to his mother, but it serves to heighten the distance and authority of the father. Kakar continues:

> The consequences of the "second birth" in the identity development of Indian men are several: a heightened narcissistic vulnerability; an unconscious tendency to "submit" to an idealized and omnipotent figure, both in the inner world of fantasy and in the outer world of making a living; the lifelong search for someone, a charismatic leader or *guru,* who will provide mentorship and a guiding worldview, thereby restoring intimacy and authority to the individual life. (p. 128; cf. Spratt, pp. 5–26)

We shall examine Gaṇeśa's submission to Śiva as a reflection of the Indian male search for authority in the next section of our discussion. For the moment it is important to notice the ways in which Gaṇeśa "submits" to his mother, attempting to remain close to her by keeping his youthful—indeed, childlike—form, and never growing up. Gaṇeśa's eternal youth matches Pārvatī's eternal adulthood. Because neither is subject to the ravages of time, they both remain temporally enshrined in a mother/son relationship. Iconographically Gaṇeśa's body is that of a plump infant. Although at least one Purāṇic source has an account of his marriage, Gaṇeśa is generally represented as celibate, a celibacy suggested visually and perhaps caricatured by his exaggerated but perpetually flaccid trunk. Finally, his insatiable appetite for sweetmeats [*modaka*]—a source of many amusing tales—raises the question (from a psychoanalytic perspective) of whether this tendency toward oral erotic gratification may not serve as compensation for his arrested development at not reaching the phallic stage as well as the severing of the maternal bond he underwent at the beheading hand of his father. Gananath Obeyesekere interprets Gaṇeśa's celibacy, like his broken tusk, as the punishment he receives for incestuous fixation on this mother (p. 471).

Gaṇeśa's iconographic form is reminiscent of an infant or young child as well as that of a *yakṣa.* Unlike the *yakṣa* figures, however, Gaṇeśa's form lacks the more mature musculature of arms and legs that these squat quasi-divine/quasi-demon creatures possess. The iconography is clear enough; Gaṇeśa is a child, a baby. So he remains, never growing into the full youthful stage of his elder brother Skanda or the maturity of his father. When shown in group settings with his parents, he is depicted proportionately as a small child to an adult. In the Purāṇas this theme of his childlikeness may be seen in the fact that the great preponderance of myths deal with the circumstances of his birth and initiation into the service of his father. Only later in sectarian and regional forms of expression, which we shall examine in a subsequent chapter, does Gaṇeśa emerge from the shadows cast by his illustrious parents into his own as an independent deity.

Gaṇeśa's celibacy links him both to his father and his mother, but for opposite reasons. He remains celibate so as not to compete erotically with his father, a notorious womanizer, either incestuously for his mother or for any other woman for that matter. As we have already noted, Gaṇeśa's celibacy is also an expression of his *brahmacārin* identity—the faithful servant to his father, the *ācārya,* as well as guardian of his parents' privacy. In relation to Pārvatī, however, Gaṇeśa remains celibate in order to stay close to her—to continue to be her little boy. In Maharashtra it is said that Gaṇeśa never marries because he is unable to find a woman as beautiful as his own mother; so he remains at the crossroads patiently waiting for such a woman to come along (Moor 1968, p. 100). In South India, Beck reports a similar view:

> There is one tale that purports to explain why his [Gaṇeśa's] images are so often found on river banks and the edges of ponds. Gaṇeśa, it is said, is waiting patiently, watching all the women who come to bathe, until he can find one as beautiful as Pārvatī herself. This is the woman he will marry. (1974, p. 11; cf. Obeyesekere, p. 471)

This view is expressed in another South Indian tale, but with a different twist.

> An anecdote about Gaṇeśa—once Pārvatī asked him whom he would like to marry; he replied, "Someone exactly like you, Mummy." and Mummy got outraged by such an openly incestuous wish and cursed him with everlasting celibacy; that's why he's still a bachelor. (Ramanujan, p. 127)

Gaṇeśa's celebacy, whether self-chosen or resulting from his mother's curse, reflects the fantasy little boys entertain before they are made aware of incest taboos about marrying their mothers to remain forever within their close protective circle of affection and power.

There is yet a further aspect of Gaṇeśa's celibacy that deserves comment. Both in his behavior and his inconographic form Gaṇeśa resembles in some aspects the figure of the eunuch. Standing at the doorway, guarding but not entering the inner chamber of Pārvatī's house or "watching all the women who come to bathe" (as he does in the story cited above), Gaṇeśa is like a eunuch guarding the women of the harem. In Indian folklore and practice eunuchs have served as trusted guardians of the *antaḥpura,* the seraglio. "They have the reputation of being homosexuals, with a penchant for oral sex, and are looked upon as the very dregs of society" (Hiltebeitel 1980, p. 162). At weddings and birth ceremonies, however, they perform an ambiguous but auspicious function:

> At marriage rites among the Bharvāds of Gujarat, for instance, a eunuch flings balls of wheat flour toward the four quarters to ward off evil spirits. And when they appear at births and marriages, they hold the power to bless as well as curse. (*ibid.*)

Like the eunuch, Gaṇeśa has the power to bless and curse; that is, to place and remove obstacles. Although here there seem to be no myths or folktales in which Gaṇeśa explicitly performs oral sex, his insatiable appetite for sweets may be interpreted as an effort to satisfy a hunger that seems inappropriate in an otherwise ascetic disposition, a hunger having clear erotic overtones. Gaṇeśa's broken tusk, his guardian's staff, and displaced head can be interpreted as symbols of castration. Anthropologist Edmund Leach notes:

> Gaṇeśa's broken tusk is a phallic emblem and . . . its detachability denotes a certain ambivalence about Gaṇeśa's sexual nature. There are contexts in which the *liṅgam* phallus, which is properly the emblem of Śiva, may serve as a manifestation of any one of Śiva's sons, Gaṇeśa included. In such a context, Gaṇeśa may be virile and potent. But there are other contexts where Gaṇeśa seems to be an effeminate eunuch. (p. 82)

This combination of child-ascetic-eunuch in the symbolism of Gaṇeśa—each an explicit denial of adult male sexuality—appears to embody a primal Indian male longing: to remain close to the mother and to do so in a way what will both protect her and yet be acceptable to the father. This means that the son must retain access to the mother but not attempt to possess her sexually. As a child, a renouncer, or a eunuch, he can legitimately maintain that precious but precarious intimacy with his mother because, although he is male, he is more like her then he is like his father. This may explain why Gaṇeśa takes on these qualities through his own choice or why he willingly accepts them as mutilations from others—even from Pārvatī herself—so long as they will guarantee his continued proximity with her.

We have already encountered Gaṇeśa's appetite for sweets, particularly in the story in which, as the moon looks on laughing, he falls off his rat vehicle and splits open his belly full of *modaka. Modakas,* or sweet wheat or rice balls, are offered to Gaṇeśa in copious quantities—traditionally twenty-one—by his devotees. Some contemporary Hindus say that he is so fat because he can never get his fill of *modakas;* and the more of them a devotee gives him, the more likely is Gaṇeśa to remove obstacles for him. Thus the god's gluttonous tendencies are turned to the devotee's spiritual advantage. In South India one anthropologist has recently observed:

> All informants who celebrated *Vināyakar chaturdī,* commemorating the day when he [Gaṇeśa] received his elephant head, wanted to satisfy his gluttonousness, only they did not all agree on what he liked best. In Tamilnad, people offer to Vināyakar Koṛukkaṭṭai, a generic name given to several cakes with sweet or salty fillings, of which the Āgamic *modaka* is one. In Karnataka, he received *kadubu,* similar to the Tamil cake but always sweet; in Andhra Pradesh, he likes *undrallu,* a sweet ball, and in Kerala, people are convinced that he is especially fond of ghee *appam,* a sweet round cake fried in ghee. In the latter state, in order to appease Gaṇapati's hunger, even *mūdappam pūjā* may be performed, where the idol is literally submerged by the cakes. (Eichinger Ferro-Luzzi 1977a, p. 546)

Gaṇeśa's extraordinary fondness for *modaka* or its local equivalents may be more comprehensible when viewed in the light of the following Purāṇic conversation in which Pārvatī explains to her two young boys, Skanda and Gaṇeśa, the special qualities of the *modaka:*

> "The gods were filled with happiness [at the birth of the two sons of Śiva and Pārvatī] and gave this sweetmeat, it is called 'great intelligence [*mahābuddhi*]' and 'ambrosia [*amṛta*].' I'll tell you its virtues, listen carefully. Anyone who merely smells it will certainly become immortal. He will become one who is learned in

> the Śāstras, clever at weapons, knowledgeable in the Tantras, a writer and painter, one who has both worldly and divine knowledge, there is no doubt, my sons." (PP Sṛṣṭikhaṇḍa 65.8–11)

In the context of this story, *modaka* is equivalent to *soma,* the immortality-bestowing seed/food that the gods and demons fight over throughout Hindu mythology. The word "*modaka*" derives from the root *mud* meaning "be merry," and it may also be used as an adjective meaning "gladdening" or "exhilarating," characteristics also attributed to *soma.* According to one myth about Gaṇeśa's rat companion it is said that the rat was drawn by the scent of the *modaka* to come out of his hole and take a bit of this wondrous food, whereupon he became immortal and Gaṇeśa's vehicle (SkP 7.3.32.2–12).

Gaṇeśa's insatiable appetite for this food and the obesity resulting from it symbolize the abundance of his life-giving power as the remover of obstacles. Devotees literally bathe or bury him in *modakas* to satisfy his hunger. This feeding of the god to appease his hunger is reminiscent of feeding the demons to prevent them from upsetting the sacrifice and turning it to inauspicious results. Feeding Gaṇeśa is both an expression of the devotee's generosity and devotion to the god and his effort to avert the god's hunger, lest Gaṇeśa turn away in anger at being unfulfilled and create obstacles for the devotee in response.

The perpetual son desiring to remain close to his mother and having an insatiable appetite for sweets evokes associations of oral eroticism. Denied the possibility of reaching the stage of full genital masculine power by the omnipotent force of the father, the son seeks gratification in some acceptable way. As long as he remains stuffed full he is content and benign, like a satisfied infant at its mother's breast. If Gaṇeśa should go hungry because of the devotee's failure to feed and worship him first before all other gods, then his primordial hostility is aroused, to the detriment of all. Feeding Gaṇeśa copious quantities of *modakas,* satisfying his oral/erotic desires, also keeps him from becoming genitally erotic like his father. This would lead to a conflict more disastrous for the gods and humans than neglecting to feed him. Gaṇeśa's obesity suggests a compulsiveness in his character. All the gods and goddesses receive food offerings of various kinds, to be sure, but Gaṇeśa must receive his first and in excessive quantities, like the demon Rāhu who sneaked to the head of the line to get his share of ambrosia before the other gods could get their portions. Gaṇeśa's impatience for food suggests an anxiety, a hunger that is never completely fed no matter how many *modakas* he consumes. He is the child forever longing for the mother's breast—that fountain of life-giving elixir he once enjoyed without distress in infancy but is now denied because of the father's intrusion. Gaṇeśa's belly seems to empty itself as fast as it fills up, as the myth of his stomach splitting open suggests. As with so many other threshold locations in which he resides, here he stands on the threshold between hunger and satiation: fat, yet unable to be sufficiently filled. As each morsel appeases his appetite, it only reminds him unconsciously of the food from his mother that he may no longer have.

Gaṇeśa's story is, in part, the story of maternal attachment, loss, and indirect but incomplete compensation. As a celibate child, and resembling the ambiguous figure of the eunuch, Gaṇeśa is one whose masculinity remains partial, trimmed, and contained. Unable to take full possession of his mother in the face of his father's beheading/castrating power, Gaṇeśa lives a threshold existence—near but not near enough—seeking his own fulfillment in dutiful service to his parents and taking pleasure in an endless flow of sweetmeats from adoring devotees. He is the mythical expression of the male wish for maternal intimacy denied in real life in the course of growing up, a fantasy in which the defeats the son must suffer at the hands of the father are compensated indirectly by an orally erotic celibate proximity to the mother.

Father/Son

The conflict between Śiva and Gaṇeśa at the threshold and the latter's subsequent submission and restoration introduce the theme of father/son aggression and invite comparison with the myth of Oedipus and the meaning Freud and his followers have derived from it for understanding human psychological dynamics.

The Oedipus story begins with Laius abandoning his infant son because an oracle predicts that his son will eventually murder him. But Oedipus survives and is raised as a prince in another kingdom. When he grows up, he searches for his origins and, in a chance encounter on the road, meets and slays Laius in an argument, not knowing Laius is his father. Later, arriving in Thebes, he solves the riddle of the sphinx and is made king; he marries his mother Jocasta and fathers two sons and daughters. For a while the kingdom prospers, but after a time a plague breaks out. The oracle prophesies that prosperity will not return until Laius' murderer is banished. After a long pursuit and many delays, Oedipus comes to know that he is the murderer of his father and the husband of his mother. Horrified at his own actions, Oedipus blinds himself and goes into exile, thus restoring the welfare of the kingdom and fulfilling the oracle of the gods.

Freud saw the truth of this myth in its dramatic expression of repressed childhood desires to bond with the mother and exclude the father. The myth directs "our first sexual impulses toward the mother and our first hatred and our first murderous impulses against our father. Our dreams convince us that this is so" (Freud, p. 262). This myth is powerful in ways others are not because it gives narrative form to the "first sexual impulses" at that very primal threshold of psychosexual development where such emotions are experienced with greatest intensity. The myth leads males, Freud thought, to identify with Oedipus' desire to express the infantile wish to be united with the mother but then are chastened by Oedipus' later agonies so that this desire is abandoned along with the related wish to murder the father. Only then do males accept identification with the father and seek sexual gratification in a mature, genitally erotic manner with another woman. For Freud:

> [Oedipus] is one in whom these primaeval wishes of our childhood have been fulfilled, and we shrink back from them with the whole force of repression by which those wishes have since that time been held down within us. (p. 296)

In the myth and drama Oedipus is a tragic figure; in the fantasy there can be no fulfillment, only an acceptance of the inevitable reality of losing the mother and the subsequent identification with the father that makes it possible for the ego to develop adequately and realistically.

The similarities between the myths of Oedipus and Gaṇeśa from a psychoanalytic perspective have been noted by a number of scholars (Goldman, pp. 371–72; Leach; Ramanujan; Spratt, pp. 124–27, 350–51; cf. Courtright 1980, pp. 75–77; O'Flaherty 1976, pp. 361ff.). Robert Goldman summarizes the links between the two myths:

> The legend of Gaṇeśa, well known to the later purāṇic literature, is a much clearer example of a story representing the primal oedipal triangle of son, father, and mother and the son's attempts to possess the mother to the exclusion of the father, an attempt that leads to violent conflict and the final symbolic castration of the son. (p. 371)

The triangle of father, mother, and son, with the son's violent contest with the father over access to or possession of the mother, are clearly parallel in the Oedipus and Gaṇeśa stories. Unlike Oedipus, Gaṇeśa does not kill his father, he is himself killed, to be revived later with a new head. Ramanujan notes this important reversal in the flow of aggression:

> The Indian and Greek/Western tales do not differ in the basic pattern: (a) Like sexes repel, (b) Unlike sexes attract across generations. But they do differ in the *direction* of aggression or desire. Instead of son desiring mothers and overcoming fathers (e.g., Oedipus) . . . we have fathers suppressing sons . . . and mothers desiring sons. (p. 133)

Another important difference in the direction of the myths is that although the Oedipus story directs us to the fundamentally tragic acceptance of the exile from the mother and submission to the superego demands represented by the father, gods, or fate, the Gaṇeśa story ends with his restoration and a new beginning in which relations between parents and child are reconciled. Gaṇeśa emerges with a new consciousness—symbolized by the new head—as the model devotee. He has borne all his misfortunes and mutilations as gifts of grace. The reward for his suffering is to receive eternal intimacy with the androgynous divinity represented by *both* his mother and father together. Iconographically he is most often represented with his father, or father and mother together, but seldom with his mother alone.

This resolution, however, is not without its price. From the psychoanalytic perspective, the symbolism of the threshold as the location where the battle occurs is significant. It is the threshold to Pārvatī's bath and bedroom, symbol of her shrine, womb, and point of sexual entry. It is the place simultaneously of union and separation. Gaṇeśa the child is coming out of the door at the moment Śiva the husband is attempting to get in. The doorway is not big enough for both of them at the same time; one must prevail, and, of course, it is the father. The resolution, at least initially, must fall in his favor. The particular type of mutilation Śiva inflicts on Gaṇeśa is also significant. As Robert Goldman points out in commenting on Gaṇeśa's beheading, "This particular mode of displaced castration is a common feature of Hindu legends. Beheading is, moreover, a regular symbol for castration in dreams and fantasies" (pp. 371–72; cf. Freud, pp. 366–69). In traditional Indian yogic physiology the head is the receptacle of both thought and sexual potency or seed. In Tantric descriptions of the process of spiritual liberation [*mokṣa*] the seed is drawn up from the sexual organs through various centers [*cakra*] along the spinal axis until it is released through an aperture at the top of the head [*brahmarandhra cakra* or *sahasrāra cakra*] (cf. O'Flaherty 1980, pp. 17–61). In some versions of the myth where Gaṇeśa already has his elephantine form, the "displaced castration" takes place on an even more obvious surrogate, the tusk. In separating Gaṇeśa's head/tusk Śiva, or one of his stand-ins, removes any potential threat of incest and thereby leaves Gaṇeśa sexually ambiguous. Leach identifies the logic of such a structural resolution within the context of Śiva and Pārvatī's relationship in terms of Sāṁkhya principles of *puruṣa* and *prakṛti* (or cosmic sexuality):

> The male principle and the female principle stand opposed; a third principle (Ganesha), a kind of impersonalized sexuality, stands in the middle and serves both to unite and to separate. The combination of male-plus-female is fertile but if the outcome is a secondary complete male, then jealousy will separate what was united. The alternative male-plus-male is sterile, and the two males will be jealous over the possession of women. The myth offers a "resolution" of the paradox. If male unites with female to produce a sterile offspring then the latter will serve as a mediation between the sexes instead of a source of hostility. The "man in the middle" must be either no sex or both sexes in alternation. (p. 93)

Although the myth may offer a resolution to (1) the psychoanalytic paradox of erotic attachment to the mother and murderous hatred for the father through resuscitation with a new head and (2) to the structural paradox by introducing Gaṇeśa as an asexual or sexually ambiguous figure between the two equally mighty and opposed embodiments of feminine procreative and masculine ascetic powers, it remains uncomfortable about portraying Śiva in such an unflattering light as a father. To camouflage the full force of Śiva's mutilating actions, the myth displaces the deed onto various surrogates: Śani, Paraśurāma, a curse, the actions of fate, and Śiva's ignorance that Gaṇeśa is his son. Similarly, when Gaṇeśa does battle with Śiva, he is also ignorant of Śiva's true identity and takes him to be an anonymous intruder even though Śiva shouts at him, "Fool, don't you know who I am? I am none other than Śiva!" (ŚP 2.5.13.33). Thus they both act out their aggressions unaware of each other's true identities. As a narrative device in the myth, the characters' mutual ignorance corresponds to the themes of forgetting and repression in psychoanalytic theory; once the son has become socialized into his identity through identification with the father, he forgets or represses his desire for the mother and his hostility toward the father. In the myth, when Gaṇeśa comes to understand that Śiva is his father—a recognition he acquires only after receiving a new head from his father—he accepts his role as the Lord of Obstacles, becomes a yogi and a dancer (like his father), and takes up various weapons to guard the doorway for both his parents to protect their intimacy from unwanted intruders.

However much the myth may want to cover up or displace the violence inherent in Śiva and Gaṇeśa's confrontation, the logic of the story requires that the rupture between them take place. Śiva must get past the doorkeeper. Pārvatī must not be allowed to remain aloof from the world and create without male participation of some kind. The lord must unite with his *śakti.* In the same way, at the entrance to the shrine, the devotee must risk doing battle with the explicit and hidden forces of external pollution and internal resistances to faith and press on into the innermost part of the shrine to experience the awesome grace inherent in contact with the deity's presence. A similar logic obtains in the realm of ritual and social life. In the rite of *upanayana* the *ācārya* must sustain the tradition by breaking the childhood attachments of the initiate and make him into a new being, born again into a male world that is linked to the past through text, sacred speech, and gesture. It is a necessity, the proper order [*dharma*] of things that this process take place. The father must take the boy out of the domestic world of women and introduce him to the world of men, this public realm of work and politics, the arena of the superego function, just as his father did for him and so on back into the ancestral past.

There is displacement of another sort in the myth also, this time seen in Pārvatī's role in Gaṇeśa's mutilation and restoration. When she creates him and stations him at the door, she exposes him to inevitable danger. What need is there of a guard unless you are expecting trouble? She tells him he must remain there admitting no one; no exception. In another version of the story, when Śani resists looking at Gaṇeśa because of the curse he is under that anything he looks on will be destroyed, Pārvatī mocks him and forces him to look at her son. Her complicity in her son's dismemberment suggests a more subtle ambivalence than the one we noted with Śiva. It is as though she has to expose him to his inevitable fate, just as the mother of the *brahmacārin* must turn her son over to the *ācārya,* and the psyche must see the mother as less than absolutely benevolent. Pārvatī is a "good" mother because she loves her son tenderly and defends him against the father's violence; she is a "bad" mother, in that she exposes him to danger and gives him an impossible task to perform. But the myth is as uncomfortable about admitting her complicity in Gaṇeśa's beheading as it is with Śiva's naked aggression. It attempts to diffuse the force of the events onto a wider set of powers and persons. When viewed in relation to the dynamics of the traditional Hindu extended family, the myth finds a structural parallel. In a family organization that contains multiple parental surrogates, the forces of infantile desire are not placed in overdetermined ways on the mother and father alone; instead they are scattered among a number of adults, leaving the child with the feeling that the pains of maturation rest with forces larger than those of the mother and father.

For Gaṇeśa there is no final death, only a temporary rupture. Śiva puts him back together in the only form in which he can exist in the world. As with the sacrifice he completes Gaṇeśa even as he destroys him. The hand that rends is the hand that mends. The story has a happy ending: when Gaṇeśa is restored and given primacy of place before all the gods, Śiva and Pārvatī are reunited, death is rationalized away, and there is opportunity for a new beginning.

After Śiva has restored Gaṇeśa with the head of an elephant, he confers on him various powers and privileges. The stories vary in details, but the pattern is important. After embracing him, performing the proper rites of childbirth, and giving him weapons, Śiva initiates Gaṇeśa into his new duties. In some versions of the story Gaṇeśa's *dharma* is to protect the status quo. Śiva speaks:

> "My son, you are born in order to destroy the demons and help the gods and Brahmins who teach the Vedas. Stand there in the path that leads to heaven and create obstacles in the rites of whoever has sacrifices performed but fails to pay the priests' fee." (LP 105.14–16; cf. SkP 1.2.27.7–14)

Other versions of the story have Gaṇeśa create obstacles for the gods or for Śiva's own devotees, who are seeking entry into heaven through Śiva's shrine and crowding out the gods (SkP 7.1.38.1–34; VāmP 28.72). This pattern of Gaṇeśa's ambivalent behavior at the threshold links him with the actions of demons and will be examined in more detail later.

In the divine scheme of things Gaṇeśa does not win recognition for battling heroically against the superior might of Śiva, but rather receives his titles and powers as a reward for submitting to Śiva. This submission theme emerges particularly clearly when Gaṇeśa allows Śiva's axe to fall on his tusk rather than to deny obedience to his father's weapon, the symbol of his authority. Śiva is forced by the power inherent in Gaṇeśa's renunciation, and with no small amount of prodding from Pārvatī, to recognize Gaṇeśa as his son and reward him with the symbols of the son and disciple. In the battle with Śiva, Gaṇeśa wins by losing. It is a passive-aggressive strategy and Gaṇeśa's submission coerces his father's generosity.

Parallels can be observed at the level of ritual performance and infantile fantasy. In the rite of *upanayana,* the *brahmacārin* submits to fasting, separation, shaving, and so on, and the *ācārya* gives him his staff and clothing, adopts him, and gives him his ritual name and instruction. The final stage in the resolution of the Indian variation of the oedipal situation comes with the identification of the son with the father, but for Indian males this identification is absolute, especially as it occurs in the relation ship of the disciple to the guru. Carstairs comments, "When confronted with this complete surrender the deity, the father and the Guru are compelled to offer help; the tyranny of early childhood reasserts itself" (p. 160). This new father/son, guru/disciple, *ācārya/brahmacārin* relationship creates a new bond of affection in the context of absolute domination by the authority figure and utter dependence of the disciple. The sexual nuances of this relationship are well hidden, but it is significant that in the myth Śiva gives Gaṇeśa his weapons and in the ritual the *ācārya* gives the *brahmacārin* the ascetic's staff [*yogadaṇḍa*]—symbols, like the broken tusk, of the detached phallus. Carstairs notes further, "There is also a powerfully repressed homosexual fixation on the father. This is shown . . . in indirect and sublimated form, in a man's feeling toward his Guru—in one context in which a warm affectionate relationship (although a passive and dependent one) is given free expression" (*ibid.*).

An important element in the symbolism of the elephant head is displacement or, better, disguise. The myth wants to make it appear that the elephant head was not a deliberate choice but merely the nearest available head in an auspicious direction or the head of one of Śiva's opponents to whom he had already granted salvation. But, from a psychoanalytic perspective, there is meaning in the selection of the elephant head. Its trunk is the displaced phallus, a caricature of Śiva's *liṅga.* It poses no threat because it is too large, flaccid, and in the wrong place to be useful for sexual purposes. In the myth of the broken tusk, Śiva does not restore it but leaves it for Gaṇeśa to carry around and to use occasionally as a weapon or a writing instrument. The elephant head is also a mask, and, as it is a mask's purpose simultaneously to reveal and conceal, it both disguises and expresses the aggression inherent in the story. So Gaṇeśa takes on the attributes of his father but in an inverted form, with an exaggerated limp phallus—ascetic and benign—whereas Śiva is "hard" [*ūrdhvaliṅga*], erotic, and destructive.

Gaṇeśa's characteristics mirror those of his father. In contrast to the erotic/heroic lord of creatures, Śiva-Paśupati, Gaṇeśa is the celibate/passive animal-headed lord. When Śiva is bold, Gaṇeśa is meek; but when Śiva stands powerless before an obstacle—as he does before the righteous King Divodāsa who rules over Śiva's longed-for city of Kāśī—it is Gaṇeśa who overcomes the obstacle (as we shall see). Leach comments on this structure of relations:

> The sexual qualities which are attributed to Ganesha depend upon context and, generally speaking, are the opposite of those attributed to his father. . . . As Shiva varies so also Ganesha varies, but in the inverse direction. (p. 82; cf. Beck 1974, p. 11)

The inverse variations Gaṇeśa exhibits in relation to Śiva carry beyond those of sexual identity into the realms of physical form and action, where these identities are displayed and played out.

The theological message of the Śiva/Gaṇeśa, *ācārya/brahmacārin,* father/son pattern can be summarized in this way: submit that you may be saved, be destroyed that you may be made whole. The sacrifical violence is not the tragic conclusion, but the necessary beginning of a passage into a new order where renunciation of the self makes affirmation from the other possible, where transforming yourself into an offering to the deity induces the god to give you rebirth into this world. The god who breaks you makes you; destruction and creating ultimately spring from the same source. Personal fulfillment comes when personal idiosyncratic attachments give way to acceptance of the transpersonal divine order, an order made apparent only at the moment in which the particular self surrenders itself. The Maharashtrian poet-saint Tukārāma expressed this theological vision succinctly (*Tukārāma Gāthā,* no. 3414, 3171):

> *If we want to enjoy God,*
> *we should lop off our head from our body*
> *and hold it in our hands*
> . . . .
> *when the body has been sacrificed to god, says Tukā,*
> *all worship has been accomplished.*

Brother/Brother

Śiva and Pārvatī have two sons, neither engendered in the normal fashion. Skanda, also known as Kārttikeya, Guha, and (in Tamil) Murukaṉ, born from Śiva's seed spilt into the Ganges, and he is raised by the six Pleades (Kṛttikās); hence Skanda has one body and six heads. The myth of his origin appears in the older Epic and Purāṇic texts in many variations; he enjoys a separate following among devotees, especially in South India (cf. O'Flaherty 1975, p. 327 [myth no. 43] for variants; see also P. K. Agrawala 1966, Clothey). Although the myths of Skanda's birth are earlier and appear to provide the model for some of the versions of Gaṇeśa's birth story, Skanda in most areas tends to be regarded as the younger son (Beck 1974, pp. 11–12). He is a handsome child, a perpetual youth, slender of body and heroic in his exploits in defense of the gods against the ravages of the demon Tāraka. Unlike Gaṇeśa, Skanda's relationship with his mother appears uncomplicated by incestuous desires, and with his father there is none of the conflict that his brother experiences. The two sons of Śiva and Pārvatī do come into conflict with one another, however, and their story evokes the theme of sibling rivalry; the competition takes different forms in several myths (Riviere). It is a continuation of the oedipal conflict, this time played out not with the father but with another male, the brother, over access to the mother. The best known of these myths is from the *Śiva Purāṇa,* in which the two brothers compete over the prize of women:

> Śiva and Pārvatī said to their two sons, "You are both good sons, equal in our eyes. An auspicious marriage will be performed for the son who returns here after having gone round the entire world." When he heard this, Skanda started off immediately to go around the world, but Gaṇeśa pondered in his mind. Then he bathed and placed two seats for the worship of his father and mother. After praising them he circumambulated seven times around their seats, and then said, "Let my auspicious marriage be celebrated now." But his parents were surprised at his remark, and so Gaṇeśa replied. "Is it not said in the Vedas and Śāstras that anyone who worships his parents and circumambulates them will derive the merit of circumambulating the earth? Such things are said in the Vedas and Śāstras; are you going to say they are false? If you do, then your forms become false, as to the Vedas themselves. So, let my marriage be arranged quickly."
>
> When Śiva and Pārvatī heard his words they were greatly astonished, but they praised their son for his clever mind. And so Gaṇeśa was married to the daughters of Prajāpati: Siddhi (Success) and Buddhi (Intellect). After some time Gaṇeśa begat two sons: Kṣema (Prosperity) born to Siddhi, and Lābha (Acquisition) born to Buddhi. When Skanda returned and found that he had

been tricked by his brother, he went angrily to the Krauñca mountain where he remains, celibate. (2.5.19.15–20,26)

The prize of a bride is curious in the light of Gaṇeśa's usual aversion to women other than his mother. Iconographically he is sometimes represented sitting between Siddhi and Buddhi, but there is little in the way of mythology about his marriage in the textual tradition. These women appear more like feminine emanations of his androgynous nature, *śaktis* rather than spouses having their own characters and stories. They are like the figure of Gaṇeśānī or Vināyakī, a feminine form of Gaṇeśa. Their appearance iconographically seems to be to provide an overall balance and pairing of gender (see P. K. Agrawala, *passim*). The prize of the wife may be interpreted in another way, in light of a variant of this myth from Sri Lanka. Gaṇeśa's mother, Pattini, offers the prize of a mango to which of her sons can go around the world first. Gaṇeśa wins by circumambulating her and eats the fruit and then gets beheaded. Obeyesekere points out that in the cult of Pattini the mango is a vaginal symbol. Hence Gaṇeśa's eating the fruit is an act of incestuous possession of the mother for which he is punished by beheading, symbol for castration, and his celibacy is his punishment for acting out his incestuous desires (p. 471).

The celibate character of his marriage is evoked by the seventh-century poet, Bāṇa, who wrote of Gaṇeśa and his bride as the fused-androgyne, lacking sufficient separateness from one another to engage in the erotic possibilities of marriage. "May the single-tusked Gaṇeśa guard the universe, who imitates his parent's custom in that his bride, it seems, has been allowed to take that half of him wherein his face is tuskless" (SRK 94, Ingall's trans.). He lives a celibate marriage; yet, according to the above myth at least, he has children; this is another way in which he is the inversion of his father, who has sex but no children—at least none engendered naturally. Reference to Gaṇeśa's children are indeed rare, this one in the *Śiva Purāṇa* being the only one known to me among the Purāṇic sources. The contemporary North Indian cult to the recently established goddess, Santośī Mā, the benign mother who gives her mostly women devotees good health and auspicious marriages, claims Gaṇeśa as her father (Howell, pp. 21–22). The myth attempts to domesticate

Gaṇeśa into the fold of family life, using the rivalry with Skanda as the occasion, just as it uses Gaṇeśa to make a father out of Śiva. It may also be because Gaṇeśa and Skanda are always in opposition in the myths in which they appear together that the logic of the opposition requires if one is celibate, the other must be married. The Skanda tradition predates that of Gaṇeśa, and Skanda's identity as a *brahmacārin* is clearly established. In those cases where there is a tradition of Skanda being married, Gaṇeśa is the one who is celibate. Here as elsewhere, Gaṇeśa is the more protean figure, capable of making a sudden about-face and moving in contradictory directions.

This story of fraternal competition may draw its inspiration from a much older tale in the Brāhmaṇas about a bet between Indra and Ruśama, who appears to be cast in the role of Indra's brother:

> Indra and Ruśama made a wager: "Whichever of us shall first run round the earth shall be the winner." Indra ran round the earth, Ruśama ran round Kurukṣetra (only). She said, 'I have conquered thee." But Indra said: "It is I that have conquered thee." They went to the gods for a decision. The gods said: "Kurukṣetra is as great at the *vedi* (sacrificial post) of Prajāpati." So neither of them won. (Tāṇḍya 25.13.3; cf. JB 2.300)

The issue in the competition between Indra and Ruśama, as in that between Skanda and Gaṇeśa, is which effort yields the greater prize. It is a conflict between two ritual strategies. On the one hand is the complex of winning the prize by conquest, reminiscent of the ancient kings who, prior to the sacrifice of the horse, would "go around the world conquering on every side" (AB 8.21–23). The theme of conquering the world, marking off its outer boundaries coalesces into *bhakti* tradition of pilgrimage, going a great distance and grasping the prize of the auspicious sight [*darśana*] of the deity. It is the heroic quest for the "center"—the locus of secret and precious power at the far and dangerous periphery of the familiar world, followed by the return home with the prize in one's hand or marked on one's soul (cf. Turner 1974, pp. 166–230). It is Indra and Skanda's quest: they are both heroes and such ventures are appropriate to their natures. The other ritual strategy is to keep the circumambulations closer to home. Kurukṣetra and Śiva and Pārvatī are the "centers" of the universe. This leap of theological imagination saves many steps and much time. In the myth of Indra and Ruśama, their efforts cancel each other out, and the gods call the contest a draw. In the second story, Kurukṣetra is the whole world. In the case of Gaṇeśa and Skanda, there is a clear winner. The myth claims equal status for devotion and pilgrimage, the *bhakti* solution is as potent and "easier" than *karmayoga.* This is the lesson the *Bhagavad Gītā* teaches. Gaṇeśa tricks his brother out of the prize and forces Śiva to reward him for his cleverness, a cleverness that is inseparable from his devotion.

The theme of sibling competition appears to have deep roots in the Indian tradition, as the ancient Brāhmaṇic story indicates, and it has not escaped notice in anthropological studies of contemporary India. Stephen Tyler emphasizes the tension built into the structure of fraternal relations in the joint family that seems to contribute to alienation between brothers:

> Brothers are not expected to be mutually supportive, but more often than not become jealous and quarrelsome, particularly when the father's authority declines or ceases with his death. . . . A younger brother is supposed to extend to his elder brother the kind of respect he gives to his father, but he often resents and rebels against this arrogation of his elder brother's status. Conversely, elder brother quickly takes offense at any flippancy or lack of respect from a younger brother. Younger brothers feel that their elder brothers attempt to make them do more than their share of the work, and elder brothers suspect younger brothers of laziness and malingering. Both siblings are quick to suspect the other of receiving a disproportionate share of family income either through paternal preference or skulduggery. (p. 137)

The competition between sons for the parent's affection comes into even clearer focus in another variation of the Gaṇeśa/Skanda story. After Pārvatī explained to Skanda and Gaṇeśa the marvelous *soma*like qualities of *modakas,* the two boys besieged her, each asking for them for himself. She said to them:

> "Your father will decide who I will give it to." When Skanda heard this he quickly went on a pilgrimage through the triple world, mounted on his peacock, but the wise pot-bellied one circumambulated his two parents. Then he stood there happily in front of his two parents, saying, "Give it to me, give it to me!" as Skanda was coming behind him. Then looking at them both,

> Pārvatī smiled and said, "All the pilgrimages and sacrifices are not worth a sixteenth part of the worship of one's parents. Therefore this son [i.e., Gaṇeśa] is worth more than a hundred sons having a hundred virtues. (PP Sṛṣṭikhaṇḍa 65.14–20)

Unlike the first version of the story, here the prize is food rather than wives—each bestows its own kind of immortality. The contest over ritual strategies—action versus devotion—remains constant in both variants, and *bhakti* is the preferred path to salvation, for it alone gives the greatest measure of nourishment.

These sibling rivalry stories repeat themes we have seen before in the relationship between Gaṇeśa and his parents, especially his mother. Gaṇeśa defeats Skanda in the contest by remaining close to his parents, honoring them, setting up a shrine and worshipping them there. He makes use of the same strategy with Paraśurāma, who, like Skanda, came back from his pilgrimage of battle and sought entry into his "parents' " presence. But Gaṇeśa got to the door before him, and, lecturing him like an elder brother about the etiquette of children not looking on the nakedness of their parents (i.e., not getting *too* close to them), he refused to allow Paraśurāma to get closer to Śiva and Pārvatī than he himself was. The classical Sanskrit court poet, Maṇḍana, writes of Gaṇeśa—this time the younger brother—asking Skanda a mocking riddle about their parents' separateness and union: "When father and mother became a single body, what happened, elder brother, to the other halves of each? The one on earth was born as every man, the other every woman" (SRK 85, Ingall's trans.). Here again, Gaṇeśa is the model devotee. Why go around the world when the center of the world, the source of the world—your parents—stand before you? As before, Gaṇeśa's submission wins him the reward. The myth portrays Skanda as well-meaning but a bit dim-witted; Gaṇeśa is not only the perfect devotee but he is also the clever ritualist-theologian who knows how to turn the rules and doctrines to his own advantage. He is a clever god, and his cleverness as the mover and placer of obstacles is an important theme we shall explore later.

The contrast in personality between Skanda and Gaṇeśa finds expression in relation to their devotees as well as their parents. In contemporary South India, where the cult of Skanda (or Murukaṉ, his Tamil name) is particularly popular. Gaṇeśa plays a more specialized role than in other parts of India. As Brenda Beck notes:

> Ganesh, the elder, is mainly seen as someone who helps overcome obstacles and inauspicious influences. Murugan (Skanda), on the other hand, has a more positive personality and is granter of favors or boons. Murugan is known to respond to a devotee's expression of affection and need. (1974, p. 12)

In the cycle of myths of Gaṇeśa, we see a series of ambivalences inherent in the realities of family life. The father and mother engender children out of the desire for the affection and prestige they confer, yet they, especially the father, see them as an intrusion into the ultimate goal of liberation from the world of desire and rebirth. The son both unites and separates his parents. With his mother the son is bound in a close emotional relationship, yet she must participate in severing this bond as she yields him up to the authority of the male world, symbolized by the constellation of asceticism and initiation into the realm of social life and by Pārvatī's creating and then endangering Gaṇeśa by making him her guardian. She is the generous "good" mother *and* the decapitating "bad" mother." The son submits to his father's arbitrary and heavy hand of authority and takes on himself the acceptable forms of cultural identity and participation—an inversion of the Western version of the oedipal conflict. Through this submission comes acceptance, recognition, and ultimately a victory of sorts over the father as the son/initiate/devotee receives the mantle of his new status and takes his ordained place in the divinely grounded order. In the myths this process is represented in Gaṇeśa's beheading and restoration as the Lord of Obstacles and Beginnings, the one to be worshipped at the outset of all undertakings, even those directed toward Śiva himself. The myths finally explore the world of sibling competition in the stories of Skanda and Gaṇeśa contending for their parents' approval. Implicit in this rivalry is the competition between different religious paths, the ascetic's path of pilgrimage and renunciation over against the householder's path of duty and devotion to one's parents and community at home. Much of the appeal of Gaṇeśa for Hindus surely stems from the capacity of his myths to evoke the inevitable ambivalences of family life at their most intense levels and to represent the tensions and resolutions of the developmental process as they occur in the context of traditional Hindu society and values.

Gaṇeśa and the Demons

In many respects Gaṇeśa is one with the demons in Hindu mythology. As we have already noted in our discussion of the myth of his origins, Gaṇeśa's story draws much of its imagery from the earlier tales of Śiva's defeat of the elephant demon Gajāsura. Gaṇeśa exhibits a pattern similar to other demon adversaries of gods and goddesses who take on animal forms. He is like Kāliya, the river serpent demon, whom Kṛṣṇa first defeats when Kāliya threatens the cow maidens, but then restores Kāliya to be his disciple. Or Gaṇeśa is like Mahiṣa, the buffalo demon, who receives salvation from Durgā after she has taken his head in battle. When Śiva defeats and beheads Gaṇeśa, he prepares the way for Gaṇeśa's elevation into the inner circle of Śiva's own divine retinue, and Śiva brings Gaṇeśa across the threshold into the company of the gods as their guardian.

Gaṇeśa's connections with the demon world appear in various ways in different myths. It is said that in the *dvāpara yuga,* the cosmic age prior to the present *kali yuga,* Gaṇeśa appeared as Gajānana, the elephant-headed one, and did battle with the red demon Sindūra. After he had defeated the demon, Gaṇeśa himself turned red (GP 2.126 ff). The tale explains why many of Gaṇeśa's iconographic representations are red in color and it also hints that Gaṇeśa took on the quality of the demon when he inherited his color, much as when Śiva took the skin of the elephant demon and wrapped himself in it.

Gaṇeśa's demon ancestry shows itself in another myth about his origins, one in which the elephant-headed demon Mālinī drinks Pārvatī's bathwater mixed with her seed/dirt and produces a son with five elephant heads. Śiva completes the creative process by trimming the four superfluous heads (Jacobi, pp. 807–8). Hence Gaṇeśa has one divine mother, Pārvatī, who androgynously provides the creative substance, and one demon mother, who brings forth the five-headed child. Śiva finishes the engendering process with an initiatory mutilation, making Gaṇeśa recognizable and acceptable to the gods. The amputation of the four heads may also be read as Śiva's cutting away Gaṇeśa's demon portion to render him fully divine.

Gaṇeśa's association with demons is hinted at elsewhere in a brief but suggestive passage in a text of ritual instructions for the worship of the goddess Jyeṣṭhā (or Nirṛtī), the inauspicous deity who instigates quarrels and the alter ego of the benevolent goddess Lakṣmī. The text describes Jyeṣṭhā as "elephant-headed" and "pot-bellied" and followed by a "retinue of obstacles" (BGS 3.9.3.4; cf. BGpS 3.9.14–19; Kramrisch 1975, p. 254). Nevertheless, coming from demon stock is not particularly disadvantageous in the context of Hindu mythology; the demons are not all bad. Of course, they do compete with the gods over the *soma* of the sacrifice and the *amṛta* at the churning of the ocean. They perform mighty acts of asceticism to win boons from the gods, which enable them to destroy the universe and undermine *dharma*. But they also sacrifice themselves as model devotees and become transformed thereby into beings of divine stature (cf. Hospital). It is not so much that the gods are all good and the demons are all bad. The demons tend to look bad because the myths about them are told from the gods' point of view (on the evil god and the good demon, see O'Flaherty 1976, pp. 94–138; Shulman, pp. 317–46). The demons play an indispensable role in the Hindu ecology of suffering and sacrifice, sometimes crossing over the boundary from one mythological category to another, from gods to demons and vice versa.

As his iconography reveals, Gaṇeśa is similar in form to the *yakṣas,* that class of semidivine, usually benevolent beings who attend the god Kubera and others and who take their places at the boundaries and bases of temples, lending their aid to maintain an auspicious environment for deities and devotees alike (see pl. 5). In the Buddhist *Jātaka* tales the *yakṣas* are the demonic giants who stand as guardians of the earth's riches. A very early image of Gaṇeśa (or perhaps his prototype) appears on the coping of the Buddhist shrine at Amarāvatī—dating from the second century of the common era—standing among other *yakṣas,* although his name does not appear on any list of these creatures (Coomaraswamy 1928a, p. 7). Gaṇeśa also resembles Kubera in functions. Kubera is the lord of wealth and king over the *yakṣas;* his retinue includes a host of auspicious beings, such as *guhyakas, kiṇnaras, gandharvas,* and *apsarases.* Kubera has a fat, dwarfish body similar to that of Gaṇeśa as well as an almost tusklike mustache; he is also associated with wild and malevolent forces underneath his benign exterior. Because of his ability to bring both auspicous and inauspicious influences, he is both praised and propitiated. Like Gaṇeśa, Kubera protects one of the directions—standing as the guardian of the northern direction—in opposition to Gaṇeśa as lord over the south. According to one reference in the *Mahābhārata,* he also has a consort named Ṛddhi (MBh 5.115.8–9). Both Kubera and Gaṇeśa are closely associated with Śiva, and they are both invoked by devotees to bring wealth, success, good fortune in worldly matters, and to ward off malevolent or dangerous powers (cf. Bedekar, *passim*).

When Śiva restores Gaṇeśa's head with that of an elephant, Śiva rewards Gaṇeśa for his sacrifice by placing him in charge of Śiva's own entourage of semidivine, semidemonic followers, the *gaṇas.* The *gaṇas* are the troops, as their name implies, who follow Śiva from place to place and carry out his orders. They are a motley looking crew of strange-faced creatures, alternately horrible and humorous, and, like their master, denizens of the wild forest. They resemble the Vedic *maruts* or *rudras,* the martial storm gods who make up the troops following Indra and Rudra. Like Siva's *gaṇas* of the Epic and Purāṇic periods, these ancient *maruts* act as the guardians of the directions and protectors of the divine palaces. We have already noted the connection between the story of Gaṇeśa's origins and that of the *maruts,* who were born from Diti's womb after Indra had cut them into seven pieces. The *gaṇas* sometimes add comic touches to life at the feet of Śiva and Pārvatī. As the poet-dramatist Kālidāsa tells it: on their wedding night when Pārvatī was reacting with all the shyness appropriate to a new bride to Śiva's amorous advances, Śiva called to his *pramathas* (i.e., *gaṇas*), the custodians of laughter, and "he caused her to laugh by the grimaces [*vikāra*] of the faces of the *pramathas*" (*Kumārasambhava* 7.95). Like the seven dwarfs of European folklore, who serve Snow White and go merrily off to work each day, the *gaṇas* always appear in the plural, anonymously, and they dutifully revere their master. They draw their powers from Śiva, or, at his bidding, from Gaṇeśa.

Gaṇeśa has another explicit connection with the demon world in his name Vināyaka. Etymologically the name is derived from the prefix *vi* and the root *nī* ("lead"); taken together they translate as "lead away." In the earliest sources in which this name appears, vināyakas are groups of malevolent creatures who lead people astray and place obstacles in their paths. However, with proper and potent ritual propitiation—detailed in some of the Smṛti texts—their mischievous influences could be controlled.

The *Mānavagṛhyasūtra,* a Vedic manual for domestic rites, details a ceremony called the *vināyakakalpa* for the propitiation of these vināyaka demons. In it the symptoms of the vināyakas's malevolent presence are described:

> Now we shall explain (the rite for the atonement of) the Vināyakas. (The names of the Vināyakas are:) Śālakaṭanalaṭa, Kūṣmāṇḍarājaputra, Usmita, and Devayajana. The person who is possessed by these (Vināyakas), show the following symptoms: He presses a clod of earth. He cuts down blades of grass. He makes scratches on his limbs. He sees water in his dream. He sees people with shaven heads (in his dream). He sees people with crested hair (in his dream). He sees people with reddish-brown garments (in his dream). He sees camels, pigs, donkeys, Caṇḍālas, etc. (in his dream) and (has other impure) dreams; (He dreams that) he strides through the air. When he walks along a path, he thinks (to himself): "Someone is following me from behind." Princes now, when they are possessed by these Vinayakas, even when they are endowed with auspicious marks, are not blessed with issue. Of women, even when they are virtuous, the children die. A learned Brahmin, even when (he has the qualities for) being a teacher, he does not gain the (official) status of teacher. During the time that the pupils study great obstacles arise for them. The traffic of merchants vanishes. The husbandry of ploughmen bears (only) few fruits. (MGS 2.14.1–21, Dresden trans.; AP 264; *Bṛhatsaṁhitā* 58.9; GarP 100.1–9; *Viṣṇudharmottara Purāṇa* 2.105; cf. YS 1.270–74; Kane 2/2, pp. 213–16)

This text identifies four vināyakas, possibly associated with the four directions, whose powers of destruction are capable of overcoming the positive influences of personal virtue in order to place obstacles in the way of those who seek an auspicious marriage, healthy childbirth, political rule, scholarly attainment, and profitable business and agriculture. They appear to cause seizures, nightmares, and paranoia. This same text goes on to specify what ritual strategies might fruitfully be used to ward off the negative influences of these vināyakas. After making the appropriate purificatory ablutions and invoking the presence of the vināyakas, the priest performs the following ritual:

> At the cross road in a village, or at cross roads in a town, or at a cross road in a market-place, after having strewn darbha grass with the points of the blades turned (outwards) in all directions, he offers with a new winnowing basket a *bali* sacrifice (consisting of) husked (rice) grains, unhusked (rice) grains, uncooked meat and cooked meat, uncooked fish and cooked fish, uncooked flour-cakes and cooked flour-cakes, pounded, fragrant substances, a fragrant beverage, a honey beverage, a Maireya (?) beverage, a Sura beverage, an untrimmed wreath and a trimmed wreath, a red wreath, a white wreath, red, yellow, white, black, blue, green, and multi-colored garments, beans, Kalmasa (a species of rice), roots and fruit. (MGS 2.13.28, Dresden trans.; cf. YS 1.285–92)

When these offerings have been made at the crossroads, the point where forces intersect, the priest recites, "May these gods be pleased with me, may they, while being pleased, please me, and being satisfied, satisfy me" (MGS 2.13.29). The purpose of these portions of food (raw and cooked, vegetarian and nonvegetarian) and praise is to keep the vināyakas at a distance, fed, and untroublesome.

Another ritual manual, probably of later compilation, reproduces essentially the same description of the symptoms of vināyaka possession, but with one important difference. Instead of mentioning four vināyakas, it speaks of a single figure, Vināyaka, the son of Ambikā (Pārvatī), who "has been appointed by Rudra and Brahmā as the leader of the *gaṇas* with the power to bring about obstacles to action" (YS 1.271). This description explictly links Vināyaka and Gaṇeśa both in terms of parentage and role. A commentary on this text, the *Mitākṣara,* adds the observation that Vināyaka's purpose is to obstruct rites in two ways: to undercut actions that have the power to accomplish certain ends and to thwart attaining the fruits of actions or rites properly performed (YS 1.271). Thus Vināyaka works at both the beginning and end of actions, putting up barriers to the proper performance of a rite—such as causing the priest to forget his lines—and obstructing access to the benefits of rites even when they have been correctly performed. Consequently his efforts erode the effectiveness of ritual action and the influence of personal virtue. It is not surprising that Vināyaka was feared or that he was accorded ritual honor before other rituals were undertaken. This is the same role *rākṣasas* play in Vedic sacrifices. The enormously authoritative law book, the *Mānavadharmaśāstra,* condemns those who offer sacrifices and worship the *gaṇas*—and it also includes these people on the list of those to be excluded from receiving a portion of the Vedic sacrifice, along with the thieves, outcasts, eunuchs, atheists, and other undesirables (*Manu* 3.164). The demon lineage from *rākṣasa, marut,* and *vināyaka* to Gaṇeśa further supports the argument that Gaṇeśa emerges from within the network of Aryan and Vedic symbolism in contrast to the view that he is an outsider from a Dravidian or non-Aryan folk tradition. In the above text for *vināyaka* propitiation, these rituals are appropriately located as a kind of preface to the section on auspiciousness-producing rites [*śānti*] to the planets to ensure successful undertakings. The larger significance of the custom of worshipping Gaṇeśa at the beginning of undertakings is one we shall explore more fully later.

An account of the destructive tendencies of Vināyaka appears in the description of Brāhmaṇic customs in South India by the eighteenth-century traveler and cleric, the Abbe Dubois, who was never excessively generous in his appraisal of Hindu religious practices. His account closely parallels those given in the classical texts:

> He [Vināyaka] is of a morose and irascible disposition, and always ready to annoy and thwart those who fail to pay him sufficient respect. It is for this reason that so much deference is shown to him, and then on grand feast days his good offices are the first to be evoked, his worshippers fearing lest he should take it into his head to disturb the feast and bring it to an untimely end. (pp. 164–65)

The latter part of this description, gathered from conversations with priests, reminds us of Śiva and his tendency to mess up the feasts or sacrifices of those who fail to propitiate him, as he did with Dakṣa.

The Purāṇic texts are uncomfortably aware of the discrepancy between the malevolent, obstacle-creating powers of Vināyaka and the positive, obstacle-removing actions of Gaṇeśa, and they attempt to disguise Gaṇeśa's demon background through the clever use of false etymologies for the name "Vināyaka." In one case, when Śiva saw, much to his surpirse, that Gaṇeśa appeared out of the mixture of his and Pārvatī's sweat and bathwater, he exclaimed to her, "A son has been born to you without [*vinā*] a husband [*nāyakena*]; therefore this son shall be named Vināyaka" (VāmP 28.71–72). This etymological sleight of hand obscures the association of Vināyaka with "those who lead astray," which is its etymologically prior meaning, and connects it with another meaning of *nāyaka* as leader or husband. Another effort at disguising Gaṇeśa's link to the inauspicious Vināyaka appears in the conversation between Śiva and Pārvatī after she made her headless son out of her bodily dirt and sent Skanda to fetch an available head for the child. As Skanda attached the head onto Gaṇeśa's shoulders, Pārvatī screamed that it was too large. But Śiva reassured her, explaining that since the head is the leader of the body and since Gaṇeśa's new head is so large [*mahat*], he shall be called Mahāvināyaka (SkP 7.3.32.15–17).

Finally, a different strategy of concealment comes into play in yet another myth of Gaṇeśa's origins from South India, one in which he is created in order to defeat the demons. The story is a variation of the Gajāsura/Jalandhara myths in which Śiva saves the universe from destruction by defeating and destroying the demon who has surpassed the powers of the gods themselves and the story of Gaṇeśa's dismembering the moon into bright and dark halves. The tale opens with the familiar predicament of the gods being pushed around by the demons:

> . . . ill used, as they were, by the haughty giant Gajamukha (the elephant-faced), who had obtained the privilege that neither a god, nor a demon, nor a man, nor a beast, should be able to kill him, (the gods) thought of Gaṇapati, as the one who might kill the tyrant, seeing that he was none of the four, but a compound. Accordingly, Gaṇapati went with all his hosts into battle, and in the height of the combat, he broke his right tooth and threw it at the enemy, who, in the consequence of this, tumbled to the ground, and suddenly became a great rat. Gaṇapati, however, not slow, sprang at once on the back of the rat, which has ever since been his vehicle. (Ziegenbalg, p. 59; cf. Jouveau-Dubreuil, pp. 41–42; GP 2.134)

Like his father destroying the elephant demon, Gaṇeśa defeats Gajamukha—a double of Gajāsura and perhaps Gaṇeśa's own alter ego—turning him into a rat, a creature similar in its ability to overcome obstacles—such as getting into tight places to find food—yet in marked contrast to the elephant-faced giant. The rat and the elephant are poles apart in size and strength within the animal kingdom, but each has the capacity both to overcome obstacles and to thwart the fruitful outcome of undertakings. The unlikely image of an elephant-faced deity riding on a rat may be comical—and a sense of humor seems to be quite intentional—but this curious pair share a common trait: both are masters at overcoming obstacles.

As one whose demon ancestry is manifest, despite efforts at a cover-up in the Purāṇic texts, Gaṇeśa is superbly qualified to be lord over Śiva's *gaṇas,* themselves a generally unruly bunch. As one of the demons brought over into the family of the great lord Śiva, Gaṇeśa mediates between the oppositional forces of the divine and the demonic. He understands the demons; he knows their ways and does not fear their powers. Like his father, who was originally an outsider within the Hindu pantheon and an opponent to the other gods, Gaṇeśa stands both outside and inside the divine worlds as he dwells at the threshold (cf. Hiltebeitel 1976, chap. 12) He both places and removes obstacles and facilitates and thwarts undertakings. He does not tolerate neglect from gods, demons, or humans; those who fail or forget to do him homage or give him propitiation find their efforts coming to ruin. Only a being who is as much a demon as a god could stand simultaneously on both sides of the threshold that separates and connects the worlds of the gods and demons. Only a being as protean as Gaṇeśa could qualify for this mediatory assignment in the arena of principalities and powers as represented to human beings through their myths and images.

Obstacles and Thresholds

Gaṇeśa is also called Vighneśvara or Vighnarāja, the Lord of Obstacles. His task in the divine scheme of things, his *dharma,* is to place and remove obstacles. It is his particular territory, the reason for his creation. Śiva gives him these responsibilites as the chief of his *gaṇas,* as he had done with other *gaṇas* in other myths, such as Andhaka and the *yakṣa* Harikeśa in reward for their exemplary asceticism (MatsyaP 178.38–40; 179). Śiva explains in one story of Gaṇeśa's birth:

PLATE 1 Dancing Ten-Armed Gaṇeśa. Eighth century. Central India. Buff sandstone; h. 125.7 cm (49½″). The Asia Society, New York. Mr. and Mrs. John D. Rockefeller III Collection, 1979.13.
Photograph by Otto E. Nelson.

PLATE 2 Gaṇeśa. Late tenth to early eleventh century. Early Chola period (A.D. 875–1070). South India. Tamilnadu, region of Tanjore. Bronze; h. 41.3 cm (16¼″). *The Nelson-Atkins Museum of Art (Nelson Fund), Kansas City, Missouri.*

PLATE 3 Gajalaskṣmī (Elephants lustrating Lakṣmī). Second century B.C. Sanchi. Detail of a pillar.
Photograph by Job Thomas.

PLATE 4 Gajalakṣmī with Gaṇeśa. Contemporary lithograph. Maharashtra.
Author's photograph.

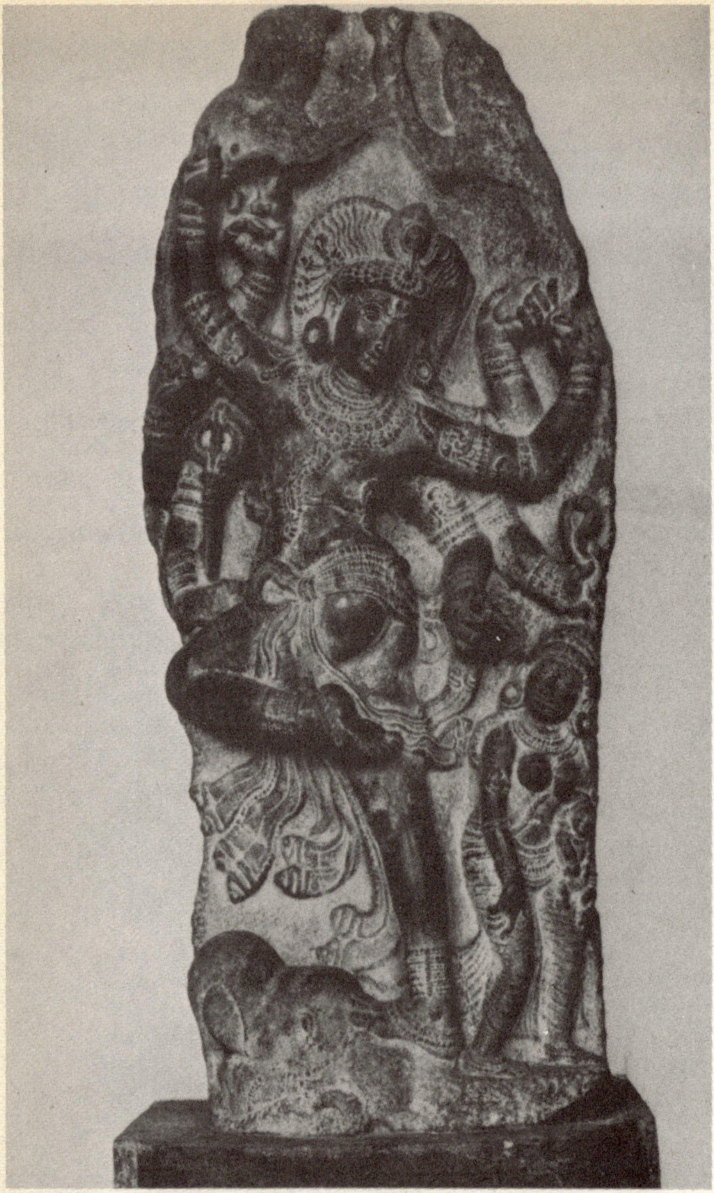

PLATE 6 Gajāsurasaṃhāramūrti (Śiva dances on the head of the defeated elephant demon). Twelfth century. Darasuram, Tamilnadu. *Photograph by Job Thomas.*

PLATE 7 Gajendramokṣa (Viṣṇu liberates the elephant king). Fifth century A.D. Daśāvatāra Temple, Deogarh, Uttar Pradesh.

PLATE 8 Gaṇeśa images of the *aṣṭavināyaka* shrines in Maharashtra. Contemporary lithograph.
Author's photograph.

PLATE 5 Yakṣa figures. Second century B.C. Sanchi. Stupa no. 1, west arch. © *American Committee on South Asian Art.*

PLATE 9 Gaṇeśa as a child, with Śiva and Pārvatī. Maharashtra. Contemporary lithograph.
Author's photograph.

PLATE 10 Worship of Gaṇeśa at the domestic altar. Maharashtra. *Author's photograph.*

PLATE 11 Gaṇeśa image in procession.
Maharashtra. *Photograph by H. P. Tipnis.*

PLATE 12 Immersion of Gaṇeśa image in the river.
Maharashtra. *Author's photograph.*

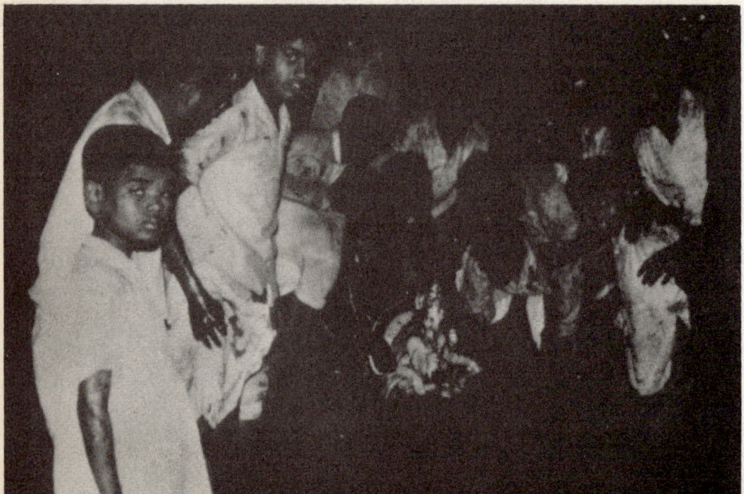

> Hear, O Pārvatī, what this son of yours will become. He will be like me in might, heroism and compassion. This son of yours will become one just like me because of these qualities. He will make obstacles that last until death for those evil and impious ones who hate the Veda and *dharma,* And those who fail to pay homage to me and Viṣṇu, the supreme lord, they will go to great darkness by the obstacles laid before them by this lord of obstacles. In their houses there shall be quarrels without end.
>
> Because of the obstacles your son makes everything perish utterly. For those who do not worship, who are intent upon lies and anger, and are committed to fierce savagery, he will create obstacles. He will remove obstacles from those who revere the traditions, knowledge and teachers. Without worshipping him, all actions and laws will become obstructed. (SkP 1.2.27.8–14; LP 105.12–16; cf. VarP 23)

In this account of his role, it appears that Gaṇeśa's energies are to be spent defending the cosmological status quo: protecting the interests of the gods, routing demons, shoring up the authority of the Brahmins, and generally looking out that the flow of sacred power moves upward toward the gods and their earthly representatives. Gaṇeśa does battle with the demons, fighting heroically and victoriously, as in the following myth in which he defeats the demon-mother Danu:

> The gods went to Mount Arbudha with Gaṇeśa in the lead. then the demon Danu, powerful and feared by all the gods, saw Gaṇeśa and created through her power of illusion many demons equal to her in size and strength, each one knowing all the skills of warfare. Then there followed a great battle and the demons which Danu had created conquered all the armies of Gaṇeśa with their various obstacles. The gods became terrified, thinking Vināyaka [Gaṇeśa] might also have been destroyed. "If he were killed in the battle, we don't know how to protect Indra," they thought. Then Śiva, Indra, and Viṣṇu drew their weapons and struck Danu and fought her back for a while. And as the gods were fighting with Danu Gaṇeśa got up from the ground, and in a rage he took the missile which Śiva had given him and cut off the head of Danu, and he utterly destroyed all her demon followers, the ones she created by her asceticism and valor, tying them with a noose. Then Gaṇeśa returned the gods their kingdoms and took away all their fear. (DP 115)

As the champion of the interests of the gods, Gaṇeśa removes one obstacle by placing another. The demon Danu was the obstacle thwarting the gods. The gods called on Gaṇeśa to remove the obstacle of the demon.

A story is told in Sarasvati Gangadhara's *Gurucaritra*—a devotional text of the Dattātreya tradition in Maharashtra that was written in 1538 and remains a chief source of *bhakti* for devotees of this deity—that Gaṇeśa prevented Śiva's *liṅga* from being stolen by the demon Rāvana, the bête noire of Rāma. Rāvana attempted to carry the precious form of Śiva away to Lanka and establish it in his capital where it would remain invincible and a threat to the gods. Śiva's devotees would also thus be deprived of the object of their worship. Viṣṇu turned to Gaṇeśa to place an obstacle to prevent Rāvana's theft of the *liṅga*. Śiva had said that if the *liṅga* were established in Lanka, it would reach down to the lowest world and remain immovable. It would be impossible even for the gods to take it back once it was installed. Taking the form of a small boy, Gaṇeśa gained Rāvana's trust. The demon asked him to hold the *liṅga* while he relieved himself and said his morning meditations. As Rāvana was thus engaged in his morning ritual, Gaṇeśa placed the *liṅga* on the ground and it at once took root. The place of the *liṅga* has become a center of pilgrimage, called Mahābaleśvara ("the great child-lord"), and serves as a center of worship for both Śiva and Gaṇeśa in northern Karnataka and southern Maharashtra (Ghurye, pp. 110–11; cf. Tulpule, pp. 352–53). In this story Gaṇeśa's cleverness saves the day for the gods. Unlike Rāma he does not confront Rāvana directly with force of arms but by the power of disguise and his own devious imagination.

In other contexts, however, Gaṇeśa reverses this pattern and places obstacles before the gods, as he does in this version of the story of the churning of the cosmic ocean:

> The gods churned the ocean until poison began to spill out. Nārada warned them that they should pay homage to Śiva, but the gods were eager to fulfill their desires and so they ignored him. Soon the poison spread to the upper regions and the gods, sages and demons fled in all directions, as they did at the time of the sacrifice of Dakṣa, and finally took refuge in Brahmā. But Brahmā could do nothing, and he led them to Viṣṇu, who was also powerless to stop the burning poison. Finally all the gods and world-guardians came to Śiva for refuge.
>
> Then Gaṇeśa said to Śiva, "Just to amuse myself I have created

> this obstacle which is difficult for them to overcome. Because of fear and illusion the gods do not worship you or me, and so they encounter terrible obstructions to their actions." Śiva then said to the gods, "Even though this world is thought to be perishable, there is also that which is imperishable. Look to yourselves. What is the use of sacrifice, asceticism, or undertaking any action, or thinking whether all is one or many? Together you attempted the difficult task of churning the ocean to obtain nectar. But you excluded and ignored me, and that is why all of you fell into the jaws of death, there is no doubt. We have created Gaṇeśa to bring every action to successful conclusion, but you did not honor him and Durgā, that is why you have become afflicted with difficulties. (SkP 1.1.9.91–10.9.75; cf. PP Sṛṣṭikhaṇḍa 67.22–56)

In this version of the myth of the churning of the ocean, the gods get into trouble partly because they are greedy for the benefits to be derived from possessing the immortality-conferring elixir—but more importantly and immediately, it is because they fail to honor Gaṇeśa, who removes obstacles from all undertakings. Even the universe itself cannot be created without first propitiating Gaṇeśa; through failing to do so, the gods encounter the obstacle of the poison. That obstacle ultimately drives them to Śiva, who uses the occasion of their distress to instruct them on the proper way to worship Gaṇeśa. This story follows the pattern of the earlier tale of Śiva's destruction of Dakṣa's sacrifice because Dakṣa excluded Śiva from it. In this story, the exclusion, together with its disastrous consequences, also has reference to Gaṇeśa—Śiva's son and the one to whom Śiva's powers extend. In causing the poison to be churned out of the ocean and threatening to devour all that has been created, Gaṇeśa—for sheer enjoyment at watching the gods squirm in their predicament—brought it forth as an obstacle to the gods in order to remove from Śiva and himself the obstacle of nonrecognition by the other gods. At one level the myth serves as a legitimation for the worship of Gaṇeśa at the beginnings of undertakings. There is no action prior to the creation of the universe, except, of course, worshipping Gaṇeśa. As one text reassuringly puts it, "Whenever there is calamity or whenever one wants to obtain his desires, he should worship Gajānana [Gaṇeśa] and all his plans will become successful, there is no doubt" (BrP 2.3.42.42–44). The story brings order out of chaos by turning the anxiety of the gods at seeing their efforts devoured by the poison into devotion to Gaṇeśa. Disaster proves to be the appropriate precondition for religious instruction.

In addition to placing obstacles for demons and gods, Gaṇeśa also obstructs the efforts of the righteous to obtain salvation when too many of them are going to heaven and crowding out the gods. The story is told of Gaṇeśa's efforts in this direction in connection with the famous Śaivite shrine of Somanātha:

> Just before the *kali yuga,* women, barbarians, *śūdras* and other sinners entered heaven by visiting the shrine of Somanātha [Śiva as lord of the *soma*]. Sacrifices, asceticism, gifts to Brahmins, and other obligatory rites ceased to be performed, and heaven became crowded with men, old and young, those skilled in the Vedas, and those ignorant of them. Sacrifice was destroyed and the earth emptied; heaven became so overcrowded that people had to stand holding their arms straight up. Then Indra and the gods became distressed at being overrun by men, and sought refuge with Śiva, saying, "It is because of your grace that heaven is crowded with men. Give us a place to live. Yama, the lord of *dharma,* is struck dumb when he thinks about their evil deeds and the seven hells which are now empty." But Śiva could do nothing, for he was the one who had granted them entry into heaven. So Pārvatī created Gaṇeśa from the dirt of her own body and said to the gods, "For your sakes I have brought forth this being to place obstacles before men so that they will become filled with great delusion, their wits defeated by desire, and they will not come to Somanātha, but to hell instead." The gods became happy and their fear of men vanished. (SkP 7.1.38.1–34; cf. Kennedy, pp. 354–56; O'Flaherty 1976, pp. 253–55)

As a sacred center, the shrine is a "place outside of and opposed to the sway of time and the corruption that time brings about" (Shulman, p. 23). Devotees who go there obtain entry into heaven regardless of sex, caste, ritual purity, or knowledge of sacred texts and rites. The shrine undercuts all other means of obtaining merit and power, such as sacrifice and asceticism. Most important, the shrine negates the negation of death; Yama becomes unemployed. This upsets the balance between gods and humans, heaven and earth, and chaos results from this excess of Śiva's grace. When the gods appeal to Śiva for help he can do nothing for he has already given his unconditional boon to the devotees who come to the shrine. It is Pārvatī who gets the gods out of their predicament by creating Gaṇeśa to stand at the threshold of the shrine and corrupt the devotees with worldly desires. As a center of pilgrimage and offerings, the shrine serves the needs of the gods, but it also potentially threatens their hegemony because the sacrednes of the shrine overcomes death and thereby causes crowding among the immortals in heaven. The shrine's sanctity must remain uncorrupted, but access to it must be made difficult; the promise of salvation to pilgrims must stand without conditions, but the realization of the spiritual benefits must, nevertheless, be hard to win. As David Shulman points out:

> No man or woman must be allowed to reach the shrine. The security of the gods depends upon the corruption of men. . . . Still, the implication of this myth is that if a man, be he righteous or evil, can succeed in getting past the gatekeeper, he is assured of salvation. The gatekeeper thus comes to represent a trial of inner strength; the devotee must overcome his fears, his doubts and his human weakness, in order to accomplish his pilgrimage. (p. 24)

Gaṇeśa, the gatekeeper, removes obstacles from the gods by placing them before humans. He does not corrupt the shrine itself, but rather corrupts those who attempt to enter it by deluding their minds with desire. He poses as the challenge to the devotee, the one who must be gotten past. The devotee who is not deluded will know that the "secret" of entering the shrine and taking advantage of its sacred power lies in "remembering" to worship Gaṇeśa at the beginning, at the point of entry to the shrine and its ritual processes. The balance between god and human depends on the devotee not recognizing Gaṇeśa as he stands at the door, just as Śiva did not recognize Gaṇeśa when he sought entry into Pārvatī's bath. The difference between Śiva and the devotee is that this time it is Gaṇeśa who holds the axe, and it is the devotee's head that, metaphorically at least, must be offered in order to get past the Lord of Obstacles. Gaṇeśa subverts humans to protect the gods, but the true and uncorruptible devotee subverts Gaṇeśa's subversion by paying him homage at the threshold, an homage Gaṇeśa is obliged to reward.

A similar theme of the corruption of humans in order to make life easier for the gods appears in the story of the righteous King

Divodāsa of Kāśī (Benares) and Śiva's efforts to regain his beloved city:

> King Divodāsa lived in Benares. At this time Śiva and Pārvatī were married and lived with his in-laws. But his mother-in-law took offense at Śiva's behavior. Pārvatī pleaded with Śiva to take her away, and so Śiva looked over all the worlds and decided Kāśī would be the most pleasant place to live. But when he saw that Divodāsa already lived there he ordered Gaṇeśa [Nikumbha] to empty it, by means of subtle deceit. Then Gaṇeśa appeared in a dream to a barber named Kaṇṭaka, instructing him to build a shrine and install his image there. When the shrine was established many came there and received gold, sons, and other boons. Then the chief queen of Divodāsa worshipped there, asking over and over for a son. But Gaṇeśa did not grant her desire, hoping to arouse the king's anger. When, after a long time, the king became enraged at Gaṇeśa for not giving him a son, he angrily destroyed the shrine. Then Gaṇeśa cursed him, and the city became empty. Then Śiva came there with Pārvatī and they dwelt in Kāśī. (H app. 1, no. 7, 57–140; BrP 2.3.67.30–65; VayuP 2.30.25–55; cf. O'Flaherty 1976, pp. 189–204; Shulman, pp. 77–78)

Like the story of the Somanātha shrine, this myth turns on the assumption that gods and humans cannot live in the same place at the same time. For Śiva to take his bride to Kāśī, he must first rid the city of its inhabitants. It falls to Gaṇeśa as the lord of obstacles to delude the righteous king, which Gaṇeśa does by creating a shrine that confers favors on all comers, especially the low-caste barber, but not to Divodāsa and his queen. Gaṇeśa denies the queen offspring and Kāśī an heir to the throne. When Divodāsa impetuously destroys the shrine, Gaṇeśa uses this occasion as the opportunity to empty the city, making way for the divine couple to take their places. In this way balance is restored. Śiva finds a home and settles down with his wife. But Divodāsa is not simply thrown out of his city to become a homeless martyr: Gaṇeśa seduces him into an enraged gesture of ritual defilement by obstructing the flow of beneficial power from his shrine to the king and his wife, meanwhile granting all boons to others. By placing the obstacle of delusion before Divodāsa, Gaṇeśa removes the obstacle of homelessness from Śiva and Pārvatī. In another version of this story, Viṣṇu and Gaṇeśa take the form of Buddhist monks and convert the king and his wife to a heretical faith, thus leading them to abandon sacrifice and temple rites and in that way incurring the withdrawal of divine favor. At last in their apostasy they abandon the city, leaving it to Śiva (GP 2.47; cf. Kennedy, p. 251).

In a South Indian version of this story, Gaṇeśa assumes a different form to accomplish Divodāsa's removal from Kāśī:

> Vināyaka took the form of an astrologer with a book under his arm. He gave the town's citizens bad dreams, and then appeared and interpreted their dreams and the position of the stars as auguring the impending ruin of the city. The people fled, forgetting to perform their rites. (*Vināyaka Purāṇam* 81.109 ff., quoted in Shulman, p. 80)

Here Gaṇeśa uses his now familiar strategy of delusion, this time by giving people nightmares and then interpreting them so that they would flee the city. The Sūtra and Smṛti texts we examined earlier make the point that one of the ways in which Vināyaka or the vināyakas appear is in nightmares and hallucinations.

In a version from a sectarian Gāṇapatya purāṇa, the story of Divodāsa becomes the occasion for a reversal of roles between Gaṇeśa and Śiva:

> Tortured by the pain of separation from Kāśī, Śiva performed asceticsim until Gaṇeśa appeared. Then Śiva said, "O Lord of Obstacles [Vighnarāja], I am beset with obstacles, therefore please free me from them. Protect me from this pain of separation. In the past you gave me a boon that by remembering you at the beginning of actions I would become like a son to you.
>
> Then Gaṇeśa made a Brahmin named Ḍhuṇḍi out of his body and said to him, "In order to bring success to Śiva, go to Kāśī and delude the people with the teachings of the Buddha." Then Gaṇeśa summoned Viṣṇu and said, "Assume the form of a Buddhist, and at my command go with Ḍhuṇḍi and corrupt the city." In the meantime Kāśī was also practicing asceticism for a thousand years and Gaṇeśa came to her and granted her the boon that her husband would be returned to her. (MudP 1.50–51)

Śiva suffers from the obstacle of separation from his beloved Kāśī, understood either as the city or his lover, and seeks refuge in Gaṇeśa, assuming the posture of a devotee of the elephant-faced lord. Gaṇeśa makes Ḍhuṇḍi out of his body, much as Pārvatī made him out of hers. Ḍhuṇḍirājā, the lord of Ḍhuṇḍi, is the name by which Gaṇeśa is worshipped at a major shrine in the middle of Benares (SkP 4.39ff; cf. Eck 1982, pp. 187–88). In each of these variations of the Divodāsa story, Gaṇeśa's role remains constant: he is the one who places the obstacle before the righteous king so that Śiva may take the city for his own. He makes use of disguises or creates other beings out of himself to delude the king. Gaṇeśa is the one who actually redresses the balance by his deft placement and removal of obstacles. Placing and removing, as it turns out, are two sides of the same action. Giving to one means taking from another.

In other contexts Gaṇeśa comes to the rescue of humans of every social and religious stature, helping them to overcome obstacles. This pattern comes into focus in several thematically related stories. In a pair of myths about kings who meet with obstacles in their efforts to expand or overcome their treacherous appetites, Gaṇeśa makes it possible for them to realize their goals.

The first tale in the pair is a reworking of the famous story of the quarrel between the warrior-king Viśvāmitra and the Brahmin sage Vasiṣṭha. Viśvāmitra had attempted to become a Brahmin but he was either seduced from his asceticism by a *gandharva* or, when he had performed his asceticism properly, Vasiṣṭha refused to recognize him as a Brahmin. Our version of this story opens with a conflict over the sage's wish-fulfilling cow that Viśvāmitra desires to take for his own:

> Formerly Viśvāmitra was a *kṣatriya* afflicted with hunger. Once while hunting he came upon the hermitage of the great sage Vasiṣṭha where he saw the beautiful wish-granting cow, Nandinī. Viśvāmitra desired the cow and tried to persuade Vasiṣṭha to trade it, offering him every sort of riches, armies, and horses. But the sage refused. Then the king stole the cow. As she was being carried off, the cow opened her mouth, and from it there poured smoke, fire, and great armies of warriors. When Viśvāmitra saw the power of the sage's cow, he thought, "I will become a Brahmin too, and attain the marvelous power he has." And so the king performed asceticism, but though his meditation was fierce he still did not attain brahminhood. Then he went to Kailāsa, and, praising Śiva and Pārvatī, asked that the obstacle to his asceticism be removed. Then Śiva taught him the proper means of worshipping Gaṇeśa, the remover of obstacles. Viśvāmitra performed the wor-

> ship [*pūjā*] and all the obstacles disappeared and he became a Brahmin, which is difficult for anyone to attain. (SkP 6.214.19–72)

Viśvāmitra desires to become a Brahmin out of jealousy for the sage's supernatural powers—in the form of armies of celestial beings issuing forth from the mouth of Vasiṣṭha's cow. When Viśvāmitra's ascetic practice fails to produce the desired results, he resorts to devotion to Śiva. Śiva then instructs Viśvāmitra (and the audience of the story) on the proper ways of devotion to Gaṇeśa, who, once appropriately honored, removes the king's obstacle to attaining Brahmin status.

In the second myth, King Somakānta finds the worship of Gaṇeśa to be salutary for curing moral as well as physical ills:

> Formerly Somakānta, the king of Devanagara, became ill with leprosy. Installing his son on the throne, he and his wife Sudharmā retired into the forest. One day while fetching water Sudharmā met the sage Bhṛgu whom she told about her husband's affliction. Then Somakānta went to Bhṛgu and asked him to cure his leprosy. Bhṛgu explained that in a previous life he [Somakānta] has been a *vaiśya* and was reckless and given to killing Brahmins. Then, in his old age he had become penitent and desired to give away his ill-gotten wealth to the Brahmins, but they all refused to accept it. So, instead he spent his fortune refurbishing an abandoned Gaṇeśa temple; and then he died soon after. Allowed by Yama to reap the rewards from this pious act, the king was reborn as the righteous king Somakānta, but finally the retribution for his earlier Brahminicide caught up with him in the form of leprosy and having wild birds devour his flesh. But Bhṛgu cured the king by sprinkling water on him while reciting the one hundred and eight names of Gaṇeśa and sent his evil nature out of his body. (GP 1.2.10)

Like Viśvāmitra, Somakānta's affliction is the consequence of having injured Brahmins. Giving all his fortune for the construction of a shrine does not create a sufficient wealth of merit to overcome the previous evil *karma,* just as Viśvāmitra's heroic asceticism fails to transform him into a Brahmin. Both are saved by the power of Gaṇeśa's presence, manifested to them through worship and recitation of his divine names. The Lord of Obstacles alone has the power to remove the obstructions that prevent the two kings from realizing their objectives; and both myths serve as examples of how the impossible can be accomplished with the help of Gaṇeśa. Of course, Gaṇeśa is not unique in his ability to rescue his devotees, many gods and goddesses do that; and many such stories of divine deliverance are told to illustrate the saving power of the deity. These two stories indicate some of the particular ways in which Gaṇeśa rules over the terrain of obstacles.

Some stories portray Gaṇeśa as a particularly clever character, a trickster, outwitting his opponents to gain the advantage—as he did with his brother in the story of their contest for a bride wherein Gaṇeśa circumambulated his parents, whereas Skanda returned breathless from running around the whole world. There are a number of stories of this type that besides being wonderful tales of wit and surprise reveal the deeper ambivalence inherent in Gaṇeśa's movements:

> The chief of the *gaṇas* led a troubled life, and he gave himself over to acts of mischief. Once when he went close to the ocean of milk he dipped his trunk into it, sucking up all the ocean including Viṣṇu, Brahmā, Lakṣmī, Ādiśeṣa, and Garuḍa. A few moments later he spat out everything he had sucked in. Hari [Viṣṇu] and his companions were spat out, thrown this way and that, and struck dumb. Regaining his senses, Viṣṇu realized that his conch was gone and he grieved because of it. Then, at that moment he heard the sound of his conch and knew that one of the *gaṇas* had it. He went to Mount Kailāsa and asked Śiva to return his conch to him. Śiva replied that he would not intervene in the actions of one of his *gaṇas* but that he could get his conch returned if he established a shrine for Gaṇeśa at Kāñcīpuram. (Dessigane et al. 1964, pp. 15–16)

This tale of the founding of a shrine is in some ways reminiscent of the story of the churning of the ocean in which Gaṇeśa obstructs the gods from obtaining the ambrosia. Here Gaṇeśa confounds the gods by sucking them all into himself and spitting them out, as a child would spit out bad-tasting medicine. The story then gives an account of the *gaṇas* playing keepaway with Viṣṇu's conch—the mighty instrument made from the demon Pāñcajanya's body—which Viṣṇu blows to strike terror into this opponents. The *gaṇas* demean the great god by treating him like a toy, and Śiva uses this occasion of Viṣṇu's vulnerability to force him to establish a shrine for Gaṇeśa in the famous temple at Kāñcīpuram.

Gaṇeśa plays similar games with holy sages and Brahmins in

the following pair of tales, the first from South India, the second from Maharashtra:

> An exceptionally hot summer set in once in South India. The whole land became parched. So Agastya (the sage) went to Śiva and requested some holy water, and the lord put Kāverī, who was worshipping him just then, into the *kamaṇḍalu,* (waterpot) of Agastya, and sent him back. Indra, who did not relish this action of Śiva, asked Gaṇapati to somehow or other upset Agastya's *kamaṇḍalu* of holy water, and Gaṇapati in the guise of a crow went and sat on the brink of the *kamaṇḍalu* and thus upset it. Agastya and the crow quarreled with each other. Then the crow assumed his original form as Gaṇapati and blessed Agastya. Moreover, Gaṇapati filled Agastya's *kamaṇḍalu* with holy water which he later distributed among devotees in South India, and that is the present river Kāverī. (Mani, p. 273; cf. Dessigane, et al. 1967, pp. 79–80; Mate, p. 10) msp. 197

Like the story in which Gaṇeśa saves the gods from fiery poison at the time of the churning of the ocean, as this myth opens, the world is being devoured by a drought, symbolic of the fire of doomsday. The only water to be found was that in the river Kāverī, who had left the world to worship Śiva. When Agastya appealed to Śiva to save the world from its distress, the ascetic lord answered his plea by filling his waterpot with the sacred river. But Indra, ever a foe to Śiva and jealous of his creative powers, persuades Gaṇeśa to spill the water. Agastya is said to have been born from such a waterpot, much as the gods were born from the churned ocean. It is also said that Agastya once drank up the ocean and uncovered the demons who were hidden there, thus enabling the gods to destroy them. When Gaṇeśa takes the shape of an inauspicious crow in order to upset Agastya's waterpot, he fulfills Indra's request; but the story takes an unexpected turn and becomes an epiphany of Gaṇeśa, who reveals himself in the midst of the spilled water, much as his father's *liṅga* emerged out of the cosmic ocean. After the spilling of the water and the revelation of Gaṇeśa, Agastya finds the waterpot running over in such abundant supply that it satiates all the devotees and there is a sufficient surplus to form the sacred river Kāverī. The theme of breakage and restoration, like the theme of beheading and adoption as it appears in the stories of the creation of Gaṇeśa or the sacrifice of Dakṣa, points to the theological and cosmological dimensions of the story: the deity appears suddenly in the midst of chaos bringing a new and more plentiful order. In this tale Gaṇeśa is the master of many surprises. He tricks Śiva by upsetting the waterpot at Indra's request, but then he tricks Indra by restoring it. He outwits Agastya through his clever use of disguise, but then he reveals himself and fulfills the sage's wish for water. Insofar as the symbols of the drought and waterpot are analogues to the fiery doomsday and watery creation, Gaṇeśa takes on a cosmogonic role as the one who distributes the water. Thus he saves the world from the fire of drought and establishes a continuing source of nourishment, both material and spiritual, in the river Kāverī as the sacred place for his self-revelation.

Many tales of Gaṇeśa's exploits of deception are funny, and they evoke much laughter when told in temples and at assemblies of devotees; but they also teach theological lessons. One such story is told by the Maharashtrian poet-saint Nāmadeva (b. 1270) about the theft of sweetmeats offered to Gaṇeśa. Nāmadeva was a Vaiṣṇavite devotee of Viṭṭhala at Pandharpur, and his story bears strong resemblance to the famous myth about the young child Kṛṣṇa eating dirt. When Yaśodā, Kṛṣṇa's mother, heard that her child was eating dirt, she scolded him for it, but he denied doing it. Then she demanded that he open his mouth and show her. She looked into his mouth and saw the whole universe displayed therein beyond his oral threshold (BhP 10.8.21–45). In the following tale about Gaṇeśa, this theme of revelation of divinity through the open mouth centers around the eating of sweetmeats rather than dirt, but it comes to a similar conclusion:

> Yaśodā made all the preparations for the worship of Gaṇeśa and placed a tray of sweetmeats [*laḍḍu,* a sweetmeat similar to *modaka*] on the altar before the elephant-faced lord. But Kṛṣṇa kept pestering her, "Mother," he cried, "when are you going to give me some of the *laḍḍu?*" Yaśodā answered that he could have some once they were offered to Gaṇeśa, and then she went into the other room to bring back some incense. Then Kṛṣṇa realized that there was no one else in the room he stole all the sweetmeats and ate them quickly. When Yaśodā returned and saw that the *laḍḍu* were gone, she angrily asked Kṛṣṇa what happened to them. He replied with animated expression, "Thousands of mice stampeded in here led by Gaṇeśa riding on a huge mouse and swept them up

with one sweep of his mighty trunk and ate them all. He was fierce and his mouse was terrifying. I was paralyzed with fear and could not call out. But now I am very hungry; won't you give me some of the *laḍḍu*?" Yaśodā was suspicious of Kṛṣṇa's story, and she demanded, "Open your mouth, for I am sure it is you who have eaten all the *laḍḍu* intended for the offerings." "But," Kṛṣṇa protested, "there were so many *laḍḍu*, how could they all fit in my small mouth? It is Gaṇeśa who stole them. You accuse me falsely." Then she began to beat the child; but when he opened his mouth she saw the whole universe filled with innumerable Gaṇeśas made out of the sweetmeat offerings. These Gaṇeśas in Kṛṣṇa's mouth said in unison to Yaśodā, "Why do you worship me? You should be worshipping your own child." Then Yaśodā fell into a trance and saw that Kṛṣṇa filled the whole universe. But then the veil of illusion [*māyā*] returned and she saw him again as her own son, and then picked him up and caressed him tenderly. (*Nāmadeva Gāthā*, no. 83, pp. 34ff; cf. Eichinger Ferro-Luzzi 1977b, p. 508)

Like the story of Aditi, this tale plays with the theme of stealing the offerings intended for the gods, only this story leads to a more auspicious conclusion. Gaṇeśa emerges here as a co-trickster with Kṛṣṇa; each plays a role to facilitate the revelation to Yaśodā that Gaṇeśa and Kṛṣṇa are embodiments of the whole universe. Yaśodā slips back behind the veil of illusion, but the divine epiphany in the story comes through to the audience. The story is also an example, at least in the region of Maharashtra, of how Gaṇeśa does not remain exclusively within the framework of Śaivism but becomes incorporated into Vaiṣṇava mythology.

Gaṇeśa's capacity for deception takes comic form in a North Indian tale about two neighbors, one rich and the other poor. One day the poor neighbor had a stroke of good fortune and became rich, and his rich friend asked him the cause of his success. He replied that on the previous night he and his wife had worshipped Gaṇeśa in their home with offerings of sesame seeds and sugar. Then while they were sleeping, in the middle of the night, a voice spoke to them saying, "I am pleased with you." When the couple asked who it was, the voice replied, "It is I, Chauth Gosain [Gaṇeśa]." Suspecting that the voice might actually belong to a thief, the wife asked what the intruder wanted. The voice asked to relieve himself; and, terrified at this request, the couple told him to use the corner of the room. Finally, at dawn, the intruder departed. When the dawn's light appeared the frightened couple found piles of gold and jewels in the corner. They felt ashamed that they had treated the god so discourteously. The rich neighbor listened intently to his friend's story and inquired in detail about what procedures of worship he had followed that had yielded such impressive results. Then, on the next sacred day for the worship of Gaṇeśa, the rich man and his wife worshipped the god in the same way his formerly poor neighbor had done. In the middle of the night, the same voice made the identical request from within the worship cabinet. The rich couple gladly invited the voice to relieve himself in the corner of the room. When the light of dawn broke the couple was astonished to find that the room was "filled with human excrement, flooded with urine, and giving forth a horrible stench!" (Mukherji, pp. 15–19).

This marvelous tale of the unexpected rewards for the humble and just retribution for the arrogant also explores Gaṇeśa's capacity to invert the expected order of things. The humble couple had worshipped Gaṇeṣa without thought of reward, but only out of true devotion, and were willing to receive any gift from his hand, even one of filth. To the rich couple who thought they could manipulate Gaṇeśa's rituals to produce material reward, Gaṇeśa gave them the "reward" the poor couple has originally expected to find. In this story Gaṇeśa's dirt manifests itself as *both* gold and its opposite.

Gaṇeśa's power to help the underdog and embarrass the powerful by making unexpected nocturnal visits is also illustrated in a story from the Mahars, a scheduled caste of sweepers in Maharashtra:

> A Mahar [sweeper] youth named Gaṇapati who used to be one of the guards over the Shaniwar Palace in Poona, was fair and elegant to look on. One of the ladies of the palace carried on intrigues with him. The misconduct was discovered, and the Peshwa put the guard to death. The ghost of the dead man kept appearing to the prince in his dreams, and would give him no peace until he made an effigy of the Mahar in the form of the god Gaṇapati and set him up at the Eastern entrance to the palace where all would do obeisance to the Mahar's name. (McKenzie, p. 73)

This story turns on the identity of name between the guard and the god, both of whom stand at doorways. The Mahar Gaṇapati became involved in a forbidden sexual liaison with a Brahmin woman at court and was killed for it, just as Gaṇeśa had lost his head for being too close to Pārvatī in a potentially incestuous and likewise-forbidden relationship. The Mahar Gaṇapati haunted his murderer until he was resuscitated, as it were, in the form of an image of the deity Gaṇapati at the threshold, just as his divine counterpart received a new form from a repentant Śiva and a place of privilege at the gateway of the gods. The story further illustrates Gaṇeśa's protean character, in that he removes and places obstacles, regardless of the social, political, or religious status of the people involved. He operates in the same way in the divine world (as we have seen), placing and removing obstacles for gods and demons alike according to the situation and his own fantasy. It is likely the myth may also be an etiological myth about the worship of a Gaṇapati image by Mahars in service in the Peshwa's palace. Here, as in the story of Divodāsa, where he appears in an image established by another low-caste devotee, a barber, Gaṇeśa breaks through conventional religious hierarchies.

The theme of obstacles and tricks appears in the story about the composition of the *Mahābhārata.* The tale speaks of how Gaṇeśa helped the poet Vyāsa to put the massive oral epic into writing. Vyāsa called on Gaṇeśa at the outset of writing the text to grant the new undertaking an auspicious conclusion:

> Vyāsa said, "Leader of the *gaṇas,* be the scribe of the Bhārata that I have formed in my mind and am now about to recite." When Vighneśa heard this, he replied, "If my pen does not stop writing for a moment, then I will be your scribe." Vyāsa said to the god, "If there is anything you do not understand, cease writing." Gaṇeśa signified his agreement by repeating the syllable "*oṃ*"; Vyāsa began to recite and as a diversion he knit the knots of the texts close together. (MBh 1 app. 1, lines 7–15, 39ff; cf. Mbh 1862 1.1.65–73)

By scholarly consensus the tale is a late interpolation into this important text that otherwise makes no significant mention of Gaṇeśa in the rest of its massive corpus. This fact accounts for why the editors of the critical edition consigned the story to an appendix to the appendix of the text. Indeed, the Gaṇeśa/Vyāsa story may reflect an attempt to get Gaṇeśa into the epic of which it is said anything that is not included within it does not exist. The story is well known to Hindu audiences, however, who generally regard it as part of the epic, as did the 1862 edition of the *Mahābhārata.* The story illustrates the obstacles or "knots" involved in the transmission from an oral to a written medium. The condition imposed by Gaṇeśa for serving as Vyāsa's scribe is that he must never stop writing, a condition that places the poet under no small amount of pressure. In return, Vyāsa makes Gaṇeśa promise that he will stop writing when there is something he does not comprehend. This gives Vyāsa time in his recitation to keep slightly ahead of his divine secretary by throwing convoluted syntactical constructions or difficult philosophical arguments—"knots"—in his way. The act of writing, the transformation from face-to-face oral communication to unmediated text, is itself a threshold activity. When the reciter disappears into the text as its author, the "knots" appear, for the text only transmits the words, it cannot convey the subtle but essential gesture and intonations that the speaker uses in communicating the text. Vyāsa knit eighty-eight hundred knots into the text; even the wise and clever Gaṇeśa had to ponder over their meaning before he could write them down and thereby claim to understand them. As Lord of Beginnings and Obstacles, Gaṇeśa is an appropriate scribe. This story appears at the very beginning of the epic. The act of writing is a matter of making a beginning, to bring word and sense into form, a form that takes on a life of its own once it leaves the pen of its author. As the text takes on an identity and life of its own apart from the author, it initiates ambiguity and creates obstacles to its understanding. Much is gained in the writing of texts; the text becomes available in a more durable way than it would if it depended solely on the recitation of the poet. But something is lost as well. The text as spoken word, with its animation from the vital breath of the poet and the immediacy of response between poet and audience, becomes disembodied and reified. This transition is evoked by the symbol of the knot. The relationship between Vyāsa and Gaṇeśa inverts the expected role regarding authorship of sacred texts. Usually it is the god or divine sage who recites and the human disciple who hears and records the sacred speech. Here the human poet dictates to the divine scribe, and they spar with each other in a battle of wits: Vyāsa trying to stay ahead of Gaṇeśa, who will only write so long as Vyāsa does not stop talking; Gaṇeśa attempting to befuddle Vyāsa as he recites under the pressure of Gaṇeśa's nonstop pen. As in many other contexts having to do with thresholds and beginnings, here Gaṇeśa *both* thwarts and facilitates Vyāsa's efforts. The epic does get written down, its sacred words preserved, but the text is full of "knots" that impede mere mortals as they struggle to fathom its meanings.

If Gaṇeśa makes it possible for Vyāsa to put the *Mahābhārata* into writing, "knots" and all, it is his forgetting to invoke Gaṇeśa that leads to the composition of another text, the *Gaṇeśa Purāṇa,* which is important for the sectarian Gāṇapatya tradition. While narrating the *Gaṇeśa Purāṇa* to King Somakānta, the sage Bhṛgu tells why the text was composed in the first place:

> Vyāsa divided the original single Veda into four, and then undertook to write the Purāṇas in order to clarify their meaning. But out of pride he failed to begin any of the verses with the worship of Gaṇeśa, and so his memory left him at certain points. When he could not understand why he lost his memory, Brahmā explained to him that it was because he had neglected Gaṇeśa. Then Vyāsa wanted to know more about Gaṇeśa and so Brahmā instructed him. (GP 1.10.2–9)

As in the other stories dealing with the misfortunes attending those who neglect Gaṇeśa, here Vyāsa's poetic lapses are a consequence of his pride and his forgetting to worship the Lord of Obstacles. Because Vyāsa forgot his rites, Gaṇeśa placed a "knot" of another sort in Vyāsa's recitations. Knots and forgettings are forms of disappearance of the text, things missing from or obscuring the text's words and meanings. As such, they become obstacles to the communication of the text and thwart the text's purpose. In the case of the *Mahābhārata* story, Vyāsa remembers Gaṇeśa and includes him when he undertakes to write down the epic; but as a consequence of the agreement they make before the beginning, the epic contains its own obstacles. In the story about the composition of the *Gaṇeśa Purāṇa,* Vyāsa's neglect of Gaṇeśa prevents the text being understandable, from being untangled, and requires that the Purāṇa be taught by Brahmā to unravel the "knots" of forgetting in the previous texts.

In looking at these myths of obstacles, we see that the pattern of Gaṇeśa's actions is fluid: he places obstacles to gods, demons, and humans; he also removes them. At the same time he *is* the obstacle who must be gotten past if one is to possess the prize. By beheading Gaṇeśa, Śiva gets past him to possess Pārvatī, the devotee gets past by remembering him at the threshold, Vyāsa uses poetic sleights of hand to slip by his scribe's relentless transcribing, and so on.

In many of the myths we have seen Gaṇeśa's movements are full of surprise and humor. In these respects he resembles the figure of the trickster. In his pioneering study of the trickster figure in the mythologies of North American Indians, Paul Radin offers his summary definition of this elusive character:

> Trickster is at one and the same time creator and destroyer, giver and negator, he who dupes others, and who is always duped himself. He wills nothing consciously. At all times he is constrained to behave as he does from impulses over which he has no control. He knows neither good nor evil yet he is responsible for both. He possesses no values, moral or social, is at the mercy of his passions and appetites, yet through his actions all values come into being. . . . Trickster himself, is not infrequently identified with specific animals such as raven, coyote, hare, spider, but these animals are only secondarily to be equated with concrete animals. Basically he possesses no well-defined and fixed form . . . he is primarily an inchoate being of undetermined proportions, a figure foreshadowing the shape of man. (pp. ix–x)

There are a number of trickster elements in the character of Gaṇeśa: he creates and destroys, he dupes others, and he is associated with animals—the elephant and rat; he has a voracious appetite, his bodily form lacks clear definition, and his bodily form undergoes redefinition through beheading and detusking. Radin identifies as one of the traits of the trickster a detachable penis he carries around in a box (pp. 18–19). Leach sees this characteristic as Gaṇeśa's closest link to the trickster: Gaṇeśa's broken tusk and severed head with the long flaccid trunk are the clearest signals of his sexual ambiguity; his placing and removing obstacles indicates his moral and behavioral ambivalence (p. 82).

These similarities are compelling; and Gaṇeśa as the child, theriomorph, placer and remover of obstacles does move about in his myths with all the unpredictableness of the trickster. Yet, we should be cautious in labeling Gaṇeśa as a Hindu incarnation of the trickster figure. There are important dissimilarities as well, and the distinction between being a trickster and simply mischievous is useful. In the trickster myths, based on Radin's sample of North American Indian tales, the world and values come into being in spite of the trickster's haphazard actions. In the case of Gaṇeśa, there is more of a method to his actions and a location from which he acts, namely, the threshold. Gaṇeśa plays a crucial role in the scheme of things. Standing at the threshold, like the keeper of the locks on the river, he serves to regulate the flow of power according to the needs of the cosmos as a whole. When the gods are too powerful, as when they get all the nectar from the churning, Gaṇeśa turns it into poison. When humans become arrogant in their ritual privilege, as in the story of the gold and excrement, Gaṇeśa turns the tables. When gods or humans or demons are unfairly victimized, he comes to their aid. As the one who himself was an obstacle to Śiva and lost his head for it, he is supremely qualified to be in the business of obstacles at the only vantage point from which to manipulate them, in the margins where the power and possibilities as well as the dangers lie. Generally speaking, tricksters tend to be small and apparently insignificant creatures, although vulgar and outrageous. Gaṇeśa's childlike qualities suggest a smallness of stature in relation to his parents, but his elephantine form also evokes royal power and authority. There are things tricksters tend to do that Gañeśa does not do: he does not mock rituals and myths nor does he undo his own logic, he does not act in ways that defy interpretation. In evaluating the appropriateness of the trickster model as applied to Gaṇeśa, we should say that Gaṇeśa makes use of wit, tricks, and surprises in his actions, that he is mischievous at times, and that he is a "cousin" of the North American Indian trickster. But, in the context of Hindu mythology where all the gods make use of disguises and sleights of hand from time to time, all are to some extent tricksters, we must resist the temptation simply to graft the title of trickster onto Gaṇeśa.

Although we should resist seeing Gaṇeśa simply as a Hindu trickster figure, he is clearly a protean, liminal character in many situations. His body has removable parts and is itself a composite of other previous forms: *yakṣa,* child, and elephant. He stands in the liminal point of crossing or the intersection between two orders of space and power. His sexuality remains ambiguous, as his relationship with his mother and father, his detachable tusk/phallus, and his similarities to eunuchs all suggest. He remains heroic and "manly" in his capacity to destroy demons although this masculinity frequently is overshadowed by his more usual mode of overcoming his opponents by outwitting rather than simply smashing them. As the keeper of the gate and the Lord of Obstacles, he has the power to bless and curse, to accept and reject the petitions of others. In this respect he resembles another famous gatekeeper, St. Peter: not the sober and austere St. Peter of the New Testament and early Christian church, but the St. Peter of folklore, who is a rather devious fellow (see Hynes and Steele). For all his protean dimensions, however, Gaṇeśa is not infinitely changeable. There are things he clearly does not stand for. He does not stand for sexiness or martial power. He is not the embodiment of boundless mercy and self-sacrifice or ascetic rigor as are some other deities in the Hindu pantheon. Gaṇeśa's territory is that of obstacles. Within that terrain he reveals and conceals himself and his actions as he sees fit.

For the devotee the act of worshipping or remembering Gaṇeśa at the outset of undertakings is both a gesture of gratitude for his protection and propitiation for his noninterference in the successful completion of the undertaking. The devotee's offering of copious quantities of *modakas* both expresses unbounded generosity in response to Gaṇeśa's accomplished or anticipated aid and bribes him not to obstruct the devotee's fulfillment of the desired goal.

Gaṇeśa's role as the Lord of Beginnings and Obstacles illustrates some notions of action implicit in the Hindu tradition. The Sanskrit word for obstacle is *vighna;* Gaṇeśa is sometimes called Vighneśa or lord [*īśa*] of obstacles [*vighna*]. The word *vighna* is itself a compound made up of the prefix *vi,* meaning "away, asunder," and *ghna,* a term appearing in compound that means "striking with, destroying," from the root *han,* "strike, kill." A *vighna* can be anything that prevents, interrupts, diverts, or impedes anything else. It is any kind of resistance. Every action or undertaking is like the flow of a river or inhaling and exhaling a breath. It has its "natural" course of action according to the *karma* of the one performing it. But, just as a river can be diverted or a breath can be held, its flow thereby redirected, the undertaking can veer away from the course intended by its author. The diversion or impediment is the action's *vighna.* The forces that come into play in relation to a given action are complex, many of them not known to the actor and some are apparently circumstantial. Hence in every action there is the likelihood of some form of resistance. The task of the actor is not to eliminate the resistance (the *vighna*), for that is impossible, but to attend to the task in such a way that its potential to impede is turned to the benefit of the actor. It is a matter of overcoming the opposition of action/resistence by including the resistence in the action, just as the sacrificer does when he offers food to the demons or the devotee does in worshipping Gaṇeśa. The ritual gesture of paying homage to Gaṇeśa at the outset of an undertaking reminds the devotee that he does not act alone in the cosmos and that his actions must fit into the larger scheme of things. By enlisting Gaṇeśa's aid, the devotee acknowledges the inevitability of obstruction, one's own limited powers of control over the destiny of the action, and the necessity of including the power inherent in the resistance—that is, Vighneśa, the deity residing within the obstacle—as an ally in the undertaking. By assuming such a posture at the outset of an action, recognizing and welcoming the resistance to the act within the act itself, the devotee becomes free to carry on with the undertaking with greater confidence so that the undertaking will fulfill its goal. Psychologically, the anxiety of initiating an action is diminished and its destiny becomes tied to the power of the god. The devotee proceeds in the belief that he is not alone, that his individual action fits harmoniously within the larger framework of all actions overseen by Gaṇeśa's ultimately benevolent presence. Therefore the devotee does not feel as vulnerable as he might otherwise. Only the god who has the power to place obstacles can be of any use in removing obstacles. Time and time again the texts stress that Gaṇeśa is accessible by means of offerings, *mantras,* and other forms of remembrance. His actions frequently appear to be contradictory. But through his ambivalent movements, he regulates the flow of divine and human power in the context of time and *karma* by putting down or picking up obstacles in the interest of maintaining an intimately harmonious cosmological balance. He remains available to all. He belongs only to himself.

The obstacle is found at the boundaries of time and space: temporally at the beginning, spatially at the threshold. These are the points of entry—the loci of highest risk and possibility—where trajectories of action headed toward fruitful resolution can be shifted off course by the slightest ritual or moral error. These temporal and spatial thresholds draw much of their symbolic richness by association with the mythologies of shrines. The paradox of the shrine is that the deity wants to keep the devotee at a distance, guarded from intrusions by impure or unprepared disciples, just as the king wants his privacy protected from every supplicant and hanger-on seeking a favor. Gaṇeśa's task, like that of other doorkeeper figures in Hindu mythology, is to keep the intruders out, as he does with the devotees at Somanātha, demons, and even Śiva himself. On the other hand the deity *must* be interrupted. His or her divine status derives in large part from the honor accorded the deity by the devotee. Where would the deity be were the devotee not there to sing its praises? So the boundary between the profane world and the sacred enclosure of the shrine surrounding the deity must be breached for divine and human persons to live out their respective religious destinies. The devotee must be humbled in the process, broken by losing his head, his ego, and his attachment to false understandings of reality as the price to be paid for intimacy with the deity. The doorkeeper embodies this paradox of the shrine, for he himself is paradoxical and plays a crucial mediatorial role. In the case of Gaṇeśa, his physical form is an invention, made up from other creatures, so that he mediates between the realms of beasts and gods and all that lies between. He mediates between his ascetic father and his mother eager for domestic life and its rewards. He is a son but in a peculiar sort of way. From his father he draws his ascetic tendencies, yet he remains an eternal child close to his mother and her shrines, either in actual location or in his longings. Gaṇeśa mediates between the cosmic forces as the symbol of the obstacle demonstrates, forces that can lead to happiness [*sukha*] or misery [*duḥkha*]. Son, child, theriomorph, doorkeeper, obstacle placer and remover, formidable and fearsome, mischievous and tricksterish, Gaṇeśa connects multiple worlds while maintaining them as discrete entities. His role in the Hindu mythological and cosmological scheme of things is crucial. He is the god of all seasons, worthy of attention before all others.

The figure of Gaṇeśa gives mythic and iconographic form to a fundamental insight about the nature of action, the realm over which Gaṇeśa rules as the creator and remover of obstacles. In commencing an act each person brings to that undertaking a complex set of motivations, awarenesses, desires—all the latent and manifest tendencies of which he or she is neither fully aware nor totally in control. This accummulated karmic inheritance makes up a screen or filter through which one looks in imagining an act and its fruits. Therefore any action is inevitably unpredictable, vulnerable as to its origins, motives, and consequences. An act is irreversible, yet its consequences can be a reversal of that which was intended when the act was undertaken. The Hindu mythological tradition repeatedly bears witness to the expected reversals taking place in any action, whether undertaken by deity, sage, mortal, animal, or demon.

In seeking Gaṇeśa's support at the moment of passing over the threshold of an undertaking, in both time and space, the devotee acknowledges—ritually and devotionally—that his or her undertakings are pervaded by vulnerability. One cannot act alone; the forces and consequences of an act inevitably, and appropriately, somehow encompass all the cosmos. It moves out in all directions of time and space, like the ripples from the pebble thrown into a quiet pond. Within the realm of *saṁsāra* all is contingent. This recognition should lead not to despair, but to wisdom, to a sagacious assessment of one's own cosmological predicament and its opportunities. Such a moment of recognition is sought when the devotee worships Gaṇeśa as the lord of wisdom and obstacles. Gaṇeśa—the one who has been broken and restored, the one rejected by his father and returned to him, the dweller on the boundary where all beings are vulnerable—can appreciate the realization that brings the devotee to worship him. Gaṇeśa's wisdom is not so much the transcendental metaphysical wisdom taught by the Upaniṣads and by Vedānta philosophy as it is practical wisdom—prudence, cleverness, wit, playfulness, and sagacity—that navigates one successfully through the perilous waters of the ocean of *saṃsāra*. In assisting or leading his devotees through these chartless expanses, as his name Vināyaka ("leader") suggests, Gaṇeśa lends power and familiarity to the intractable process of action and consequence. Except for those relatively few Hindus who are his sectarian devotees, Gaṇeśa is not a deity of transcendental realization—that is Śiva's role. Instead he rules the concrete world of action and its fruits, success and failure, triumph and pain. He is the god with his feet planted firmly on the ground, in the midst of the world, and available at the door, just as you step into the reality of a world made vivid by the shrine and its rituals.

4 The Worship of Gaṇeśa

In our explorations of Gaṇeśa thus far, we have concentrated on mythology as the context in which to get acquainted with this remarkable deity. With this narrative context now sketched, it can serve as the background for the next stage of our inquiry. At this point it is appropriate to ask the questions: How do Hindus worship Gaṇeśa? What are the major rituals and settings by which Hindus express their affection for Gaṇeśa? In this chapter we shall take a close look at two major forms of religious response to Gaṇeśa—in private and public settings. The first is worship performed in the home, or *pūjā;* the second is the annual public festival in the diety's honor, or *utsava.*

Information on the worship of Gaṇeśa can be found in as many different places as his images. Ritual instructions are located in some of the Sanskrit Purāṇas embedded in and around the myths. These instructions usually reflect the patterns of Brāhmaṇic practice and sometimes Tantric traditions. In contemporary India ritual manuals may be purchased in inexpensive paper editions that offer instructions for worshipping Gaṇeśa with or without the aid of a Brahmin priest. There is considerable latitude in permissible and recommended patterns of worship, depending on the means, desires, or the traditions of the worshipper and his family. Yet, one has to look beyond the ritual texts to gain an understanding of the devotion Hindus express for Gaṇeśa. An obvious place to look is at the actual performance of the rites and forms of devotion. Because patterns of worship vary from one caste group, region, and family to another, it has not been possible for me to observe the full range of ritual practices to Gaṇeśa; so the following discussion of worship will be limited to research conducted primarily among the Brahmin community in the central region of Maharashtra, an area called the Deśa, in the cities of Ahmadnagar and Pune. Gaṇeśa enjoys considerable popularity in this part of Maharashtra. A few brief side-glances will be taken at the ritual practices among intermediate castes in Maharashtra and Karnataka (for the latter drawing on the field research of Suzanne Hanchett). The focus of our inquiry into ritual will be that of contemporary practice. In the following chapter we shall explore the history of the sectarian tradition of devotion to Gaṇeśa in Maharashtra and the antecedents to the contemporary public festival.

As with other deities in Hinduism, there are many contexts for the worship of Gaṇeśa. Acts of private prayer and meditation, communal singing of devotional songs, calendrical rites and vows, pilgrimages to sacred shrines, and the annual public festival to Gaṇeśa together make up the whole fabric of means by which Hindus articulate their relationship to him. The approach I have adopted is threefold: to describe the major ceremonies in their social contexts; to analyze exegetically the important symbols, gestures, and ritual transactions that Hindus perceive to take place between them and Gaṇeśa; and to assess the social and religious roles of these patterns and cycles of worship in the larger configuration of Hinduism in its Maharashtrian context. The center of my focus will remain the rituals themselves and their internal textures of meaning.

Recently a great deal of excellent research has been done that focuses on how rituals and festivals in India generally serve as dramatic expressions of social processes, often reinforcing the prevailing social structure by inverting it periodically. This allows for the release of accumulated tensions and is followed by the reassertion of the social structure's fundamental authority (cf. Babb; Hanchett; Marriott; Östör). Similar processes can be seen at work in the case of Gaṇeśa and his worship. My point of departure and goal here lie in a somewhat different direction. My grounding methodological assumption is that religious practices must be understood on their own terms: they have their own internal logic and coherence. Religious actions constitute their own world of assumptions, purposes, expectations, and satisfactions on the part of those who perform them. These religious actions must be seen in relation to the claims they make for themselves (their own ideology) rather than seen simply as window dressing for a more fundamental reality of a social or political nature—a reality the actors are not aware of but which the observer has access to by means of models drawn from the social sciences. Although such an approach might seem an obvious choice for a historian of religions, other recent studies undertaken by anthropologists raise similar methodological questions. For example, in his analysis of the indigenous ideology of the Bengali festivals of Durgāpūjā and Śiva-gājan, Ákos Östör responds to the "orthodox" tradition of anthropological analysis:

> My aim is to study the festivals themselves, without positing any direction from society to religion . . . the question is what these categories are in indigenous cultural terms. Thus we are led to the ideologies of the festival participants, and beyond to the system of meanings that ideologies and actions express. In the festivals themselves we see society realized in a certain way that may not be the same as "caste," "kinship," or "politics." (Östör, p. 11)

For the purposes of this study, we shall look at Hindus on those occasions on which they devote their whole energies to Gaṇeśa through words, gestures, actions, moods, and assumptions so that we may catch a glimpse of them in the midst of that world, whatever other worlds of caste, society, and politics they may also live in during these and other times. As Östör argues, festivals are a social and symbolic process in their own right, to be understood in terms of their own rules and assumptions.

Gaṇeśa is often said to be the most popular deity in the Hindu pantheon. He enjoys nearly universal adoration because he is the one who removes obstacles from new undertakings, protects worshippers, and provides access to the other gods and goddesses. Before commencing acts of formal worship, life-cycle ceremonies, pilgrimages and other journeys, courses of study, openings of new businesses, or simply beginning the routines of the day, Gaṇeśa is to be honored with varying degrees of elaboration—from the brief *mantra,* "*Oṃ śrī gaṇeśāya namaḥ* ("Homage to Lord Gaṇeśa"), to the much longer prayers in vernacular languages of Sanskrit, such as the *Śrī Gaṇapati Atharvaśīrṣa,* a Sanskrit Upaniṣad celebrating Gaṇeśa as the embodiment of the ultimate *brahman* (see Appendix). Whatever other deity a Hindu may worship, whether as part of his household shrine [*kuladevatā*], as the guardian of the village [*grāmadevatā*], or as that god or goddess who has the place of special honor in the devotee's life [*iṣṭadevatā*], Gaṇeśa is the one to be worshipped first. He stands at the doorway and allows the devotee access to the other deities and whatever blessing may flow from them. Consequently, Gaṇeśa looms large in Hindu worship, whatever devotion may be paid to other deities. Among orthodox Brahmins of the Smārta tradition, popularized by the ninth-century philosopher, Śaṅkara, Gaṇeśa takes his place among the fivefold divinity, the *pañcāyatana,* along with Śiva, Viṣṇu, Sūrya, and Devī, to be worshipped in the household shrine on specified occasions.

Gaṇeśa's image may be seen almost everywhere in India, in a variety of forms. He may appear, like his father, as a rough stone covered with red paint located near the boundaries of a village or the intersection of roads. He may be found atop doorways of homes and shops, in niches at the thresholds of temples, just inside the doorways but before the devotee reaches the dwelling place of the regnant deity of the shrine. Framed copies of inexpensive lithographs adorn shops and tea stalls, along with pictures of other deities the proprietor and his clientele may venerate. Schoolchildren frequently write the Gaṇeśa *mantra* at the top of their examination papers, and books on religious subjects often include the same *mantra* at the top of the title page, along with a drawing of Gaṇeśa's image. In most households an image of Gaṇeśa may be found on the southern side of the family altar, protecting the other gods of the household from inauspicious influences emanating from the dangerous south, the abode of demons (see Kane, vol. 2/2, p. 717; Das, pp. 20–22).

Gaṇeśa's crucial and pivotal location, both spatially and temporally at the beginnings, assures him a welcome and a gesture of homage. In contrast to this pattern of adoration, however, relatively few Hindus regard Gaṇeśa as their primary deity of devotion [*iṣṭadevatā*], and the sectarian side of Gaṇeśa's worship remains, in Bhandarkar's phrase, a "minor religious system" (pp. 147–49). Instead most Hindus focus their attention on one of the forms of Viṣṇu, such as Kṛṣṇa, Rāma, Hanumān, Śiva, or Devī, or on one of the myriad regional and local deities, deities that in Maharashtra include Viṭṭhala, Dattātreya, Bhavānī, and Khaṇḍobā. There is no contradiction in viewing Gaṇeśa as the embodiment of the ultimate reality [*brahman*] in the context of honoring him at the outset of an undertaking but not worshipping him as the center of one's religious affections and obligations at other times.

Gaṇeśa's threshold location and patterns of action as the remover of obstacles have led poets and devotees to compose invocatory prayers, found appropriately at the beginnings of texts or dramas, that celebrate the elephant-lord's auspicious form and call on him to lend his benevolent presence and grant success to what is to follow. The tenth-century poet Somadeva, author of the *Kathāsaritsāgara* (*The Ocean of Story*), a collection of fanciful tales, invokes Gaṇeśa in his form as a dancer to protect the hearers of the tales from obstacles as they listen:

> May Gaṇeśa, in the advancing night as he dances his tumultuous dance with his trunk raised up and making a whistling sound and spraying forth light and nourishment to the stars, protect you. (KSS 109.1)

> May Gaṇeśa, who throws up his trunk in play around which fly a constant swarm of bees like a triumph pillar covered with letters erected to announce the destruction of obstacles, protect you. (KSS 68.1)

> We honor Gaṇeśa who disperses clouds of obstacles as he fans away with his flapping ears the clouds of bees that fly from his trunk. (KSS 114.2)

The images of Gaṇeśa as the twilight dancer, the triumphal pillar evoking the *liṅga*, and as fanning away bees, all point to his close association with the symbols of his father whom he serves.

In Maharashtra the most popular devotional song [*āratī*] to Gaṇeśa is attributed to the seventeenth-century Vaiṣṇava Brahmin saint Rāmadāsa, asserted by some scholars to be the preceptor of Śivājī, the founder of the Maratha empire and the "father" of contemporary Maharashtra. The song vividly evokes Gaṇeśa's appearance and conveys the experience of *darśana* or the auspicious presence of the deity transmitted through the medium of sight:

> Maker of happiness, remover of miseries, whose grace extends love to us, and does not leave a trace of obstacle remaining, you have a layer of red lead around your whole body and a necklace of pearls shines brightly around your neck.
>
> Victory to you, victory to you, O god of auspicious form. At your sight [*darśana*] all desires of the mind are fulfilled.
>
> O son of Gaurī, you have a jewel-studded ornament, ointment of sandalwood paste, red powder and saffron, and a diamond-inlaid crown. They all look beautiful on you. Anklets with tinkling bells make a jingling sound around your feet.
>
> Victory to you, etc.
>
> You have a large belly, you wear a yellow silk garment, you are praised by Śeṣa [the demiurge]. Your trunk is straight, your tusk bent. O three-eyed one. This devotee of Ṛama, waits for you in his home. O god who is revered by all the great gods, be gracious to us in times of difficulty and protect us in times of calamity.
>
> Victory to you, etc. (Bhat, sect. 3, p. 374)

Other invocations identify Gaṇeśa as the divine Puruṣa, the embodiment of the cosmos; the underworlds are his feet, the continents are his thighs, and the sacred pilgrimage centers are contained in his belly (LP 81.31–35). The identification of Gaṇeśa with the Vedic Puruṣa, the divine persons whose sacrificed parts make up the universe, becomes an important theme in the rites of installing the image of Gaṇeśa on the family altar during the domestic worship (as we shall see).

A somewhat different and more elaborate set of homologies is advanced in a long invocation to Gaṇeśa by the thirteenth-century Maharashtrian poet-saint, Jñānadeva (or Jñāneśvara), in his *Jñāneśvarī,* a commentary on the *Bhagavad Gītā* that extols devotion to god and teaches the path of liberation through devotion leading to knowledge [*jñāna*]. Jñāneśvara begins his text with a panegyric to Gaṇeśa, identifying the elephant-faced lord with the totality of sacred texts and knowledge:

> The Vedas in their perfection are as the beautiful image of the god, of which the flawless words are the resplendent body.

The Smritis are the limbs thereof, the marking of the verses shows their structure, and in the meaning lies the veritable treasure-house of beauty.

The eighteen Purānas are the rich ornaments, and the theories propounded in them are the gems, for which the rhythmic style provides the settings.

The fine metrical form is his many-coloured garment of which the composition is the fine shining texture.

So the epic poems and dramas in it, read with delight, are as jingling bells giving out the music of the sense.

The various principles carefully expounded in them and the aptness of the world expressing them appear as precious jewels set in the bells.

The wisdom of Vyāsa and the others is the waistcloth, its tassled end gleaming with purity.

The six systems of philosophy are the six arms, and the different theories propounded in them are the six weapons held in his hands.

The art of reasoning is the hatchet, logic the goad, the Vedānta philosophy is the luscious sweetmeat [held in the hand].

In one hand is held the broken tusk, symbolizing the rejection of the teachings of the Buddha, refuted by the Vedānta commentaries.

Then the doctrine of the Universal Spirit is the lotus-like hand of blessing; the establishment of religion is the hand of reassurance.

Pure discrimination is the straight trunk, wherein dwells the highest joy of supreme bliss.

Impartial discussion is the pure white tusk; [Ganesh is] the small-eyed elephant-god, remover of obstacles, [representing the subtle eye of wisdom.]

I regard the two systems as his ears, and the bees [hovering over his temples] as the sages who taste of the nectar of their own teaching.

The themes of duality and non-duality come together on the temples of his elephant-head as lustrous corals.

The fragrant flowers adorning the crown of the head are the ten Upanishads, containing in full the honey of knowledge.

The A of the Om is the legs, U is the large belly, and the M is the great circle of the head.

When these three are united, the sacred word is formed. Through the grace of my preceptor, I salute this, the primal cause of all being, the Om. (*Jñāneśvari,* Pradhan trans., 1.3–20)

In this long invocatory prayer, Jñāneśvara calls forth the rich visual imagery of "seeing" the whole tradition of sacred text, poetic meter, philosophical wisdom, refutation of heresy, and religion itself as the "form" of Gaṇeśa. Written and spoken word, religious discourse itself, has its visual, physical form [*rūpa*] in Gaṇeśa's iconic appearance. As a metaphorical device and a theological affirmation, this invocation identifies Gaṇeśa with the totality of the Advaita Vedāntic vision of *brahman* as *sat-cit-ānanda,* being-consciousness-bliss, for Jñāneśvara, even though he himself was a devotee of Kṛṣṇa. This invocation makes only oblique reference to the myths of Gaṇeśa, but it presumes familiarity with them and redirects their meaning from the narrative to the metaphorical level. The broken tusk becomes the weapon used to defeat the influence of the Buddhist heresy rather than the one Gaṇeśa used to destroy the demon adversary he transformed into his rat vehicle. The setting for the defeat of the opponent is not the field of bloody combat but the field of discourse and argument in which the opponent is defeated by persuasion rather than by force of arms. The overwhelming impression conveyed by the invocation is visual: turning text, word, and intellectual tradition into a form, an image, that can be disclosed by the deity and apprehended by the devotee. In this way the words of the invocation draw out the visual experience of *darśana,* the auspicious self-disclosure of the deity through its visual form.

Moments of Danger and Power

Besides these invocational prayers and songs, to be recited according to one's inclinations, Gaṇeśa receives special worship at fixed times during the Hindu religious year. Each lunar month of the year is divided into two parts: a bright half [*śuklapakṣa*] when the moon waxes and a dark half [*kṛṣṇapakṣa*] when the moon wanes. The bright half brings with it ascent and auspiciousness, and Hindus regard it as a more appropriate time to begin new undertakings in the confidence that they will prosper. The dark half is inauspicious, a time of decline, when the possibilities of chaos and failure are greater and new projects are to be avoided.

The fourth day of the dark half of each month is called *saṁkaṣṭacaturthī* ("dangerous fourth"). It is a day when it is particularly inauspicious to begin any new undertaking. A vow [*vrata*] to worship Gaṇeśa on this day during each dark half of the month may be performed in the hope of averting difficulties and avoiding obstacles. Such a vow includes offering *modakas* and other foods to Gaṇeśa, fasting, worship, feeding one's preceptor or, traditionally, twenty-one Brahmins. A myth associated with this vow says that Śiva was able to defeat the wicked demon Tāraka on this day because he had worshipped Gaṇeśa before going into battle (Kane, vol. 5/1, p. 436; see also Ghurye pp. 99–100; Underhill, p. 69). The observance of *saṁkaṣṭacaturthī* as a day of concentrated inauspicious power by worshipping Gaṇeśa with fasting—food may be eaten only after the moon rises in the evening—and other acts of devotion points to the ambivalence of the god's character as one that both creates and removes obstacles. As the creator of obstacles, which he does especially in his form as Vināyaka, he must be propitiated in order for worshippers to avert calamity—just as one would give the demons food to satiate them and thus distract them while the performance of the sacrifice or other sacred rite is taking place, thereby to keep the demons from stealing food intended for the gods. One also worships Gaṇeśa on this inauspicious day because he is the one empowered to overcome obstacles, to render the time that is by nature inauspicious powerless to harm the devotee. The basic ritual posture the devotee takes is one of seeking protection by giving devotion to the deity through offerings of food, self-restraint, and praise; in turn the devotee receives the benefits of Gaṇeśa's obstacle-averting power in the broadest contexts of his life.

The fourth day of the bright half of the month is called *Vināyakacaturthī* ("Gaṇeśa's fourth"). In contrast to *saṁkaṣṭacaturthī,* this day generally reflects Gaṇeśa's positive side, his powers to grant success in undertakings. On this day it is particularly auspicious to start new projects; its mood is happy and energetic. On this day of each lunar month, Gaṇeśa usually receives special recognition in the form of offerings, prayers, and songs. In Maharashtra, the most important annual festival honoring Gaṇeśa takes place on the *Vināyakacaturthī* that falls in the month of Bhādrapada (August/September). It is sometimes said that this day is Gaṇeśa's birthday, his day of auspicious beginnings. It is on this day that his image is taken to the home to be installed and worshipped on the family altar. Although Bhādrapada *Vināyakacaturthī* is in general the most auspicious day associated with Gaṇeśa, as the day sacred for the commencement of the festival and all that follows it, paradoxically it is also the most inauspicious of days in one respect. It is on this day Gaṇeśa cursed the moon because it laughed at him when he stumbled and split open his belly, which was overstuffed with *modakas* received from his devotees. According to some versions of this story, Gaṇeśa not only cursed the moon to wax and wane but also extended his curse to include all who looked at the moon on this day, causing them to suffer from false accusations of theft made against them during the coming year. The reason for this association between the calamity of false accusation and Gaṇeśa's curse of the moon is given in the myth of Kṛṣṇa and the *syamantaka* (wish-fulfilling) jewel. The myth is attributed to the *Skanda Purāṇa* and is retold as a *kathā* (sacred story) on the occasion of Gaṇeśa's worship on the fourth of Bhādrapada (*Vināyakacaturthī*). This complicated story is an important myth of Gaṇeśa in Maharashtra. It is summarized as follows:

> Once there was a Yādava named Sutrājit who, after performing much asceticism to Sūrya, the sun, received a boon. Sutrājit asked for the *syamantaka* jewel (a precious gem said to yield eight loads of gold per day and protect one from all dangers) from around Sūrya's neck, the jewel that yields all wealth and protects against all calamities. Adorned with this magical gem, Sutrājit then went to Dvarka [Kṛṣṇa's celestial city] and so dazzled its inhabitants that they took him to be Kṛṣṇa himself. Fearing that Kṛṣṇa might learn of this imposture, Sutrąjit gave the jewel to his brother Prasena. Later Kṛṣṇa, Sutrājit and Prasena went hunting together, and Prasena was killed by a lion, who took the jewel. Then the lion in turn was killed by a bear named Jambavanta who gave the jewel to his lovely daughter. When Kṛṣṇa and Sutrājit returned from hunting, Sutrājit accused Kṛṣṇa of killing his brother and stealing the jewel. Kṛṣṇa returned to the forest and reclaimed the jewel from Jambavanta's daughter and gave it back to Sutrājit.
>
> Then later, while Kṛṣṇa was away, another Yādava named Satadhanva, jealous of his magical possession, murdered Sutrājit and stole the jewel. When Kṛṣṇa returned to avenge his murder, Satadhanva gave the jewel to Akrura who took it to Kāśī and used its wealth-bestowing properties to build temples and sponsor sacrifices, thus bringing much good fortune to the city and removing its diseases and suffering. Meanwhile, Bālarāma, Kṛṣṇa's brother,

upon seeing Kṛṣṇa's return thought he had only come for the jewel and accused him of being greedy, and so a quarrel broke out between the two brothers.

Distressed over these turns of events, Kṛṣṇa went to Nārada and asked him why things had been going so badly for him and why he had suffered these two false accusations. Nārada replied that it was because he had seen the moon on the night of Bhādrapada *Vināyakacaturthī,* a cursed night which causes people to experience the calamities of having false accusations made about them. (Javadekar, pp. 18–24; see also Gupte 1919, pp. 61–66)

This entire myth of Kṛṣṇa serves as a setting in which a second myth is related in response to Kṛṣṇa's question as to why it is inauspicious to look at the moon on the night of *Vināyakacaturthī.* Nārada's reply both tells a story and gives instructions on how Gaṇeśa's worship is to be performed:

Once Brahmā offered worship to Gaṇeśa and was rewarded with the boon that nothing in his creation would be obstructed. Later Gaṇeśa went to Candraloka (the world ruled over by the moon) and stumbled and fell to the ground (and, according to some variants, spilling his bellyful of *modakas*). When the moon laughed at his misfortune, the god cursed him that no one would look upon the moon's vain and arrogant face; and if they did they would be falsely accused by others and suffer the misfortune that would follow. When the moon could no longer be seen by anyone the world began to wane. The gods and sages asked Brahmā to approach Gaṇeśa and ask him to relent in his curse. The gods began to worship Gaṇeśa on the bright fourth [*Vināyakacaturthī*] and fast on the dark fourth [*saṁkaṣṭacaturthī*]. The moon worshipped him also and apologized for his arrogance. Pleased with their devotion, Gaṇeśa relented in his curse, modifying it that only anyone seeing the moon on the *Vināyakacaturthī* of Bhādarapada would be visited with the obstacle of false accusation. He gave further instructions of how he is to be worshipped with flowers, food, stories, clothing, and feeding Brahmins. (Javadekar, pp. 24–29; see also Gupte 1919, pp. 66–68; Russell and Lal, vol. 4, pp. 39–40; Kane, vol. 5/1, pp. 146–47)

The Bhādrapada *Vināyakacaturthī* is also called, in some areas, *dagadi cauth* ("stone-throwing fourth"), stemming from the practice that, if one sees the moon on that night by accident one should throw stones onto his neighbors' roof to avert any calamity arising from the curse. The reason for this ritual is obscure.

Underhill suggests that it is a way to draw "abuse upon [oneself] and so to avert the evil." (p. 69) In the view of this text, it is better to have a neighbor angry at you rather than god. Another possible interpretation of the story is that the throwing of stones in the ritual parallels the gods throwing away the *syamantaka* stone in the myth, thus removing any suspicion of greed such as Kṛṣṇa suffered in the story. This act of symbolic renunciation is a gesture to counteract the effects of an inadvertent glance at the moon on this most inauspicious of nights. This complex set of myths and ritual practices centering around the curse and the moon further underlines the ambivalence of Gaṇeśa. On his most auspicious day of the year, he can act in ways that both create calamity for his devotees, if they see the moon, and free them from calamity, if they worship him according to the practices set forth in the story.

Gaṇeśa Caturthī, *"Gaṇeśa's Fourth"*

There are many contexts for the worship of deities in the Hindu tradition. The most socially restricted level is that of the domestic household where members united by ties of kinship assemble to pay devotion to the deities that are of particular significance to the family. The caste or caste group is another context for worship in which communities united by bonds of caste gather to honor a deity who is of special importance to them. This latter pattern is more representative of the village than the city. In the city, especially with regard to the worship of Gaṇeśa, it is occupational groups—such as railway workers, cigarette makers, and others—and voluntary associations—formed in neighborhoods, around schools, and around libraries—that collect money from their constituencies to purchase an image of Gaṇeśa and put on various programs of religious and cultural interest for the populace. In Marathi, these groups are called *sārvajanik māṇḍals* ("public groups"). There are also occasions when an entire village or several neighborhoods in the city join together for worship or a festival.

In the case of Maharashtra, religious observances in honor of Gaṇeśa occur over this entire spectrum. In the cities and villages, at the domestic level, particularly among Brahmins, the most important occasion for the worship of Gaṇeśa is the *pūjā* performed on *Gaṇeśa Caturthī,* the fourth day in the bright half (*Vināyakacaturthī*) of the month of Bhādrapada (August/September). Although this context for worship is the most socially restricted, ritually it is the most complex. At the most inclusive level of participation, there is the public festival to Gaṇeśa in which entire villages or a substantial proportion of a city's population may take part. The central ritual event in this context is the procession of images of Gaṇeśa through the streets and their immersion into an available body of water, be it the ocean, a river, or a tank. Worship in these contexts takes place in a rough temporal sequence. The domestic ceremonies occur on the day of *Gaṇeśa Caturthī* with the installation of the image on the family altar as the central event. Attention then shifts to the larger communities in which images of Gaṇeśa are set up as the foci for various performances open to the public. These include singing of devotional songs, dramatic performances, dance, films, lectures, and speeches by various public figures. This context represents the major innovation in the festival tradition instituted by Bal Gangadhar (Lokamanya) Tilak in the 1890s (more will be said about this in Chapter V). These occasions for worship in a community context take place on successive nights over a period of ten days until the fourteenth day of Bhādrapada *Ānantacaturdaśi.* These first two contexts merge to form the public procession of the images of the deity in a grand, tumultuous—but carefully choreographed—display of devotion, play, tension, and social cohesiveness. This sequence is more typical of the urban areas; in the villages the middle part of the ritual process, the neighborhood and voluntary association celebration, is less in evidence, and the cycle moves directly from the domestic setting to the all-village procession.

Domestic Worship

The central event in the worship of Gaṇeśa in the Hindu household, at least among Brahmins, is the establishment of a clay image on the domestic altar on *Gaṇeśa Caturthī.* It is endowed with life, worshipped as an honored guest in the home for a period of from one to ten days (varying according to the family's tradition), and it is then taken out of the home and immersed in a nearby river or other water source where it quickly dissolves. This immersion may be a fairly private affair, or, as frequently is the case both in villages and in cities, it may coincide with the public immersion procession.

Most simply stated the word *pūjā* means "worship." It derives from the Sanskrit meaning to adore or respect. *Pūjās* are richly and varied sets of religious expressions in honor of a particular deity or group of deities. They form one of the most pervasive genres of ritual performance in the Hindu tradition. Their appearance historically coincides roughly with the eclipse of Brāhmaṇic sacrifice and the rise of temple worship during the first few centuries of the present era. The lore on *pūjās* is enormous: whole sections of Purāṇas, ritual manuals, and oral traditions. The status *pūjā* enjoys is the basic formal means of relationship between Hindus and their deities that is reflected in the claims made for the benefit [*phala,* "fruit"] that one derives from performing such a rite of worship or for listening to someone else perform it or from financing its performance if one is not able to participate.

Pūjās range in character from relatively simple acts of private devotion and hospitality to the deity by means of words, gestures, and offerings to an image or symbol [*mūrti, vigraha*] that in some way "embodies" the reality of that deity. They can be multileveled performances lasting days and encompassing the participation of legions of priests, families, and neighborhoods, villages, and cities. *Pūjās* bring together the human and divine worlds at specific times and places according to prearranged utterances, actions, and ritual objects. All these events in turn rest on a network of shared beliefs, assumptions, myths, and linguistic and gestural strategies. In other words *pūjās* create or invoke their own worlds of meaning.

At the center of the phenomenon of *pūjā* is transaction between the worshippers and the deity or deities. The latter is represented by some object, image, or abstract design in which the deity is understood to take his or her place during the course of the rite and for some specified time thereafter. The worshipper adopts the posture of host, servant, and devotee. Through the performance of *pūjās,* the deity and devotee move closer together into a special intimacy with one another: the deity receives homage and food; the worshipper gains spiritual and existential enhancement. The prevailing metaphor for *pūjā* is that of hospitality and servitude. Both deity and devotee become dependent on one another and receive benefits from their mutual interaction.

Gaṇeśa's *pūjā* shares many features common to *pūjās* to other deities. As a ritual process, *pūjā* draws on the symbolism of the Brāhmaṇic sacrificial tradition, with its prominent use of Vedic *mantras* and the hymn to Puruṣa (ṚV 10:90) that elaborates the creation of the cosmos out of the sacrificed form of the divine person, Prajāpati. *Pūjā* incorporates elements from traditions of hospitality, highly valued in the Dharmaśāstras; the deity is treated in a manner similar to the ways one would honor a guest in the home, indeed, a royal guest. The *pūjā* also incorporates aspects of ceremonies of installation of images of deities in temples as well as principles of internalization and manipulation of the cosmos through the use of *mantras* typical of Tantric ritual traditions (see Kane, vol. 2/2, pp. 739ff.). There is great latitude in the degrees of ritual elaboration in this *pūjā* to Gaṇeśa. The analysis undertaken here draws from two textual sources, both popular ritual manuals available to anyone wishing to perform the rite (Javadekar, N. Joshi). The *pūjā* as I saw it performed among Deśastha Brahmins in Ahmadnagar was an elaborate performance, making use of the services of a family priest [*purohita*] who chanted much of it in Sanskrit while giving ritual instructions in Marathi to the head of the household [*yajamāna*] who performed a series of ritual gestures. I have made a translation and commentary on this *pūjā* elsewhere; here it will be more appropriate to present the major episodes in the ritual and explore their meanings in relation to the picture we have derived so far of Gaṇeśa (Courtright 1974, pp. 99–198; cf. Barnouw). Ritual manuals recommend the services of a Brahmin priest, but if one is not available or exceeds one's means, then the rite can still be performed with the aid of the manual and some coaching from a priest. One manual advises the potential worshipper, "according to what is convenient, by reciting this *pūjā* four, eight, or fifteen times with the help of one who already knows it, you should be able to perform it for yourself and narrate it for others" (N. Joshi, p. 46).

Many varieties of possible *pūjā* formats and texts are available to Hindus according to the intensity of their devotion or their means to afford the necessary ritual items to be offered and priests to be paid. However, what appears to be common to all *pūjās* is their goal: to bring about an enhanced level of intimacy between the worshipper and the deity. This intimacy is realized through a series of transactions. The worshipper prepares a sacred arena and provides an unfired, "raw," clay image and establishes Gaṇeśa's special presence in that image by invoking the life force [*jīva*] and vital capacities [*indriya*]. This process of invocation or establishment [*pratiṣṭhā*] involves the transferring of both the worshipper's own and the cosmos's *jīva* and *indriyas* into the inert clay image, thus bringing it to life. It is as if Gaṇeśa were condensed from his universal presence in the cosmos into a particular and accessible form in a time and place coinciding with that of his devotees. The worshipper then honors Gaṇeśa-in-the-image by bathing him (the clay image itself is not bathed because it would dissolve, but a betel nut serves as the surrogate image for the purposes of bathing) and by feeding, clothing, and giving the god gifts and an entertainment of songs; in short, honoring him as one would the most valuable and royal of guests. Gaṇeśa reciprocates by giving his obstacle-removing powers to watch over the family during the coming year. After he has enjoyed the offerings of food, Gaṇeśa "returns" them to the family to be shared as *prasāda* or leftover spiritual food. In consuming this food, the family members take into themselves existential enhancement or a tangible experience of this intimacy with the deity that is the goal of the ritual's performance. This divine food, or *prasāda,* is an important religious element in the ritual. The word *prasāda* comes from the Sanskrit prefix *pra,* meaning "down," and the root *sad,* meaning "sit." In its barest meaning *prasāda* is a settling down, growing clear, or becoming satisfied. Specifically, in relation to ritual, *prasāda* is that food presented to the image of a deity or that left for one's *guru* or that which is available to the devotees to consume (Monier-Williams, p. 696). In eating this leftover food, the devotees take into themselves the substance that has been in closest proximity to the presence of the deity and thereby receive spiritual nourishment. *Prasāda* is the edible symbol of the "real presence" in the image; an assurance to those who eat it in the company of the god that their undertakings will be successful and encounter no obstacles. In this way *pūjās* create their own realities. They mark these occasions of enhancement in time by fixed calendrical dates; in space by an altar, usually a low table called a *cauraṅg,* or simply by an area marked out on the floor and by a home purified of contamination by destructive influences. Through special speech, gestures, forms of nourishment and ornamentation, the human and divine meet each other halfway, giving and receiving mutual support.

How does this religious reality come about? What are the means by which the *pūjā* creates a world of its own within, yet transforms the world of ordinary experience? What methods or strategies and what assumptions about reality are employed to realize this special context for the divine-human interplay that brings worshippers and deity together year after year, generation after generation, at the appropriate season? A useful way to address these questions is to examine the constituent episodes and transactions that make up the ritual, pausing along the way to exegetically examine the ones that precipitate major turns in the ritual process.

The name of the specific *pūjā* to be analysed here is the *Śrīpārthivamahāgaṇapatipūjā,* the "worship of the great Gaṇeśa in auspicious earthen form." The *pūjā* can be viewed structurally in terms of the threefold diachronic or processural form: entry into the ritual sphere, transformation of the conditions of reality between deity and devotee, and exit into the world outside the ritual. This tripartite scheme, originally suggested by Van Gennep and elaborated by Turner, may be applied to many rituals (Van Gennep; Turner 1969).

Before the rite can begin, the space of the household in which it takes place and the worshippers must be brought into a maximal state of purity. This is done by cleaning and whitewashing the home or, more often, that part of the house in which the image is to be kept. Worshippers bathe, and the patron of the ritual, the *yajamāna* or male head of the household, wears a silk lower garment [*sovaḷē vastra,* or *mukṭā*], usually red, and a shawl around his shoulders. Silk is the purest of cloth; red has frequent associations with Gaṇeśa, it being the color of many of the images in his shrines in Maharashtra. The clay image, which has been fashioned by a sculptor, usually of the smith caste, is brought into the home and placed in the area prepared for it. The altar is marked off as a sacred space with patterns made with colored powder [*rāṅgoḷī*]. It is the women of the household who draw these designs, similar to ones frequently drawn on the threshold of the house on other sacred occasions. They also assemble the special foods, flowers, leaves, spices, water, milk, fragrant substances, and other ritual paraphernalia and place them in various containers to resemble the setting for a meal in front of the altar. The image is brought into the home by the family and is placed within this sacred enclosure, usually on a low table called a *caurаṅg* that is associated symbolically with a throne. At the time the image is placed on the altar, it is inert substance, a mere curio. It possesses no special sanctity until it is established with vital breath [*prāṇa*].

The setting is imbued with the symbolism of kingship. The deity is guest, king, and lord; to receive him into one's home is the ultimate expression of hospitality. Behind the image is placed a picture of Gaṇeśa's self-created [*svayambhū*] forms as they appear in the eight major Gaṇeśa shrines in Maharashtra, the *aṣṭavināyakas* (see pl. 10). A brass lamp is lighted next to the image. The patron sits facing the image and the Brahmin priest, sitting to the right of the image, recites the Sanskrit *mantras* and, should it be necessary, instructs the patron in the appropriate gestures and utterances he is to make at each stage of the *pūjā*. Family members and guests sit behind the patron, also facing the image, as a sort of audience to the proceedings. The ritual involves the contributions of three different persons (or roles): the priest, who provides the sacred speech and ritual instructions for the proper moves at each step of the ceremony so that it may be effective; the patron, who performs the gestures of offerings and service and accrues the benefits of the rite for himself and his family; and, finally, Gaṇeśa himself, who receives the family's hospitality and in return enables the household members to achieve greater intimacy with him and gives substance to this transformation through the gift of sanctified food [*prasāda*] that the family consumes together at the conclusion of the rite (cf. Kane, vol. 5/1, p. 146; see pl. 10).

The *pūjā* formally begins at the time designated by the priest according to calculations based on the ritual calendar [*pañcāṅga*] or in keeping with the convenience of the family. The patron sips water [*ācamana*] and regulates his breathing [*prāṇayama*]; he then addresses Gaṇeśa and all the other gods in an honorific manner [*namaskāra*]. Then the patron (or the priest on his behalf) announces to the deity who will appear in the image the nature of his commitments to the rite and his intentions to perform it properly. This part of the ritual is called the *saṁkalpa* and, according to one version of the ritual manuals for this *pūjā,* it is to be recited as follows:

> On this holy day in my humble way, with as much preparation as possible, in order to gain the fruits designated in the revealed texts [*Śruti*], the remembered texts [*Smṛti*], and the traditional texts [*Purāṇa*], and in order to obtain sons, grandsons, wealth, knowledge, victory, success, fortune, life, and all other wished-for things in this as well as in future births, and in order to propitiate the deity Siddhivināyaka [Gaṇeśa], I shall perform the worship of Gaṇapati, reciting verses from the hymn to Puruṣa and from texts of the tradition, while performing the giving of water [*arghya*], etc. —here the sixteen *upacāras* or "ways of service" to be performed during the ritual are listed. (Javadekar, p. 1; cf. Courtright 1974, p. 127; N. Joshi, pp. 49–50)

The *saṁkalpa* expresses the intentions of the worshipper and defines the relationship between the worshipper and the deity, sets the boundaries on what is to take place within and beyond the boundaries of the rite, and articulates the goals of the worshipper and the deity. If the ritual performance is completed according to the proper conventions and if the worshipper is filled with faith in the deity, then the goals or fruits of what is desired should be realized.

Once the intention of the worship has been declared, the patron, with the help of the priest, performs a series of preparatory gestures that make sacred the various implements to be used and the person using them fit for the central transaction of the ritual, the *prāṇapratiṣṭhā* (the investiture of the image with vital breath). First the patron calls on the goddess Bhū (earth), in whom the world is supported, to support the patron; while touching the ground three times with his left heel he commands the demons and harmful spirits [*piśāca* and *bhūta*] to flee from the sacred enclosure of the ritual so that the worship of Gaṇeśa to be performed may be accomplished without obstruction. Calling on all the gods to protect the rite, the patron symbolically measures out the area where he sits by placing the span of his thumb and forefinger on the ground in front of the image, in this way he makes it sacred and suitable for continuing the ritual. This set of gestures is called *āsanavidhi,* the preparation and purification of the seat.

Reciting verses from the *Puruṣasūkta* (ṚV 10:90), along with single-word *mantras,* the patron touches his heart, the top of his head, the tuft of hair at the crown of his head, his chest, his two eyes and the subtle third eye between them. Then, with his hand raised above his head, he makes a snapping sound with his thumb and second finger. These two ritual episodes are called *ṣadaṅganyāsa*, the investing of the six limbs, and the *digbandhana*, the closing up of the quarters. Through these gestures the patron identifies the various parts of his body with those of the deity and the universe, thereby bringing into a single center the microcosm and macrocosm. A similar series of identifications takes place in the *Puruṣasūkta* itself when the dismembered pieces of the sacrificed Puruṣa are identified with various parts of the universe. In this way the patron becomes redefined, brought out of the merely human realm into the sacred arena he will share with Gaṇeśa for the duration of the rite. Like the deity he has invited, the patron is now homologous with the cosmos. A similar process follows with respect to the major implements used in the *pūjā*. The water vessel [*kalaśa*], whose contents will bathe and nourish Gaṇeśa during the ceremony, is identified with the pitcher of the Vedic sacrifice, and it becomes transformed symbolically into the cosmos itself. The priest recites:

> Viṣṇu resides at the mouth of the pitcher, Rudra in the neck, Brahmā at its base, and the group of the mother goddesses in the middle. All oceans and the earth with its seven continents reside in its belly. The *Ṛg Veda, Yajur Veda, Sāma Veda,* and *Atharva Veda,* along with their appended texts [*vedāṅgas*] are in the vessel. In it is the *gāyatrī* chant with Sāvitṛ as its deity which gives prosperity and peace. May these who remove all sins come here for worship. O Gaṅgā and Yamunā, Godāvarī and Sarasvatī, Narmadā, Sindhu and Kāverī [the seven mother/river goddesses, be present in this water]. (N. Joshi, p. 53)

A similar pattern is followed for consecrating the other ritual implements: the conch, bell, and lamp. On each of these items the patron places flowers and *akṣata,* unhusked rice grains rubbed with red powder [*kuṃkuma*]. *Akṣata* is used in many ritual settings and is not unique to Gaṇeśa. Like the rice thrown at weddings, it symbolizes food and seed, the emblems of nurture and generation. When rubbed with red powder, its generative potential is enhanced. The combination of red and white colors indicates transition toward a pure or auspicious state (Beck 1969). Throughout the ritual when the deity is offered any food, clothing, or ornaments, he is again sprinkled with *akṣata.* In this transaction the patron is the giver of this power-bestowing substance and Gaṇeśa the recipient. This is a reversal of the condition of the world outside the rite in which the diety is the giver of success and well-being and the patron is the recipient.

After a transitional gesture of purification [*śuddhikaraṇa*], the patron offers sacred *dūrvā* grass, upon which, according to mythological tradition, the immortality-granting *amṛta* was spilled at the time of the churning of the ocean. Then he sprinkles water on the ritual implements and himself for purification [*prokṣana*]. Now the moment has arrived for the investiture of vital breath [*prāṇa*] into the image. In some *pūjās* this step is replaced by a simpler ritual episode of *sthāpana,* "placing" the image onto its throne (Javadekar, p. 2). Traditionally a Brahmin priest is necessary for this investiture or *prāṇapratiṣṭhā.* A brief exegetical excursus on the symbols of breath and investiture is in order here.

The word *prānapratiṣṭhā* is a compound made up of two parts: *prāṇa,* breath or life force, and *pratiṣṭhā,* establishment or support. The latter word is derived from the prefix *prati,* toward or upon, and the root *sthā,* stand firmly or abide. The term *pratiṣṭhā* expresses the pervasive Indian religious and existential impulse, from the Vedic period onward, for what Jan Gonda calls "the firm and ultimate ground to rest upon, an imperishable and immovable support of existence, for sky, earth, for themselves, for the universe" (1954, p. 1). According to different taxonomies of reality, the precise character of this support [*pratiṣṭhā*] is by turns identified with a foothold or food (metaphoric), the earth (physical), the master of the house (social), Vedic meters (linguistic), the breath or womb (biological), layers of the sacrificial altar (ritual), speech, *brahman* (metaphysical), and space (elemental). (BĀU 4.1.12; ChU 5.19–24; ŚB 4.3.1.22).

To be established or grounded in support is to be a stabilizing power for good, maintaining the conflicting powers of the cosmos in a state of balance. It is a matter of life and death, for the dead are *apratiṣṭhā*—without support, those who have no bodies and stand nowhere. The descendents of the dead must give them support by providing them with "bodies" made of rice [*piṇḍa*] that both feed them and place support beneath them, thus giving them a place on which to stand in the cosmos (see Knipe). One's own standing can be destroyed by means of a curse, but it can be recovered through other compensatory rites (ŚB 1.6.1.18). To be grounded is to have a world and to be secure in the midst of flux, to have power over forces that threaten one's security; indeed, to achieve a profound rest and well-being. The notion of ground, support, or standing firm, is an expression of the ultimate soteriological goal of Hinduism: standing firmly beyond flux [*mokṣa*]. The vehicle or context for this support is the vital breath that is brought into the image, with the aid of *mantras*, from the patron who already has brought breath to the clay image through the conduit of sacred *dūrvā* grass.

In the *Chāndogya Upaniṣad* the five senses quarrel among themselves as to which of them is superior [*śreyas*]. Unable to resolve their dispute, they approach Prajāpati who tells them, "He, who upon departing from the body, leaves it looking the worst, he is the best among you" (ChU 5.1.7). Speech, eye, ear, and mind then left the body; but, however limited it became after losing one of the senses, it remained alive because it still had breath. "Then," the text continues, "*prāṇa* prepared to depart, tearing up the other senses as a spirited horse might tear out its tethering stakes. They then all gathered around him, saying, 'Stay with us. Don't leave. You are the best among us.' " (ChU 5.1.12). Then all senses took their firm support [*pratiṣṭhā*] in *prāṇa* (ChU 5.1.13). In the equation of the cosmos with *ātman*, the text sees the air as the *prāṇa* of the universal self [*brahman*], just as the wind came forth out of the *prāṇa* of Puruṣa (ChU 5.1.13; ṚV 10.90.13). Hence *prāṇa* is that upon which both the cosmos and the individual stand. The breath is the sacrifice of one's own self to *brahman;* it is the sacred oblation, the equivalent of *soma* (ChU 5.19.1). *Prāṇa* is the primal animating power upon which the self and the cosmos find their common support, their *pratiṣṭhā*.

Continuing the ritual sequence, the priest recites a verse identifying the seed syllables [*bīja mantra*], the condensed and potent sounds of Hindu ritual, which will serve as the vehicles for placing the *prāṇa* into the image. As the priest recites the *mantras,* the patron holds two sprigs of *dūrvā* grass touching the image. Then the priest says, "This *prāṇa* [of the patron] is the *prāṇa* of the god [*devasya prāṇa iha prāṇaḥ*]." In this way the distributed *prāṇa* of the cosmos, which includes that of the ritual patron, becomes condensed into the inert clay image bringing it to life. A similar pattern is followed in invoking animate life [*jīvā*] into the image. In that moment the separation between the patron and the deity dissolves as they share common support in *prāṇa.* It is a moment of profound religious and metaphysical meaning, the crux of the liminal phase of the rite.

The two vehicles for this transfer of *prāṇa* and *jīva* into the image are the *mantra* and the *dūrvā* grass, sound and substance. *Mantra* can be seen as *prāṇa* condensed into speech, a conveyer of sacred power. According to Gonda, a *mantra* is a "word(s) believed to be of 'superhuman origin,' received, fashioned and spoken by the 'inspired' seers, poets and reciters in order to evoke divine power(s) and especially conceived of as creating, conveying, concentrating and realizing intentional and efficient thought, and of coming into touch or identifying oneself with the essence of the divinity which is present in the *mantra.*" (1963, p. 259). It is as though *mantra* is that sound/speech appropriate to the realm of *brahman* in which self and god, knower and known, giver and recipient of *prāṇa* recognize their fundamental indivisibility and eternalness. This reality is actualized when the *mantra* is recited.

The *dūrvā* grass acts as a conduit across which passes the animating power of the *prāṇa,* activated by the *mantra,* by the patron to the image, from giver to recipient. *Dūrvā* is thought to be especially favored by Gaṇeśa and some informants claim it has medicinal properties in addition to religious ones. It resembles the ancient *kuśa* grass of the Vedic sacrifice. According to one version of the myth of the churning of the ocean, when Garuḍa rescued the ambrosia from the thieving hands of the demons, he flew up with the vat in his claws and some of it spilled out, falling on some *dūrvā* grass below. Hence *dūrvā* became the receptacle of the immortality-bestowing ambrosia, the spilled leftovers of divine creative power (Östör, p. 68). By virtue of this contact with the original and uncompromised substance of the universe, *dūrvā* has come to possess important capacities for transmitting the power of *prāṇa.*

Within this framework of assumptions, what appears to be taking place in the ritual is a process in which the patron first reconstitutes himself as the divine Puruṣa and gives his *prāṇa* to the deity, who thereby comes to reside in the image as a kind of symbolic dismemberment recalling that of Puruṣa and inverting the human-divine hierarchy. Gaṇeśa receives his own *prāṇa* as one dependent on the largesse of the patron. Thus he is committed to return the favor by the beneficent use of his power to remove obstacles for the patron and his kin. Patron and divinity participate in a carefully bounded and prepared divine world, contributing to one another's identities and sharing in common awareness and power. The image of Gaṇeśa, in some sense of the term, becomes "alive." Some informants claim that the image actually changes: it becomes lustrous, taking on more intense radiance of color. Others say they saw the image actually enlarge slightly. This perceived transformation of the material form of the image does not take place for the devotee in any other context than that of religious belief and expectation. Is it a matter of magical or alchemical change? As one informant put it, "Of course, magic is not magical to the magician." For those who come to the rite prepared for a transformation to take place between themselves and the deity, the ritual effects it. Other Hindus take a more skeptical attitude and suggest that such claims of the material transformation of the image belong to the realm of superstition. The most important transformation to take place in the ritual, they argue, is the increase of *bhāva,* or religious sentiment or experience. This increase in *bhāva* can be achieved without the use of images [*nirguṇa*], but for some the presence of the image as a receptacle of divine presence [*saguṇa*] can be a useful aid to religious realization. The *pūjā* provides the location where the divine intersects the mundane, pervading it with special presence and enlarging the sense of what is possible. The sacred, in the form of the enlivened image, becomes the cosmic center, expanding in all directions and redefining the limits of the real. From the perspective of ordinary experience outside the assumptions of the ritual, the enlivening of the image is the liminal episode wherein the power of the divine presence converges on the ritual enclosure that is so vulnerable to contamination. From the perspective of the intentions of the rite itself, that which appears so transitory from the outside—the enlivened deity—is *the* secure and grounded center of the cosmos. That some devotees "see" the image become lustrous and enlarge bears witness to their faith and the grace of the deity.

With the *prāṇa* now established in the image, so far as the intention of the ritual is concerned, Gaṇeśa's full presence has been made manifest. Dwelling in his image, he has passed, along with the patron whose breath he also breathes, from inert matter into living presence. This phase of the *pūjā* most clearly articulates the transformational character of the ritual. Those polarities that may have seemed most separated—earth and deity—have now become one another. After the investiture of the *prāṇa*, the image is not to be moved until the *uttarapūjā* (final worship) when the *prāṇa* is released from the image and dispersed again into the cosmos as a whole.

Once the breath is established, the traditional sixteen *upacāras* ("ways of service") are performed. These ritual procedures honor the image as one would receive a guest, indeed, the most honored of guests. Each of these *upacāras* is accompanied by the recitation of a stanza from the Vedic hymn to Puruṣa (ṚV 10:90), thereby establishing the homology between the image of Gaṇeśa and the cosmos. With each recitation the patron places a few grains of unhusked rice grains [*akṣata*] and *dūrvā* grass at the feet of the image to quicken the process. Other *upacāras* invoke the deity's presence [*āvāhana*], offers him a seat [*āsana*], wash his feet [*pādya*], and offer water at the reception of a guest. The last two water offerings are made to a betel nut, symbolizing Gaṇeśa, at the foot of the image because the image is made of materials that will be dissolved or disfigured. Then a sip of water is offerred to the image [*ācamana*], followed by bathing the betel nut with the five sacred fluids [*pañcāmṛtasnāna*]. These five nectars are milk, curd, clarified butter, honey, and sugar; each is poured in turn and followed by the sprinkling of a few grains of *akṣata*. Collectively these substances, along with the water for bathing, which are also poured during the ritual, make up what is called *tīrtha*. The same word is used to mean a sacred spot in a river and a crossing place between the human and divine realms. In the ritual it is the patron who gives the deity these perfect fluids for his bath; in the world it is the god who provides the bathing places, the *tīrthas*, for his devotees in the form of rivers having sacred qualities. This bath of sacred fluids is followed by a sprinkling of water [*abhiṣeka*], which completes the bathing portion of the *pūjā*.

At this point in the rite, the image is dressed and adorned with jewels and perfumes: a garment [*vastra*], an upper garment and sacred thread [*upavastra*], scented sandal paste and other fragrant substances [*gandha*], offerings of flowers [*puṣpa*] and incense [*dhūpa*], and the waving of a lamp is performed before the image [*dīpa*]. These make up the first thirteen of the sixteen *upacāras* and serve to honor Gaṇeśa through the bathing, dressing, and ornamenting of his body, much as one would an honored guest. With the recitation of the Vedic *mantras* evoking the cosmic person, Puruṣa, the linkage between the divine and human worlds is reiterated at each point.

Next comes the offering of food [*naivedya*]. The foods to be offered are *sāttvika* (the most pure). Offerings of fruit, *modakas* (sweet flour balls especially favored by Gaṇeśa), various sacred leaves, betel nuts, and a coin are presented by the patron to the image while the priest recites the verse from the hymn to Puruṣa. The patron pays homage to the *prāṇa* present in the offerings. This festive meal offered to the deity and sanctified by its proximity to the image will be returned at the end of the *pūjā* to the worshippers as the *prasāda* (food of grace) to be shared by members of the family in the presence of the deity. Technically the *prasāda* is the leftovers of the deity's meal; but, because the food has been in contact with a being of higher stature than the worshippers and has gained transcendent status and power, it becomes sacred to the worshippers. By eating the *prasāda* the worshippers tangibly take a part of the deity's presence into themselves (cf. Babb, pp. 31–68; Östör, pp. 42–70).

Following the feeding portion of the *pūjā,* the patron performs a symbolic circumambulation around the deity [*pradakṣiṇā*] and gives one final gesture honoring the image [*namaskāra*]. The patron stands in front of the image and turns around three times, reciting a *mantra* from the Puruṣa hymn, and he then says, "Sins that I have committed in this birth and previous births now vanish with each step of my circumambulation to the right" (N. Joshi, p. 69).

After these formal *upacāras* have been completed and the image suitably adorned, fed, and honored, the patron's family collectively participates in the *pūjā*. As a lamp is waved before the image by the patron, the family together sings a popular devotional song [*āratī*] in Marathi, such as the one by Rāmadāsa quoted earlier (see p. 165). Camphor is then lighted and burned before the image and passed among the worshippers who pass their hands through the flames and smoke and bring them close to their eyes and foreheads in order to take in the purifying properties of the flame that has been made sacred by its proximity to Gaṇeśa. The patron offers an additional twenty-one sprigs of *dūrvā* grass, various leaves and flowers, and prayers. The prayer [*prārthanā*] has a more devotional tone and reflects a more intimate and emotional attitude toward the deity than the more formal and transactional language of the earlier Sanskrit episodes in the *pūjā*. Addressing Gaṇeśa as the "Protector of the Poor, Reservoir of Compassion," the patron says, "Highest Lord, you are my refuge, there is no refuge apart from you. Take compassion on me and protect me . . . the worship I have given you without *mantras*, ritual, devotion, O Lord of the Gods, may it become perfect" (N. Joshi, pp. 70–71).

At this point, as the ritual draws to a close, attention turns to the priest who is now worshipped. The patron offers the priest a portion of the *prasāda*, specifically ten of the twenty-one *modakas* offered to Gaṇeśa. He offers further gifts of a scat, flowers, betel nut, sandal paste, oblations, and a small amount of money [*dakṣiṇā*]. With the *pūjā* now completed, its performance lasting about forty-five minutes, the family and assembled relatives share the *prasāda*, which may then be followed with a feast. The priest may depart at this time to perform the same rite elsewhere for another client family.

For the remaining days while the image is seated in the household shrine, it will be worshipped morning and evening with simple recitations, devotional songs, offerings of flowers and incense, and with ritual lamps. The ethos of service and hospitality to the image remains as long as it stays in the house. It may not be moved or its surrounding ritual space violated by polluting objects. When the number of days for Gaṇeśa's visit have passed, a period of from one to ten days depending on family traditions, a simple ritual [*uttarapūjā*] of divesting the image of its special status is performed. Then with sprigs of *dūrvā* grass dipped in honey, the patron symbolically closes the eyes of the image and thereby disperses the *prāṇa* in the image, which reverts back to its prior condition. The patron recites a sort of benediction, "May all groups of deities now depart, having accepted this worship of the earthen image of Gaṇeśa, in order that all desired objectives [of the rite] may be realized and that they may return again" (*ibid,* p. 72). Then members of the family, alone or in procession with others, take the image to a nearby water source and immerse it. It dissolves quickly and returns to its formless state. This final rite is called *visarjana* (immersion). The *visarjana* brings around full circle the process begun with the forming of the image out of clay and its installation in the home. The life of the image moves from formless clay to iconographic representation to animation and empowerment to dispersion and return to formlessness. In this respect it replicates the cosmos itself. As the devotees lower their clay images of Gaṇeśa into the water, they shout together, "*Gaṇapati Bāppā Morayā, pudhacyā varṣī lavkar yā!*", that is, "Beloved Gaṇeśa, Lord of Morayā (Morayā Gosāvī, the founder of the lineage of Gaṇeśa saints in Maharashtra), come again early next year!" At the level of popular religious practice, the *pūjā* is an occasion for heightened awareness of Gaṇeśa and all that is associated with him, a time of optimism and celebration.

To summarize this complex ritual process, we see that the domestic *pūjā* to Gaṇeśa follows a three-part processural pattern: (1) the deity becomes present in the form of the image, (2) he graciously resides in the household for a period of time, and (3) he returns to a primordial cosmic state when the image is immersed. This process takes place in the context of a highly developed ceremonialism that draws on ancient traditions of hospitality to guests for its dominant symbolism and ritual actions. In this ritual context the deity and patron, together with the priest, engage in a complex relationship of interdependence. The patron provides the deity with breath, life, and food; the deity reciprocates by giving the patron and his family the grace of his presence and general wellbeing. This pattern of worship is not unique to Gaṇeśa, rather it represents one group of variants of a large and pervasive form of Hindu religious life. *Pūjās* to Durgā in Bengal, Sarasvatī in Uttar Pradesh and Bihar, among other deities in India, make use of disposable clay images. These *pūjās* also stress the cycle of hospitality, auspicious presence, and distribution of divine presence into the cosmos as a whole. As Durgā is for Bengalis, Gaṇeśa is the patron deity for the Marathi-speaking people. At the most comprehensive level of its symbolism, the Gaṇeśa *pūjā* presents a microcosm of the rhythms of the macrocosm: from formlessness into form, with its animating power followed by dissolution back into formlessness; creation, maintenance, and destruction leading to new creation. In terms of popular religious practice, the *pūjā* is an occasion for drawing closer to Gaṇeśa with all the joy and hope associated with his obstacle-removing capacities. As the deity takes his place within the immediate and mundane frame of reference of the family, he enables them to step outside of the mere immediacy of its domestic world and share a time of special and transcending intimacy with its god. As the image of Gaṇeśa sinks beneath the water and returns to its undifferentiated state, the devotees experience both sadness and relief. Sadness that this deity who has become an honored member of the family has gone away, and relief that the complex ritual demands of his visit have been fulfilled. It is out of this complex religious and emotional mood that devotees are able to say, in an attitude of hope mixed with confidence, "Beloved Gaṇeśa, Lord of Morayā, come again early next year!"

The Public Festival

The worship and celebration that takes place outside the domestic context of *pūjā* is called *utsava* (festival). It is an open event with a more inclusive range of participation. In cities at least there are two dimensions to Gaṇeśa's festival, and they are observed in temporal sequence: the religious and entertainment programs that are put on by various associations or *māṇḍaḷs,* (Sanskrit, *maṇḍala,* circle or assemblage) and the festival procession in which all groups and families carry their images in procession in order to immerse them in the river, the *visarjana.* The festival traces important dimensions of its present form to the end of the last century when it was revived and popularized in Pune by the nationalist leader and journalist Bal Gangadhar (Lokamanya) Tilak. Tilak saw the festival as a vehicle for facilitating greater solidarity among Hindus and opportunities for teaching the Hindu masses the need for realizing aspirations for self-rule. This part of the story of Gaṇeśa and his worship will be explored more fully in the next chapter. For now our purpose will be to concentrate on the contemporary form of the public festival and see how it relates to the pattern of domestic worship we have just considered.

The location for our observations of the public festival is the city of Ahmadnagar, located seventy miles northeast of Pune in the central Deśa region of Maharashtra. Culturally linked to Pune and its traditions, Ahmadnagar is a medium-sized city, a market center for cotton and sugar and rapidly growing light industry. Its growth has been slow and steady, restricted by limited water resources and transportation facilities. As a district headquarters, it is a center for banking, administration, and hospitals. It has two colleges, and a number of private secondary schools. It also has a major military installation nearby. Historically the city was an important Muslim political and cultural center. It was the capital of Nizam Shahi dynasty in the seventeenth and eighteenth centuries; portions of the old city fortifications remain, as do a number of sites: shrines, schools, a palace, and a fort—some of them protected as historical landmarks. Conquered by the Marathas and later by the British, the city's Muslim character has been largely eclipsed. Today the city has a large non-Brahmin population, and the Brahmins are mainly from the Deśastha subcaste. The Muslim population, constituting about one seventh of the population before 1948, now amounts to less than one tenth. There is a small but affluent Jain community in the city with a temple to Parśvanātha and a meditation center for monks. Jains support the Gaṇeśa festival by contributing money for the purchase of images and festival programs. Ahmadnagar looks to Pune as its cultural center, and many in Pune tend to think of Ahmadnagar as a rather rustic place. The city proved to be a good location for observing the public dimensions of the Gaṇeśa festival. The festival is the largest single public religious event in the year, with upwards of one hundred thousand people participating at one stage or another of the festival cycle. Yet, the city is small enough to enable an outsider to get around to the various groups that provide leadership and participation in the festival to gain some sense of the festival as a whole. To conduct a similar study of the festival in Pune or Bombay would require a team of several scholars, and could, no doubt, be an undertaking of enormous value.

There are not a great number of Hindu temples in the city of Ahmadnagar itself, probably owing to its Muslim history. Two temples are preeminent as dwelling places of the two guardian deities [*grāmadevatā*] of the city: Hanumān at the northern gate of the old city wall (now well inside the contemporary city) and Gaṇeśa the guardian of the southern gate. The Gaṇeśa temple is located in one of the oldest neighborhoods of the city, Māḷivādā, traditionally the area of the Māḷi or garland-maker castes, and today a center of non-Brahmins. The temple is locally known as the Māḷivādā Gaṇeśa Mandir. Legend has it that the temple's image once began to sweat profusely, indicating the superabundance of power residing within it. Only after the performance of many rituals was this excessive power brought under control. The name of Gaṇeśa that is specific to the image of this temple is Vighnaharta, Destroyer of Obstacles. The temple is an important center for Gaṇeśa in the city and its environs. In a special enclosure behind the main image of the temple is kept the *utsavamūrti* (festival image). It is carved from wood and brightly painted, depicting Gaṇeśa riding a horse and plunging a lance into a tiger-demon. It is a posture reminiscent of Durgā slaying the buffalo demon, Mahiṣa. Each year during the festival procession, this image is profusely decorated with banana leaves, flowers, and garlands and placed on a bullock cart at the lead position. As the protector of the city and the remover of obstacles, this Māḷivādā Gaṇeśa is patron to the city and its inhabitants. The priest [*pūjārī*] of the temple rides next to the image and a *māṇḍaḷ* consisting of devotees accompanies the cart and image in the festival procession. There is also a small privately supported Gaṇeśa temple, maintained by a prominent Brahmin family, on the street through which the festival procession passes on its way out of the city toward the river for the immersion of images, but it does not appear to play an important role in the public part of the Gaṇeśa festival.

The associations or public groups [*sārvajanik māṇḍaḷs*] that gather together to celebrate the festival fall into three categories: neighborhood groups, occupational groups, and voluntary associations. Neighborhood groups or *māṇḍaḷs* draw their membership informally from among those who live on the same street or area of the city. The larger proportion of members are young men and boys; hence they frequently name their associations "youth" [*taruṇ*] *māṇḍaḷs*. The members of the *māṇḍaḷ* canvass their neighborhoods for contributions toward the purchase of an image to be set up in the neighborhood, covered by a temporary canopy [Marathi, *māṇḍav;* Sanskrit, *maṇḍapa*], in front of which various religious and cultural events will take place. The more money a group can raise, the greater notice people take, and status will accrue to the group. Neighborhoods feel greater solidarity during the Gaṇeśa festival season. In one area of the city where Hindu and Muslim inhabitants live closely together, a *māṇḍaḷ* including members of both Hindu and Muslim religious communities was formed and an image carried in procession. The pattern was reversed during the Muslim festival of Moharram. This pattern of intercommunal religious observance however is an exception to the more general rule that Muslims do not participate in the festival and have not done so since its revival under the leadership of Tilak at the end of the last century, a point we shall explore more fully in the next chapter.

To the extent that a particular neighborhood may be made up from a single or cluster of related castes, the *māṇḍaḷ* has a caste dimension to it. In one neighborhood where mainly scheduled castes live, there is a statue to Jyotiba Phule, the nineteenth-century opponent of caste exclusiveness and adversary of the Brahmin elite in Pune. A Gaṇeśa image is set up in front of this statue each year by a neighborhood *māṇḍaḷ*. In its songs and programs, the group emphasizes that Gaṇeśa is Gaṇapati the lord [*pati*] of all the people [*gaṇa*], and so is a kind of patron deity of social equality and anticaste ideology characteristic of the official rhetoric of the nation. Because Gaṇeśa does not have specific associations with a particular caste—apart from his cultic following in the region near Pune among Brahmins (as we shall see)—but belongs to all, there are no particular caste interests to be served in promoting his devotion. Gaṇeśa is an emblem of a new image of community that transcends caste. This appears to be the pattern in the cities of Maharashtra; in the villages, however, Gaṇeśa's festival is a more recent innovation and is tied to the emergence of non-Brahmin castes into greater prominance after land reform laws were enacted in the 1950s.

Occupational groups are *māṇḍaḷs* whose membership is based on place of employment. Employees contribute, frequently with more substantial support of the ownership or management of the company or industry, toward the purchase of an image and its installation and programs. In Ahmadnagar *māṇḍaḷs* drawn from employees in the state bus and railway services, cigarette manufacturers, weavers, and other groups have sponsored images and programs. Recently there has been an increasing "commercialization" of the festival as businesses have sponsored images and associated their names and products with Gaṇeśa, a trend that many of the more orthodox Hindus find vulgar and out of keeping with the religious character of the festival.

The third category of *māṇḍaḷs* is that of voluntary organizations. These include school committees, travel and pilgrimage groups, wrestling and athletic clubs, youth organizations, and social service groups. Some political groups from the traditionalist end of the spectrum, such as the Rashtriya Svayamsevak Sangh (R.S.S.), have sponsored *māṇḍaḷs* and participated in the processions from time to time. *Māṇḍaḷ* membership is generally restricted to men, although women participate indirectly by making ritual preparations, and they join in devotional singing and attend other programs sponsored by the *māṇḍaḷ*. This type of *māṇḍaḷ* seems to be the successor to the *meḷā* or voluntary group of singers that were instrumental in promoting the Gaṇeśa festival under Tilak's leadership. During the period of intense efforts toward obtaining independence under Gandhi's leadership, such festival organizations underwent decline, but since the early 1950s, there has been a steady increase in popularity of this type of voluntary organization sponsoring Gaṇeśa images.

There is a wide variety in the iconography and programs of the different *māṇḍaḷs*. Most are traditional: Gaṇeśa's image shows him in his conventional postures holding various ornaments. Some *māṇḍaḷs* simply place the image under a canopy and decorate it according to their tastes and means, rather like the pattern observed in the domestic context. They sponsor traditional devotional songs [*bhajana*] and song-sermons [*kīrtana*] open to anyone. Other *māṇḍaḷs* depict Gaṇeśa by placing him in the midst of tableaus taken from Purāṇic myths. Their members put on dramatic skits, again drawn from traditional religious lore, or they sponsor a concert of classical music.

Other *māṇḍaḷs* are more innovative in their iconography and programming. Images of Gaṇeśa may be placed in secular cultural and political settings: Gaṇeśa sitting on the moon next to a spacecraft, Gaṇeśa as a disco dancer, Gaṇeśa surrounded by drawings of political figures, which calls attention to current events. The programs sponsored by these groups also depart from the traditional offerings in their programs. In place of devotional songs, one finds film music played over loudspeakers, plays and skits of a political and frequently satirical character performed, and romantic and comic films of recent popularity rented and shown. These innovations are more common in larger cities, such as Pune and Bombay, and may represent a religious and cultural expression of modernization or Westernization. The *māṇḍaḷs* that sponsor such programs draw the largest crowds; young people find them most appealing, the older and more orthodox Hindus objecting to this departure from what they consider the more religious and educational character the festival used to have.

Apart from these programs and iconographic innovations designed to entertain the crowds, other associations, principally those associated with education and culture, sponsor programs more in keeping with what they take to be the original vision behind the festival. These *māṇḍaḷs* sponsor elocution contests for students and lectures and panel discussions on current issues by distinquished citizens. For example, during the 1970 festival in Ahmadnagar, the district library sponsored a series of lectures on such topics as: family planning, student unrest, bank nationalization, border disputes between Maharashtra and Karnataka, and the necessity of national unity. As a public institution in a secular state, the library board did not want to sponsor a specifically religious function, nor did they want to overlook the "cultural" character of the festival and the opportunities it provided for educating those who would come to visit the various *māṇḍaḷ* programs. Sponsoring an explicitly secular program in the midst of a religious festival was an appropriate way for the library to carry on educational outreach to a larger audience than might be possible otherwise. This approach is in keeping with the spirit of Tilak's intentions for the festival when he revitalized it (as we shall see).

As the week of the festival progresses, each evening becomes more filled with *māṇḍaḷ* programs, and the city's neighborhoods and marketplaces take on a carnival atmosphere. In Ahmadnagar, during the evenings of the festival, the police reserve the streets for women and children early in the evening, allowing them the opportunity to go around to see the various exhibits and collect the *darśana* of the many Gaṇeśas on display. People pass by the images, admire the workmanship and imagination that goes into the displays, meet friends and neighbors, and generally enjoy themselves. Many of the *māṇḍaḷs* are organized by teenagers and young adults who seem to enjoy the attention their efforts attract from adults. Although it is obviously a religious occasion, it is also festive and playful. Later in the evening the streets are open for men to go around and visit the images, which they frequently do in groups from various neighborhoods, and to take in films and other programs.

In the contemporary public festival, two countervailing themes can be seen in those exhibits that depart from the traditionally religious subject matter: national unity and religious parochialism. One *māṇḍaḷ* exhibit in 1970 seemed to express both these themes. On a temporary stage was placed a large traditional image of Gaṇeśa facing the audience. To the deity's right, painted on the backdrop was a larger than life-size portrait of John F. Kennedy standing in front of a cathedral. Behind Gaṇeśa was a similar portrait of Jawaharlal Nehru standing in front of the modern Lakṣmīnārāyaṇa temple in New Delhi and to the diety's left was a portrait of Zakir Hussain, the late president of India, standing before a mosque. Along the front of the stage was written in Hindi (the official national language), "*ham sab ek haiṃ*. We are All One." This festival display expressed the ideology of Indian and international pluralism. The three men portrayed both secular political and religious affiliations. Placing Gaṇeśa in the midst of them expressed the view that he oversees the largest and most inclusive *gaṇa,* that of international integration of politics and religion.

At the same time associating these three members of a political pantheon with the specific worship of a regional deity within Hinduism also expressed more parochial religious sensibilities. In this context the word *gaṇa* means something closer to the notion of "us" versus the "others [*mleccha*]"—originally the British and Muslims, but now that the British are gone, this attitude is mostly focused toward the Muslims. Some young men see Gaṇeśa as the lord of a revitalized Hindu tradition that is assertive and "manly"—traditional non-Brahmin values—and see themselves as belonging to his legions [*gaṇa*]. As the Gaṇeśa festival season brings a heightened sense of unity among Hindus, it also brings with it greater fears of communal conflict. Its celebration places a heavy burden on city and district police officials. At times police officials have exercised their powers of preventive detention to stop persons known for their volatile communalist views from taking advantage of the festival situation to foment communal unrest. Muslim informants have spoken of the anxiety they feel during the Gaṇeśa festival season because of the aggressive mood some Hindus exhibit. The procession route along which images are carried carefully avoids streets on which mosques are located.

In terms of the intensity of participation and sheer energy, the culminating event of the festival is the procession of trucks and bullock carts with images mounted on top that pass through the streets of the city to the riverbank where the images are immersed and the festival comes to a close. This is the occasion when all the efforts of households and *māṇḍaḷs* come together like a river, the great procession courses through the narrow streets of the city on its inexorable way to the water. The procession is a time of collective celebration—for some even ecstasy—with dancing, singing, acrobatics, and throwing sacred powder [*gulāl*] on the celebrants and crowds. It is a grand spectacle for those who observe it from the sidelines and balconies along the parade route. Emotions run high at this time of greatest unity and collective enjoyment. It is also a dangerous time because the unity that is sought is so fragile; irritations and conflicts must be suppressed at precisely the moment when one is least inclined to suppress anything (see pl. 11).

The crescendo of "collective effervescence"—to borrow Durkheim's expression—does not come as a spontaneous outburst at the last moment. Careful preparations help to provide support for this important but delicate social and religious moment. Months in advance, meetings take place among police, district officials, representatives of all the *māṇḍaḷs* seeking participation in the festival parade. Permits must be obtained for setting up images and sponsoring programs. Participants are required to wear identification tags to assist police in crowd control. Positions in the procession—after the festival image from the Māḷivāḍa Gaṇeśa temple at the head of the parade—are assigned to *māṇḍaḷs* on a first-come, first-served basis. This is in contrast to the festival processions in villages where the places celebrants take in the procession frequently reflect their position in the village social hierarchy.

In the early morning of the procession day, *Ānantacaturdaśi*—ten days after *Gaṇeśa Caturthī*—the *māṇḍaḷs* arrive with their Gaṇeśa images placed on platforms atop bullock carts or truck cabs. They are profusely decorated with flowers, leaves, cloth streamers, some with electric lights; on many there is a banner to identify the name of the *māṇḍaḷ* and to indicate the number of years it has appeared in the procession. Police officials help the *māṇḍaḷs* line up and settle disputes that flare up over whether one group has crowded ahead of another. A wide variety of *māṇḍaḷ* arrangement is in evidence, but a typical *māṇḍaḷ* consists of a bullock cart with a lavishly decorated image and an attendant to drive the cart. Sometimes a prominent member of the *māṇḍaḷ* or a young girl representing Gaṇeśa's *śakti* rides beside the image. In front of the bullock cart or truck, members of the *māṇḍaḷ* walk and dance through the streets. The dances are performed by groups—some using rhythmic instruments and others maypole arrangements—called *lezhīm* and *goph* dances. Some of the wrestling club *māṇḍaḷs* perform acrobatic feats along the procession route. Some *māṇḍaḷs* provide full bands to accompany them.

Many of the *māṇḍaḷ* carts carry bags of *gulāl,* a fine red powder, which the person sitting next to the image or driving the cart throws in great handfuls onto the crowds and celebrants, a practice reminiscent of the squirting of colored water during the Kṛṣṇa festival of Holī. The vermillion color of the powder corresponds both to the color of Gaṇeśa's images and the powder rubbed into the unbroken rice grains [*akṣata*] offered to Gaṇeśa during his *pūjā.* In a larger symbolic context, red is the color of vitality because of its association with blood, and it generally represents a symbolic transition in an auspicious direction (Beck 1969). *Gulāl* symbolically distributes Gaṇeśa's graceful presence much as does the *prasāda* of the *pūjā. Gulāl,* however, also appears to be a weapon, as when young boys delight in dousing one another, and anyone else within range, with it during the procession.

The procession in Ahmadnagar lasts about eight hours, covering a distance of slightly more than a mile. It assembles at the eastern end of the city and winds its way through the central market area and out the west side of the city to the Sina River where the images are immersed. There does not appear to be any special religious significance to the route; the procession does not detour past the Māḷivādā temple, nor does it circumambulate the city, such as one finds in some South Indian temple festivals. The general atmosphere of the festival is one of merriment, even ecstasy, as trancelike movements seem to animate some during their dancing and drumming. By the time the *māṇḍaḷs* and their images arrive at the river bank, the mood has subdued somewhat, at least in part owing to the exhaustion of the celebrants. At this point in the festival, the final episode takes place: the immersion of the images in the river.

The immersion ritual is simple. Final gifts of coconut, flowers, and lighted camphor, accompanied by the singing of *āratīs,* are offered to the image. The *māṇḍaḷs* and families that have brought their Gaṇeśas to the riverbank, either in procession or on their own, bid their farewells to Gaṇeśa, shouting the familiar "*Gaṇapati Bāppā Morayā, pudhacyā varṣī lavkar yā!*" ("Beloved Gaṇeśa, Lord of Morayā, come again early next year!"). Then a few members of the *māṇḍaḷ* or family carry the image far enough into the river to immerse it, where it quickly dissolves. The festival is over. The cycle of Gaṇeśa's appearance in animate form and his return to the dispersed universe is accomplished. The celebrants return to their homes in a mood of exhilaration mixed with exhaustion and relief (see pl. 12).

The Gaṇeśa festival is a fairly recent innovation in some villages in Maharashtra and the state of Karnataka to the south. Its observance has frequently been introduced through the village schools in recognition of Gaṇeśa's association with learning and as a festival particularly loved by children.

In her study of festivals and social cohesion in a village in northern Karnataka, Suzanne Hanchett describes the Gaṇeśa festival in a rural context (pp. 1517–22). At the level of village society, any cooperative effort requires the solidarity of the village with each individual and group doing its part. Prior to the early 1960s this village had one annual festival procession in honor of Narasiṁha, one of the incarnations of Viṣṇu. The image was carried through the streets of the Brahmin neighborhood on a temple car with members of various castes arrayed in procession according to their status in the village. Riding or walking closest to the car and its deity were the Brahmins. Non-Brahmins held the ropes and pulled the vehicle through the streets, and the lowest castes pushed the car from behind with long heavy poles. As a procession, the festival simultaneously expressed the village's cooperative solidarity and its social hierarchy.

With the coming of land reform in the 1950s and 1960s, many non-Brahmins in the village improved their economic position from being the tenant farmers of Brahmin landowners to that of landowners themselves. In 1969 a non-Brahmin patron introduced the Gaṇeśa festival into the village as the second village-wide processional festival. A Brahmin priest from a nearby village was hired to install an image of Gaṇeśa in the hall of the village Cooperative Society, the symbolic center of non-Brahmin economic and political strength. Members from the lowest or scheduled castes decorated the canopy for the image, as they do in their role as decorators for festivals and weddings. Contributions of funds came mainly from non-Brahmins; Brahmins rarely contributed. A dramatic skit criticizing corruption in government, which was written by a local non-Brahmin playwright, was the program performed during the week of the festival. On the day of the procession, Gaṇeśa's image was placed on a bullock cart rather than being pulled by hand as with the Narasiṁha festival. Non-Brahmins danced in front of the cart and sang devotional songs. As the procession moved through the Brahmin neighborhoods, some Brahmins came out of their homes to make offerings to the deity. The procession then continued through the market area to the river where the image was immersed.

This form of the Gaṇeśa festival reflects the fragile solidarity of the village, which recognizes the ritual importance of the non-Brahmins and their festival. In a context that is least violent and most conciliatory, the changing social and economic circumstances of the non-Brahmins, especially in relation to the Brahmins, are given ceremonial representation. At the same time the festival reinforces solidarity within the non-Brahmin community that sponsors it. Gaṇeśa gives symbolic expression to many of the aspirations of non-Brahmins: education for their children as the route to advancement, wealth, and flexibility in contact with the world beyond the village. The festival provides a dignified and apparently traditional, yet actually fluid, setting within which to express changing social relations. As Lord of Obstacles and Beginnings, Gaṇeśa belongs to everyone. Of late he has been particularly gracious to non-Brahmins in enabling greater success and advancement for them.

As a complex religious, symbolic, and social performance, the Gaṇeśa festival accomplishes many things. In both its domestic and public dimensions, the festival brings Hindus closer to Gaṇeśa. He comes close to them, receives their homage, distributes his graceful presence, and infuses their lives with enthusiasm and optimism. This is the intention of the festival on its own terms, and it is the reason most Hindus give when asked why they participate in the festival—to honor Lord Gaṇeśa and receive his blessing.

In social terms the festival accomplishes a heightened level of solidarity among people. At the domestic level the family draws together in relation to the image, receives *prasāda* together, shares a feast and sacred time together, and then it returns Gaṇeśa to the primordial source from which he emerged. This solidarity is not to be equated with social equality; the hierarchy of the family—or of society—is not overturned, but rather reinforced. In realm of the public festival the various *māṇḍaḷ* exhibits and programs sometimes bring people of different classes together in a common place and soften the edges of social stratification to some extent. This seems to be the case particularly in the urban context where the boundaries of social hierarchy are more difficult to identify and maintain. In the village the festival has been a vehicle for one caste group to advance its status; or more precisely, to achieve ritual confirmation of the status it has already achieved economically and politically. In both city and village the festival temporarily creates a liminal situation in which concern for maintaining human differences recedes while the awareness of the common relationship to the deity—who, after all, belongs to everyone—is enhanced. People tend to feel a greater amount of good will toward one another during this festival. In a related way the festival opens up the structures of everyday life and relieves its pressures, suffusing it with new routines and life.

The festival does foster social solidarity, but it also heightens the awareness of differences within the society. During the festival communal tensions run higher; the minority Muslim community feels more intimidated. It would be a mistake, however, to leave the impression that the festival is a tinderbox of communal hostilities. It is rather a barometer of communal pressures. When the Hindu and Muslim communities have been under stress for other reasons, economic or political, violence may be more likely to flare up during the festival. Generally careful anticipation and preventive measures by police officials have contained the liminal character of the festival and kept it from turning into chaos. The time may be vulnerable, but so also are people more vigilant.

Some Hindus, particularly conservative Brahmins, complain that the festival has declined in quality and religiosity as it has increased in the numbers of participants. They object to its secular character, to the use of popular movies in place of devotional singing, and to the iconographic innovations and what they take to be the obscene behavior of celebrants in their dances during the procession. Older Brahmins recall nostalgically the earlier years of the festival when Tilak attempted to transform it into an occasion for social uplift. This criticism may also mask another complaint many Brahmins have. To some extent these criticisms may also lament the relative decline in Brahmanical influence in the festival and in the Brahmins' status in Maharashtrian culture, society, and economy generally. During this century the festival has ceased to be the province of the Brahmin community. More and more Gaṇeśa belongs to all the people, each group responding to him according to their own tastes and values.

The festival, like the deity it honors, mediates a number of oppositional relations. The festival both honors traditional religion and celebrates change. The symbol of Gaṇeśa standing on the moon makes the statement that technology and modernity are not inimical to traditional religion. It mediates religious particularism and universalism. Although Gaṇeśa is a Hindu god, with a particular mythology and cult, he nevertheless reaches out and embraces not only all Hindus but also all religions, symbolized by the *māṇḍaḷ* exhibit on religious unity. The festival mediates the private and public worlds. The image progresses from the household with its specific religious traditions into the public streets to join with others in recognition of Gaṇeśa's power to embrace everyone. For Maharashtrians, whose own language and culture lies between the Aryan north and the Dravidian south, Gaṇeśa as a mediator has irresistable appeal. It is appropriate that his festival should be more popular in Maharashtra than anywhere else in India. He is the Maharashtrians' patron deity, a reflection of their image of themselves. He is wise, heroic, fun-loving, down-to-earth, and desirous of wealth and the good life. Gaṇeśa brings the realm of the sacred closer to the earth; and, for at least the duration of the festival, he establishes it there.

5

Gaṇeśa in a Regional Setting: Maharashtra

Gaṇeśa enjoys status in the Hindu tradition in all regions of India; he is also a Buddhist deity, although more often portrayed as a demon, in Southeast and East Asia (Getty, pp. 37–87). He inspires a particular following, however, in the Marathi-speaking region of western India called Maharashtra, or the "Great Country." In shifting the focus of our inquiry from myth to religious practice, it is important to sketch how Gaṇeśa fits into the identifiable cultural, social, political, and religious context of Maharashtra.

Maharashtra as a Cultural Region

As a political and territorial unit, Maharashtra has only existed since 1960 when Bombay State was divided along linguistic lines into the two states of Gujarat and Maharashtra. This act of political redistricting merely confirmed the cultural and linguistic facts that a viable unified region had existed for several centuries. Occupying about one hundred thousand square miles, Maharashtra falls roughly into two parts: a strip of coastal jungle between the Arabian Sea and the Western Ghats, called the Konkan; and a dry, rugged plateau region called the Desh [Deśa].

The chief factor in creating a distinct Maharashtrian cultural and religious tradition has been the Marathi language. Emerging into written texts around the thirteenth century, Marathi has produced a remarkable range of religious and poetic literature. Marathi is the southernmost Indo-Aryan language, and it exhibits grammatical and vocabularly influences not only from Sanskrit, but also from Kannada, the Dravidian language spoken immediately to the south of Maharashtra. The distinguished historian of Marathi language and literature, Professor Shankar Gopal Tulpule, comments on the role of Marathi in relation to the Indo-Aryan and Dravidian language families:

> Maharashtra and its language, Marathi, occupy the central position between the North and the South, or between the Indo-Aryan and the Dravidian, and can be regarded as the connecting link between these two different cultures and families of language. (Tulpule, p. 313)

Maharashtra's character as what the late anthropologist Iravati Karve terms a "culture-contact" region is also evident in Maharashtrian social structure (Karve 1968, p. ix). A number of castes from Karnataka to the south and the Telugu-speaking region to the southeast have spread Dravidian practices into the region. For example, several Brahmin castes have a tradition of cross-cousin marriage, a common pattern in South India; but among other Brahmin castes, principally the Citpavan or Konkanastha subcaste, the north Indian pattern is followed. In its marriage patterns and childbirth traditions, Maharashtra more closely resembles customs and practices more frequently attested in South India (Karve 1968a, pp. 161–65; Trautmann).

Some have described Maharashtra as a "rustic," "conservative," or "parochial" society. (Bharati, p. 113; Cashman, p. 3) Unlike Bengal, with its cultural and economic center in Calcutta, Maharashtra lives in its towns and villages. Although it is geographically within the state of Maharashtra, the metropolis of Bombay has its own distinct polyethnic character, made up of Gujarati, Parsi, and South Indian communities in addition to its Maharashtrian population. During the dynasties of the Peshwa rulers in the seventeenth to nineteenth centuries, it was Pune that served as the administrative and cultural center. During the British period Pune also served as the administrative center for Bombay Presidency when the monsoon rains lashed Bombay. As we shall see, Pune has had a particularly close relationship to the fame and fortunes of Gaṇeśa in the region as well. For the great majority of Hindus in Maharashtra the towns and regional centers serve as the foci of economic and religious life. Maharashtra is a culture contact region because of its strategic location between the Aryan north and Dravidian south. Within its borders there are few religious centers of subcontinental significance, and the uncertain rainfall in the Deśa region has precluded large-scale migrations of peoples from other areas. These two factors may contribute to its reputation as a provincial and rustic place.

Maharashtra enjoys a relatively homogeneous population. The social structure can be divided roughly into four major groups: Brahmins, five percent; Maratha-Kunbi (agricultural castes), forty percent; artisan castes that closely identify with the Maratha-Kunbi group in values and religious practices, twenty-five percent; scheduled castes, ten percent; and Muslims, five percent. The strongest cultural influence has come from the large aggregation of agricultural and artisan castes that form the non-Brahmin group. It was from this group that Śivājī drew his army of mountain and guerilla fighters with which he mounted a successful conquest of much of central and northern India during the latter decades of the sixteenth century. With this military heritage as part of their history, known to them in a mythologized form, the Marathas have seen themselves as a *kṣatriya* or warrior community, although this perception has not always received ritual confirmation by Brahmins. The British too tended to see them as one of the "martial races" of India along with the Sikhs, Jats, Rajputs, Pathans, and others (Cashman, p. 7).

With the death of Śivājī in 1680 political power quickly became divided between his Maratha-caste descendents in Kolhapur in the mountains and his Brahmin administrators, the Peshwas, centered in Pune. Although the Peshwas were initially appointed by the monarch, their rule became solidified and hereditary and gradually eclipsed Śivājī's heirs. Although Brahmins by caste, the Peshwas demonstrated many of the traditional *kṣatriya* values associated with Śivājī and the Marathas.

The religious traditions of the region have contributed immeasurably to the Maharashtrian sense of cultural unity. The principal vehicle for this has been the *bhakti* tradition of the poet-saints, a tradition that flourished from the end of the thirteenth to the seventeenth centuries and that brought forth such men as Jñānadeva, Nāmadeva, Tukārāma, Eknātha, and others, from a variety of castes. These poet-saints poured out their religious enthusiasm primarily to Viṭhoba or Viṭṭhala, the deity of Pandharpur, who is frequently termed an incarnation of Kṛṣṇa. The tradition of pilgrimage to Pandharpur observed by great numbers of devotees, called Vārkarīs, has given Maharashtra a vital and genuinely regional religious character (Deleury; Karve 1962; Vaudeville).

The god of Pandharpur is an embodiment of love and devotion. He elicits much the same religious fervor that Kṛṣṇa evokes in North India, but the erotic emphasis of the latter gives way to a more ascetic form of devotionalism in the case of Viṭṭhala. The lyrics of the poet-saints celebrate his accessibility to all devotees, regardless of caste and ritual status. They preach against ritual elitism and admonish their singers and hearers to adopt ascetic devotionalism and religious syncretism centered in personal mystical realization. The pilgrimage to Viṭṭhala's shrine draws devotees from all parts of Maharashtra. He appeals to all castes, but the greatest share of his devotees comes from the non-Brahmin castes.

Another major regional shrine is the one to Khaṇḍobā, at Jejuri, thirty miles southeast of Pune. Khaṇḍobā is a sword-wielding horseman whose mythology identifies him with Sūrya, and sometimes Śiva, of the Sanskrit tradition. He is also worshipped in the form of a *liṅga*. He is the patron deity of farming and herding castes. His devotees manifest a vigorous and aggressive form of popular religiosity (Mate, pp. 162–87; Sontheimer; Stanley).

Other sacred centers in Maharashtra include a shrine at Gangapur to Dattātreya (celebrated in the Marathi narrative, *Gurucaritra*), one to the goddess Bhavānī at Tuljapur, and another to the goddess Mahālakṣmī at Kolhapur. The Śaivite centers at Tryambak and Bhimashankar and Pedh's shrine to Paraśurāma—mythic founder of the Citpavan Brahmin subcaste from which came the Peshwa rulers and many within the religious, political, and intellectual elite of Maharashtra from the eighteenth to the twentieth centuries—figure as significant regional religious centers. Against this background of the general cultural and religious character of

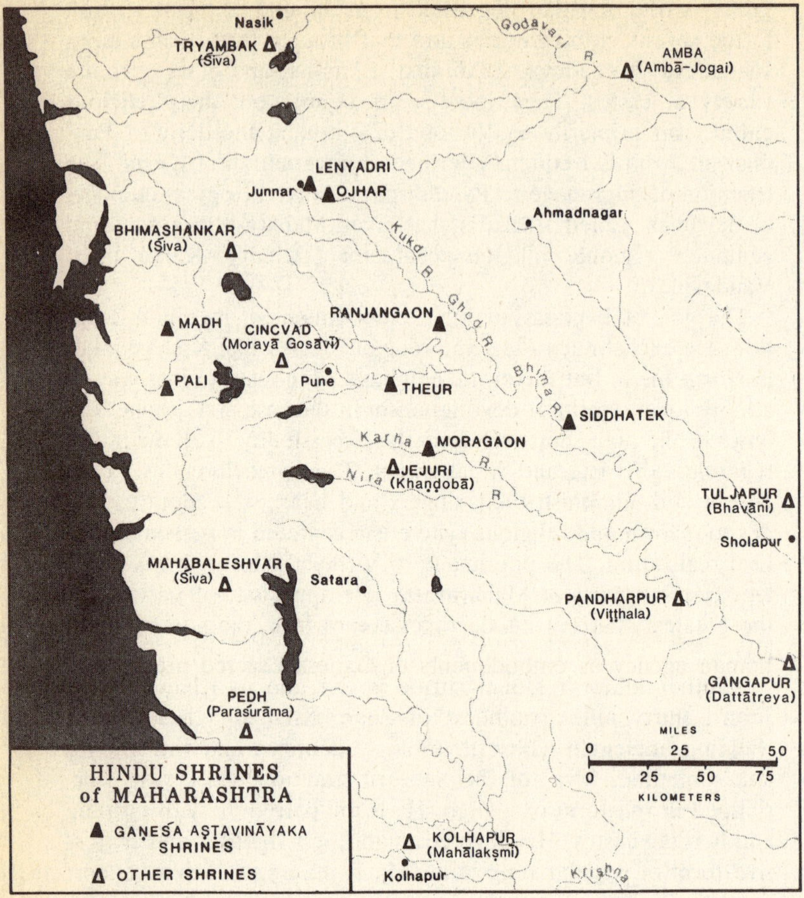

Maharashtra, it is possible now to place Gaṇeśa as a deity and a tradition that have their own distinctive regional character.

Sacred Centers to Gaṇeśa

Gaṇeśa lives in his images in shrines special to him all over Maharashtra and throughout India, shrines in which he grants his auspicious appearance [*darśana*] to devotees who visit him there.

Unlike the temples to Śiva or to other deities in which Gaṇeśa serves as a threshold guardian, in these shrines his is the central image and other deities occupy subsidiary positions. Shrines to Gaṇeśa in Maharashtra fall roughly into three categories. The most important are the *aṣṭavināyakas*—the eight shrines to Vināyaka (Gaṇeśa) that together make up a sacred complex about which more will be said later. The second group comprises the more than seventy-five shrines of varying size and affluence that are actively served by ritual functionaries [*pūjārīs*] and enjoy local reputations as centers of Gaṇeśa's sacred presence (Gadgil, 2.1–59). The third category includes the indeterminate number of small roadside shrines and images at the boundaries of villages. Usually made of rough stone and smeared with red paint, these may play important roles during festivals but do not receive the regular service of priests. Most of the images in both the *aṣṭavināyakas* and other shrines in Maharashtra are called *svayambhū* ("self-existent"). That is, they are not carved by image makers and installed by priests. Instead they are rocks that bear a striking resemblance, in the eyes of the faithful, to the head of an elephant. Like the *śālagrāma* stones of Vaiṣṇavism and the *bāṇaliṅga* of Śaivism, *svayambhū* images appear without human agency as embodiments of Gaṇeśa's sacred presence in the world and require no rites of sacralization [*prāṇapratiṣṭhā*] for their sacredness to be apparent to his devotees. They are "naturally" sacred. Temple myths tell of occasions on which Gaṇeśa appeared to someone in a dream and instructed the person to dig beneath a certain tree and find "him" in the form of a *svayambhū* stone. This *svayambhū* tradition links the worship of Gaṇeśa with very ancient Hindu modes of apprehending sacred power.

The shrines mark places where events of divine significance occurred in the mythic past or where Gaṇeśa defeated a demon or saved a god or devotee from being defeated by some obstacle. They are places in which Gaṇeśa is said to have appeared to gods and humans in order to lend them his saving presence and obstacle-removing powers. Etiological legends associated with these shrines tell how his devotees prospered in material and spiritual ways as a result of calling on Gaṇeśa in his form at a particular shrine. The legends also celebrate the power to be derived from knowing the deity's sacred lore, specifically his *mantras*. As with all Hindu shrines, tales abound of the fruit [*phala*] of merit [*puṇya*] to be picked by the faithful at these fertile centers of religious power. Many themes in these temple myths differ little from myths of other deities; however, the Gaṇeśa stories call attention again and again to the this god's special territory: the terrain of obstacles and their removal. This is his special work in the interactions of gods and humans that is celebrated in relation to the concrete places in which these mighty deeds were done.

Many myths of Gaṇeśa that specifically identify themselves with a specific shrine are variants of well-known Epic and Purāṇic stories. At one small temple in the ancient village of Adoś, near Nagpur, for example, the story is told that when Brahmā was creating the universe he brought forth a beautiful water nymph [*apsaras*], named Tilottamā, whom he then attempted to seduce. As he chased her, his lust for her became so intense that he spilled his seed on the ground, and from it sprang up three demons. The demons quickly grew so powerful that they destroyed the triple world and imprisoned all the gods. But the gods called on Gaṇeśa who told them to sit under a certain *śamī* tree with Śiva and Pārvatī at its base. Then Gaṇeśa emerged from the *śamī* tree and slew all the demons (Cendavankar 1965, pp. 82–83). The very tree from which Gaṇeśa emerged forms part of the shrine that presently stands on that spot. The myth draws on Purāṇic tales of Tilottamā (e.g., *Skanda Purāṇa* 6.153.2–27; cf. O'Flaherty 1973, pp. 248–94) but reworks them with a different narrative turn, one in which it is Gaṇeśa who saves the gods and the universe from the disastrous consequences of Brahmā's incestuous lust. The linkage between Gaṇeśa and the *śamī* tree recalls Epic and Purāṇic symbolism of the *śamī* tree as the one from whose wood the sticks [*araṇīs*] for kindling the Vedic fire were made. Agni is said to leap out of the fire sticks as they are kindled (MBh 9.46.12–20). In this story Gaṇeśa takes over Agni's role. Thus the local legend joins together the specific shrine and its territory with the "great tradition" of the mythological lore recorded in the Sanskrit texts by relating them both to the particular image. This phenomenon is widespread in Hinduism, an example of what David Shulman calls the "localization" of the divine (pp. 40–89).

Other temple legends tell of Gaṇeśa's supremacy over the other great gods of the Hindu pantheon. In the shrine at Siddhatek, one of the *aṣṭavināyaka* centers, this story is told:

> When Brahmā began creating the universe, two demons, Madhu and Kaiṭabha, appeared out of Viṣṇu's ear and began to disturb Brahmā. Viṣṇu tried to kill the demons, but they proved too powerful. Then he went to Śiva, pleasing him with devotional songs, and asked his help. Śiva scolded him, saying that if he had worshipped Gaṇeśa in the first place he would not be in this predicament. Śiva then gave Viṣṇu the *mantra* of Gaṇeśa. After a long search for the auspicious place to recite the *mantra,* Viṣṇu came to Siddhatek and worshipped Gaṇeśa there. Hearing Viṣṇu's devotion, Gaṇeśa appeared there and destroyed the demons. (Gadgil, 2.43–4)

This story turns on the realization that the power of the demons to make trouble for the gods arises from the gods' own ignorance of the greater power to be derived from knowing Gaṇeśa and his *mantra.* Their suffering stems from ritual error. Gaṇeśa's rise to prominence in the story, as in the tradition itself, depends on his ability to displace the other deities and emerge as the one capable of accomplishing what they had failed to do.

A similar battle between the gods and demons is said, according to the temple tradition of the shrine at Ranjangaon, again an *aṣṭavināyaka* center in Ahmadnagar district, to have taken place on the very plain on which the temple stands. Indeed, its existence is a commemoration of Gaṇeśa's triumph over the forces of chaos in that place:

> Formerly the demon Tripura worshipped Gaṇeśa and received the boon that he would conquer the universe. Quickly Tripura defeated Indra and captured the triple world. He extinguished the sacred fires and prohibited worship of the gods. Then Nārada told the gods to take refuge in Gaṇeśa. Śiva worshipped him and received the *mantra* that made him able to defeat Tripura on that spot. (Gadgil, 2.8–9)

This myth illustrates Gaṇeśa's capacity to play both sides of the game between the gods and demons. Tripura received the boon from Gaṇeśa that made possible his conquest of the triple world in the same way that Śiva later receives the *mantra* in order to defeat him. Gaṇeśa first creates an obstacle for the gods by giving Tripura the power to conquer the triple world, but then he removes it by granting Śiva his all-powerful *mantra.* In the same way, having removed the obstacle of powerlessness from Tripura at the beginning of the story, at the end he obstructs him by aiding Śiva. Here, as in many other myths about Gaṇeśa in his role as a threshold guardian, he regulates the passage of power back and forth between the contending parties or forces. In this myth it is between gods and demons; in others it may be between gods and humans, gods and gods, or humans and humans. Like the operator of a lock on a river, Gaṇeśa moves the levels of power up and down according to which agent is seeking passage. All must pass through him, whatever their business may be, if they are to have their efforts come to fruition. This mythic reality takes on compelling concreteness and immediacy for the devotee through its association with a particular shrine where the sacred cosmos intersects the human world.

Many myths associated with local shrines to Gaṇeśa call attention to how he grants the desires of those who worship him there. Two stories illustrate this pattern. The first is from a small and ancient temple in the village of Kalam, near Nagpur. The story is a variant of the ancient tale of Gautama's curse (KSS 17.137–48; MBh 13.41.12–13; ŚB 3.3.4.18; cf. O'Flaherty 1973, pp. 85–86)

> Out of lust for Ahalyā, the wife of the sage Gautama, Indra impersonated Gautama and made love with her. When Gautama realized this he cursed Indra's phallus to fall off and have his body covered with a thousand female sexual organs [*bhaga*]; hence he became known as Bhagendra. Then Bṛhaspati, the preceptor of the gods, went to Gautama and received the *mantra* of Gaṇeśa. He gave Indra the *mantra* and told him to worship Gaṇeśa in the form of Cintāmaṇi at Kadamba [Kalam]. Indra brought the Ganges to the shrine in order to bathe [*abhiṣeka*] the image. His curse was thus removed and his manhood restored. The sacred river [*tīrtha*] and image that Indra worshipped there remain in that temple to this day. (Cendavankar 1965, pp. 106–9; cf. GP 1.29.10–12; Preston, p. 104)

The myth rearranges elements in the story to call attention to the power of Gaṇeśa's *mantra,* image, and shrine as vehicles capable of overcoming the curse Gautama had placed on Indra for seducing his wife. In the second story it is the power of the vow [*vrata*] to Gaṇeśa that is celebrated. At the temple of Mahāgaṇapati (Gaṇeśa) in the village of Titvala, near Bombay, this story is told:

> When King Duṣyanta married Śakuntalā, he promised to bring her to his palace in a grand procession. But when he did not come for her after a while she became deeply perplexed. At that moment

> the sage Durvāsas arrived there, but she did not notice him. Enraged at this lack of respect for him, he cursed her that her husband would forget her forever. Then her preceptor, Kaṇva, told her to make a vow [*vrata*] to Gaṇeśa to overcome the obstacle of Durvāsas's curse and Duṣyanta's forgetfulness. Śakuntalā came to Gaṇeśa in his shrine and declared her vow to him. He was pleased with her devotion and caused Duṣyanta to remember her. (Cendavankar 1965, pp. 14–28)

These various temple myths are broadly etiological in character. They function to "localize" the divine power associated with Gaṇeśa and explicitly link the particular place, image, and ritual traditions with the mythological lore of "great tradition" Hinduism by reworking well-known stories to fit them into the framework of Gaṇeśa devotion.

Although there are many Gaṇeśa shrines distributed throughout the region of Maharashtra, the Gaṇeśa tradition is centered on eight shrines that together make up a complex known as the *aṣṭavināyaka*—eight Vināyaka (Gaṇeśa) shrines. These are all located in the region around the city of Pune. In the sacred geography of the Gaṇeśa tradition, they form a *maṇḍala* from the surroundings of Pune and the temple to Gaṇeśa in the nearby village of Cincvad, where the shrine is associated with Morayā Gosāvī, the patriarch of the cult [*sampradāya*] in Maharashtra. These eight shrines rose to prominence during the rule of the Peshwas in Pune during the seventeenth to nineteenth centuries, and they continue to flourish today.

All eight of these shrines contain *svayambhū* (self-existent images) that are said to have appeared to devotees "naturally" in the form of elephant-faced stones. Devotional literature and temple guidebooks admonish pilgrims to visit all eight of the shrines as part of a single pilgrimage [*yātra*], claiming that the merit to be obtained from receiving the auspicious sight [*darśana*] of the eight images far exceeds that of a visit to a single shrine. The pilgrimage to all eight shrines constitutes a circumambulation [*pradakṣiṇā*] of the boundaries of the sacred cosmos that is permeated by the presence of Gaṇeśa.

Three of the eight shrines lie to the east and southeast of Pune: Moragaon, on the Karha River; Siddhatek, on the Bhima River; and Theur, on the Mula-Mutha River. To the north of Pune are the shrines at Ranjangaon, one on the road leading to Ahmadnagar, the rock-cut shrine at Lenyadri, and the other, Ojhar, located on the Kukdi River. Lying to the west, in the coastal mountains, are the shrines at Madh and Pali (see pl. 8).

Although the tradition stresses the unity of these eight centers, the temple at Moragaon is regarded as the most important. It attracts the greatest number of pilgrims, and enjoys a generally greater level of religious prestige than the others.

Moragaon is located on the Karha River about sixty miles southeast of Pune. The pilgrim enters the temple from the north, facing the shrine located at the south end of the temple enclosure. The arrangement recalls the significance of the south as the dangerous region over which Gaṇeśa stands guard. Just outside the main shrine are images of Nandin, Śiva's bull vehicle, and Muṣaka, Gaṇeśa's rat vehicle. They guard the entrance and look devotedly toward Gaṇeśa's image inside. The shrine is laid out in a rectangular form and traced within it is the outline of a tortoise. It lies at the center of vertical and horizontal axes. Vertically the shrine intersects the triple world, having Kailāsa (Śiva's heavenly abode) above; Śeṣa in Pāṭālaloka (the serpent and the underworld) beneath; and Bhūloka (the earth) in the middle. The center of the Bhūloka is Mayūrapura (Moragaon). On the horizontal axis the temple is laid out with gates to the four directions, each containing images of Gaṇeśa attended by pairs of gods and consorts in portal niches. Each gate simultaneously represents: a form in which Gaṇeśa appeared in one or another cosmic age, an aspect of the divine principle [*brahman*], and one of the four life goals [*puruṣārtha*] detailed in the *dharma* tradition. On entering the shrine the pilgrim performs worship at each of the four directional Gaṇeśas.

According to tradition the pilgrim should begin such a pilgrimage on the first day of the month of Bhādrapada (August/September), taking one day for each of the directional images and then arriving before the shrine at the center on the fourth day [*Gaṇeśa Caturthī*], the most auspicious day in the Hindu year for the worship of Gaṇeśa. In this way the pilgrim moves spatially toward the central shrine on the most sacred day; hence spatial purity and temporal auspiciousness converge most advantageously for the devotee in the moment of contact with the sight of the image [*darśana*]. As one enters the temple, keeping the main shrine on the right according to the practice of circumambulation [*pradakṣiṇā*], the first image encountered is Ballāḷvināyaka, the form in which Gaṇeśa appeared when he defeated the demons Śaṅkarāsura and Kāmalāsura who had stolen the Vedas and hidden them at the bottom of the sea. Ballāḷvināyaka is attended by Rāma and Rāmeśā (Sītā). This portal symbolically opens onto the realms of *dharma* and honors the domain of Viṣṇu-brahman or the absolute principle of reality as it is manifested in the forms of Viṣṇu.

To the south, the second stop for the pilgrim, is the image of Vighneśa, the Lord of Obstacles. He is flanked by Śiva and Umā (Pārvatī). This gate represents the principle of *brahman* in its form as Śiva and oversees the domain of *artha* (accomplishment). At the western gate is the image of Gaṇeśa in his form as Cintāmaṇi, the fulfiller of all desires. He is attended by Kāma and Ratī, the god and goddess of pleasure. It is the domain of *asat-brahman* (the absolute principle that is beyond manifestation) and the domain of *kāma* (enjoyment). At the northern gate stands Gaṇeśa in his form as Mahāgaṇapati, the supreme lord, attended by Mahī (earth) and Vāraha (boar *āvatāra*). This is the realm of *sat-brahman* (the absolute principle that manifests itself in the world) and the domain of *mokṣa* (release from rebirth). When the pilgrim makes this four-sided journey along the outer limits of the shrine, he traces the boundaries of Gaṇeśa's cosmos, as he does when he performs a pilgrimage to all eight of the *aṣṭavināyaka* shrines together. This homage to the portals [*dvārapūjā*] serves as ritual preparation for the most significant part of the pilgrimage, the auspicious viewing [*darśana*] of Gaṇeśa's image in the central shrine.

The main shrine consists of an assembly hall [*sabhāmaṇḍapa*] in front of the shrine. The *svayambhū* image is located in a small sanctuary beneath the temple tower. This small enclosure "wombhouse [*garbhagṛha*]" is the locus of the most intense concentration of Gaṇeśa's sacred presence. To the right and left sides of the image stand Gaṇeśa's two consorts, Siddhi (Success) and Buddhi (Intelligence); they are his *śaktis* (the feminine emanations of his creative powers). In front of the image also stand Gaṇeśa's rat and a peacock [*mayūra*], a creature usually associated with Gaṇeśa's brother, Skanda. In this shrine, however, it is said that Gaṇeśa defeated the peacock and converted him into his own devotee (Mate, pp. 14–15).

The shrine at Moragaon is particularly celebrated in the *Mudgala Purāṇa,* dating from the fourteenth to sixteenth centuries. This text devotes various sections to recitation of the mighty deeds Gaṇeśa performed in eight different incarnations in respective cosmic ages. These stories tell of his many battles with the demons in defense of righteousness [*dharma*] and extol the powers associated with sacred places. One such tale associated with Moragaon is that of Gaṇeśa, in his form as Guṇeśa, the lord of the qualities [*guṇa*]:

> Formerly the righteous king Cakrapāṇi had no issue. He performed asceticism to Sūrya, who appeared to him and told him that his wife, Ugrā, would bear him a son. However, Cakrapāṇi's seed was too powerful for Ugrā to carry, and the embryo leaped from her womb into the ocean where it was raised by a Brahmin couple. When the child had grown the Brahmin couple returned the young man to his father, and Cakrapāṇi named his son Sindhu, meaning "Ocean." Leaving his kingdom to his son, Cakrapāṇi retired to the forest. After performing asceticism for a thousand years, Sindhu received the promise from Sūrya that he would conquer the triple world and have *amṛta* [the elixir of immortality churned from the ocean of milk] forever. But Sūrya warned him that he would lose the *amṛta* if the container holding it were to break. As Sindhu's power increased he became more corrupted and intoxicated with sensual pleasures, even to the point of enjoying smashing the images of the gods in the temples. Sindhu then put all the gods into prison. But the gods cried out for Guṇeśa's help. The lord of obstacles quickly appeared in his fierce [*vikaṭa*] form and quickly defeated Kāmalāsura, the general of Sindhu's army, cutting his body into three pieces. Assembling an army of Śiva's attendants [*gaṇas*], Guṇeśa battled Sindu's army and defeated it quickly. Guṇeśa cut open Sindhu's body and emptied it of its life-giving *amṛta.* The gods and *dharma* were then restored and Brahmā gave his two daughters to Guṇeśa in marriage. With this obstacle to the gods overcome, Guṇeśa vanished, and Brahmā and the other gods established a shrine at Moragaon to commemorate Gaṇeśa's appearance in this form. (Cendavankar 1964, pp. 2–7; cf. Mate, pp. 11–14; *MudP* 6.1–45)

In addition to the sanctity of the shrine itself, there is the nearby river Karha along which are a number of sacred places or *tīrthas* where pilgrims come to bathe and expiate sins. These *tīrthas* mark places where Gaṇeśa's obstacle-removing powers are especially present. Indeed, the shrine and its *tīrthas* fuse together in the expectations of the pilgrim so that the term *tīrtha* refers both to the sacred places at the river and the shrine. The *tīrtha* is understood to flow mystically through the shrine itself. Above the doorway to the temple, commanding the pilgrims' attention as they pass through enroute to the image, is a Sanskrit stanza addressed to Gaṇeśa, the lord who dwells at the blissful destination of the pilgrims' mystical realization. The external terrain of the shrine and the internal landscape of the devotee's mystical awareness ideally converge in the act of crossing the threshold. The stanza reads:

> You dwell on the bank of the *turīya* [the river near the shrine and the fourth state of consciousness according to the Upaniṣads] which gives the greatest happiness [*paramasukha*], beyond the realms of the dull-witted, in the innate places of your own bliss [*ānanda*]. You are the lord of the peacock [Mayūreśvara]. Thus I meditate on you, the progenitor of Śiva, Hari [Viṣṇu], Ravi [Sūrya], and Brahmā.

The following myth celebrates the *turīyatīrtha* at Moragaon. It is a story of primal sin and expiation and follows that pattern of myths associated with Gaṇeśa in which his powers overcome obstacles where all else has failed:

> Formerly, when Brahmā created Kāma, the latter struck Brahmā with desire. Then he lusted for his daughter, Sarasvatī; but his desire for her weakened him and he was unable to continue creating the universe. He went to the gods for help in seeking penance for his sin. Viṣṇu created the Ganges, Śiva the Narmadā, Sūrya the Yamunā, and Devī the Sarasvatī rivers; but none of their waters could clense Brahmā of his sin of incest. Then the gods together called upon the *turīyatīrtha* to appear. Brahmā bathed there and his sin was removed and his powers restored. Brahmā put the sacred waters in his water pot [*kamaṇḍalu*] and went to worship Gaṇeśa at Moragaon. As he entered the shrine he stumbled and spilled his pot causing the waters to fall nearby. He tried to collect the water again into his water pot, but Gaṇeśa prevented him. So it remained there and became the Karha River. (Mate, pp. 9–10)

In this myth of the origin of the *tīrtha* at Moragaon, Gaṇeśa splendidly plays out two of his best roles: he saves the universe from destruction when all other efforts have failed, and he tricks

Brahmā out of the waters that saved him from the impotence caused by his sinful lust. This latter sleight of hand—or more accurately, sleight of foot—recalls the myth in which Gaṇeśa took the form of a crow and upset the sage Agastya's waterpot and sent him in search of the sacred waters that turned out to reside at a *tīrtha* to Gaṇeśa. This myth combines elements of etiology and epiphany: it both recounts why the spot is sacred and reveals Gaṇeśa's divine obstacle-removing powers.

The shrine at Moragaon is served by a Brahmin priest [*kṣetropadhyāya*] who performs a series of daily rituals. He "awakens" the image each morning with the worship of sixteen *upacāras* ("ways of service"), which include offerings of bathing, food, flowers, incense, and prayers. At midday, a simpler ceremony [*pañcopacāra*] is performed. At evening, the priest concludes the day's ritual activity by reciting a series of praises and "retiring" the image for the night. At two other times during the day, a priest of the Gurav, a non-Brahmin Śaivite caste, performs more informal rites to Gaṇeśa's image called *prakṣālana.* All food offered to the deity is vegetarian. Devotees may also arrange for the priests to perform special ceremonies of adorning the image [*alaṃkārapūjā*]. These ritual patterns are generally followed at the other *aṣṭavināyaka* shrines as well. They reflect Brāhmanical practice and resemble more general Hindu temple worship patterns.

The shrines to Gaṇeśa in Maharashtra, especially the *aṣṭavināyakas,* no doubt have been sacred to Hindus for many centuries, perhaps even prior to their association with Gaṇeśa. In their present forms, however, these shrines and their temple structures date from the period of Maratha and Peshwa rule, in the seventeenth century, as evidenced by grants of land received for their support (Preston, pp. 114–22).

The Peshwa rulers in Pune supported the *aṣṭavināyaka* shrines with particular commitment because Gaṇeśa was the patron deity of their kinship lineage, their *kuladevatā,* and because their kingdom prospered under Gaṇeśa's benevolent guidance. The shrines at Moragaon and Theur were the ones most frequently visited by the Peshwa rulers, particularly Balaji Bajirao and Madhavrao I (Preston, pp. 115, 121).

In addition to their financial support of the shrines in the region, the Peshwas lavishly celebrated the annual festival to

Gaṇeśa on *Gaṇeśa Caturthī,* the fourth day of the bright half of the month of Bhādrapada (August/September). This festival was held in Pune at the palace rather than at one of the shrines. A clay image of Gaṇeśa was installed temporarily, as it was in many Brahmin homes in Pune, and probably followed the general pattern discussed in the previous chapter. Many Brahmins were invited to the palace festival to be fed; then the image was taken in procession through the streets of the city where it could be seen by the populace and immersed in the river.

After 1818, when the British defeated the Peshwa dynasty, they continued the tradition of supporting sacred shrines and temples, largely out of a desire to ensure the tranquility of their subjects. The palace tradition of the annual festival, however, fell into disuse, and the ceremony continued on only in the contexts of individual households, primarily among Pune's Brahmin community. By the end of the century, however, the festival was to undergo a rebirth in Pune under the leadership of Bal Gangadhar Tilak, known to his followers as Lokamanya—revered by the people. Tilak infused the festival with new meaning and purpose and launched it on a course that would give it much of the character it presently exhibits.

Sacred Persons and Traditions: The Gaṇeśa Sampradāya

Gaṇeśa's emergence into prominence as a deity within the Hindu pantheon was in no small measure accomplished by those devotees who through the centuries looked on him as the center of their religious lives. No one knows how old this tradition of worship is, but a reasonable guess, based on Purāṇic and other textual sources and archaeological evidence places the emergence of an identifiable cult of Gaṇeśa between the sixth and eighth centuries, although some authorities place it closer to the tenth century. (Bhandarkar, p. 148; Ghurye, pp. 70–81; Grierson 1914, p. 175). The area of Vidarbha, in eastern Maharashtra, appears to be among the earliest locations of Gaṇeśa worship. Vidarbha is midway between North and South India and was an important crossing point for cultural and religious influences. As evidence for the presence of the Gaṇeśa tradition in this area, Preston locates a Gaṇeśa temple at Kalam (Kadamba), near Nagpur. Copper plate inscriptions indicate that the temple was flourishing there by at least the fifth or sixth century (pp. 105–5).

The Gāṇapatyas describe their group as a *sampradāya.* The term derives from the Sanskrit word, *sampradā,* meaning to give or hand down by tradition. A *sampradāya* is defined as, "a particular system of religious teaching, a religious doctrine inculcating the worship of one particular deity" (Apte, p. 969). The Gāṇapatyas patronize Gaṇeśa above all other deities in the Hindu pantheon. Such a tradition appears to have existed for Gaṇeśa from at least the tenth century A.D., probably longer. A hagiological text from about this time, the *Śaṅkaravijaya* of Ānandagiri, gives us a picture of some aspects of Gāṇapatya thought and practice. The *Śaṅkaravijaya* celebrates the victories of Śaṅkara, the famous proponent of Advaita Vedānta, during the course of which he encountered in debate and defeated various religious and philosophical opponents. Ānandagiri describes the views and doctrines [*mata*] of six different groups of Gāṇapatyas, each one having iconographic and ritual patterns, and views taught by different masters of *ācāryas.*

Girijāsuta taught devotion to Mahāgaṇapati, the creator of the cosmos who remains after its cyclical dissolution. He has a single tusk and embraces his *śakti.* Meditation on Gaṇeśa in this form, Girijāsuta claimed, would bring the devotee ultimate bliss. Another preceptor, Gaṇapatikumāra, worshipped an image of Gaṇeśa with turmeric powder. His view of Gaṇeśa as the ultimate deity was based on the Vedic reference to Gaṇapati (ṚV 2.23.1) in which he is described as the lord of the hosts of gods. Devotees to this form of Gaṇeśa branded themselves on their arms and face with the mark of Gaṇeśa's tusk. Other groups of devotees worshipped him according to different iconographical and ritual traditions—Navanīta, Svarṇa, and Saṃtāna Gāṇapatyas—although all claimed to follow the teachings of *śruti* (revealed Vedic authority).

A sixth group of Gāṇapatyas, led by one Herambasuta, followed the so-called left-hand Tantric path. They are devotees of Gaṇeśa in his *ucchiṣṭa* or impure form. The word *ucchiṣṭa* refers to foods left over from the sacrifice or offering to a deity. It may also refer to food left in the mouth, hence impure. In offering leftover foods to Gaṇeśa, the Ucchiṣṭa Gāṇapatyas reverse the symbolism of Brāhmaṇical orthodoxy, a pattern consistent with Tantric inversions of orthodox practice. Herambasuta lays out the basic tenets of his doctrines to Śaṅkara as follows:

> The true teaching of the Ucchiṣṭa Gāṇapatis is called Hairamba [i.e., that taught by Heramba]. . . . They meditate on Gaṇapati as follows: four-armed, three-eyed, each hand holding a noose, axe, and a gesture relieving fear, with the tip of his trunk he sucks up wine. Such is the form of Gaṇapati worship.
>
> The image the Hairamba Gāṇapatis worship is one who is seated on a great throne, in whose left lap sits the goddess (Devī) whom he embraces while the tip of his trunk touches her sexual organ [*bhaga*].
>
> I have become content that there is no other view [*mata*] that can compare with this one. According to the teaching of the left-hand path, Gaṇapati and Devī are part of one another; just as, though the self [*jīva*] is smaller than the lord [*īśa*], even so they are one. This is my view. Having taken up both ways of thinking [the orthodox and the Tantric] I have put the mark of this sect on my forehead and left off all other marks. Now I have made the *sandhyā* and all other Brāhmaṇical rituals optional, I have drunk from the well of highest knowledge. So, I am born into bliss and have acquired the knowledge of the three worlds.
>
> Furthermore, according to my view, there are two teachings to be followed: first, all men born of different castes are of one caste; second, the women of all castes are the same as the men. There is no sin if there is intercourse between men and women [of different castes], or separation either, because there is no rule that one woman belongs to one man. If they are united in intercourse while she is menstruous, there is greater bliss [*ānanda*] to be experienced, because there is much blood flowing. There is no such arrangement as marriage and all classes [*varṇa*] are the same. The act of enjoyment should be taken by any man who, having Heramba Gaṇapati in his mind, takes a woman as his *śakti*. (*Śaṅkaravijaya,* chap. 17)

Somehow Śaṅkara fails to be persuaded by Herambasuta's arguments. He responds by saying that the Ucchiṣṭa Gāṇapatya's teachings are contrary to the Vedas and that liberation [*mokṣa*] comes only through renunciation. For those who remain in the world, sacrifice, worship, and adherence to *dharma* are the appropriate paths to follow. This Tantric interpretation of Gaṇeśa devotion does not belong to the mainstream of the tradition; the preponderance of the literature reflects the orthodox assumptions and practice. Indeed, Gaṇeśa came to be accepted, along with Viṣṇu, Śiva, Sūrya, and Devī, as one of the fivefold [*pañcāyatana*] group of deities worshipped by Smārta Brahmins of South India. To what extent the origins of Gaṇeśa worship can be traced to South India remains unclear, but the elephant-headed deity enjoyed veneration by Śaivites there from early times.

Several major Sanskrit texts enjoy central authority among Gāṇapatyas. The most important is the *Śrī Gaṇapati Atharvaśīrṣa* or *Gaṇapati Upaniṣad* (see Appendix). This is a late upaniṣad attributed to the *Atharva Veda.* The text identifies Gaṇeśa with the all-pervading *brahman* and celebrates the powers of the deity to overcome all obstacles. Another important Gāṇapatya Upaniṣad is the *Gaṇeśatāpanīya Upaniṣad.* Two sectarian Purāṇas, the *Gaṇeśa Purāṇa* and the *Mudgala Purāṇa* contain a great deal of mythological and ritual lore pertaining to Gaṇeśa. The *Gaṇeśa Purāṇa* is probably the older of the two, dating, according to Hazra, from between the eleventh and fourteenth centuries (1951, p. 97). Included in the text of the *Gaṇeśa Purāṇa* is the *Gaṇeśa Gītā* (chaps. 138–48 of the *Uttarakhaṇḍa).* It is patterned after the *Bhagavad Gītā;* indeed, ninety percent of its verses are nearly identical to it (Yoroi, p. 4). In the *Gaṇeśa Gītā* Gaṇeśa plays the role Kṛṣṇa plays in the *Bhagavad Gītā.* He teaches the inquiring prince, Vareṇya, that he, Gaṇeśa, is the supreme lord, the embodiment of *brahman,* and that by worshipping him, Vareṇya may find the sure path to liberation. In this theological respect, the two *Gītās* are very similar. The devotional path taught by the *Gaṇeśa Gītā,* however, displays a somewhat different emphasis in its assertion that the mystical union achieved in worship leads to liberating knowledge [*jñāna*] (GG 1.6.17). The text also contains a number of features that reflect modes of Gāṇapatya ritual practice. It proclaims, for example:

> Whoever recites (it) once or twice or thrice (a day): even by seeing this (man) who becomes identical with *brahman,* a man is released. . . . He who, being well prepared, recites (this) at all times, becomes (like) Gaṇeśa. There is no doubt (here). He who recites (this) on every fourth (night of a lunar fortnight), with devotion, is also fit for release. (GG 11.42.47, trans. in Yoroi, p. 74; cf. AP 71.313; BhavP 1.29–30; GarP 139; MatsyaP 260.52–55; SkP 1.1.10.87–1.1.11.22, 6.214.68–72)

The *Gaṇeśa Gītā* then goes on to link devotion to its lord with the performance of his festival, which is the major sacred event available to his devotees:

> If a man, full of devotion, makes of earth in the month of Bhādra in the bright half, on the fourth (night), the four-armed figure of Gaṇeśa, (and) which is with his mount and with his weapons, praises (him), according to the prescribed rules, (and) recites, indeed eagerly; then Gaṇeśa, having been pleased, gives him the highest enjoyment: sons, grandsons, wealth, food grains, an abundance of cattle, treasure and the rest. To him who desires knowledge, knowledge will belong; he who desires happiness, will obtain happiness; he who had a desire will gain other desires: (then) they proceed to release at the end (of their time). (GG 11.49–52, trans. in Yoroi, p. 75)

When properly adored, Gaṇeśa emerges as the giver of all gifts and the remover of all obstacles, whether they be material or spiritual. All goals achieve harmonious realization through his transformative power.

The *Mudgala Purāṇa,* the second Purāṇa sacred to the Gāṇapatyas, is probably from a later period than the *Gaṇeśa Purāṇa* and shows more familiarity with Maharashtrian sacred sites, particularly the shrine at Moragaon. Both Purāṇas play an important role in Gāṇapatya literature; a number of commentaries and abridgements of their contents have been written in Marathi to make them more accessible to wider audiences.

Gāṇapatya literature in Marathi is extensive but only a few texts deserve special mention: Karhadkar's *Gaṇeśa Gītāṭīka* (1692), Yadumanika's *Sanjivāni* (1725), Deva's *Vināyaka Mahātmya* (1751), Gosavinandana's *Jñānamodaka,* Ganesayogindra's *Yogeśvara* (c. 1775) (Tulpule, p. 418).

The tradition of sacred persons associated with Gaṇeśa in Maharashtra begins with Morayā (Moroba) Gosāvī (1610–59). He is widely regarded by Gāṇapatyas in the region as the greatest devotee of Gaṇeśa. He was the founder of a dynasty of saints at Cincvad, near Pune. Indeed, his devotion to the deity was so pervasive that he came to be regarded as a living incarnation of Gaṇeśa, as did his descendents for seven generations. Traditions of Morayā Gosāvī's birth place him either near Cincvad or the region of Bidar (southeast of Pune) and of a Deśastha Ṛgvedi Brahmin family. The hagiological tradition at Cincvad has it that

Morayā's father, one Vāmanbhaṭ, and his wife came to Moragaon on pilgrimage and settled there. Because they had no son, Vāmanbhaṭ performed penance at Moragaon until he received a vision [*darśana*] of Gaṇeśa. For twelve years he performed asceticism there, but still remained childless. Gaṇeśa then appeared to him in a dream and told him he would not receive a son. Undaunted, Vāmanbhaṭ persisted in his ascetic rigor for another forty-eight years, both a Moragaon and Siddhatek. Finally, Gaṇeśa appeared to him again, saying, "I am pleased by your devotion, and even though you will not have a son, I will take birth myself [through your wife]" (Deva and Bhingarkar, p. 3). So Gaṇeśa became incarnated in the person of Morayā Gosāvī. He was raised as a pious Brahmin, trained in the Vedas, initiated into the Daśanāmi order of monks. Morayā then went to the Gaṇeśa shrine at Theur. There he went into a meditative state for forty-two days, after which Gaṇeśa appeared to him and enabled him to experience the *turīyavastha,* the fourth or highest state of consciousness. Morayā then returned to Moragaon, but his reputation as a saint drew crowds to the shrine in such numbers that he was unable to meditate. Consequently, he moved to a small shrine near the village of Cincvad.

On the fourth day of each bright half of the lunar month [*caturthī*], Morayā Gosāvī went on a pilgrimage back to Moragaon, a three-day walk from Cincvad. After taking the *darśana* of the image of Gaṇeśa there and worshipping the deity, he then returned to Cincvad. On one occasion when he made his monthly pilgrimage to Moragaon, he arrived after dark to find the gate to the shrine locked, thus making it impossible for him to have the deity's *darśana.* Sitting under a sacred wishing tree [*kalpavṛkṣa*], he meditated on the form of the deity. Gaṇeśa responded to his meditations and came out of the shrine to give him his *darśana* on that spot. This story is frequently told among Gāṇapatyas to illustrate both the power of Morayā Gosāvī's spiritual life and the grace of the deity (Deva and Bhingarkar, pp. 4–5).

Another story illustrating the special bond between Morayā Gosāvī and Gaṇeśa tells of the time Morayā Gosāvī was worshipping at the *tīrtha* in the Kartha River near Moragaon. While pouring water into the river [*arghya*] as part of his ritual routine, Morayā Gosāvī reached into the river and picked up a stone in the shape of Gaṇeśa. He began to worship that image, and he brought it to Cincvad to worship it when he became too old and weak to make the arduous monthly journey to Moragaon and back. The image remains at Cincvad and is carried in procession to Moragaon twice a year to have the *darśana* of the image at Moragaon, after the practice of Morayā Gosāvī himself.

Morayā Gosāvī had a son named Cintāmaṇi (d. 1658) who succeeded his father as the incarnate form of Gaṇeśa at Cincvad and came to be known as the "Deva," a name that would serve as a surname for the later descendents to the present day.

In 1659 Morayā Gosāvī declared to his son, Cintāmaṇi, his intention to pass from the human world. One hagiography of the Cincvad temple recounts the story as follows:

> Then Morayā told Cintāmaṇi his decision to enter *samādhi*. Cintāmaṇi constructed a cave on the bank of the Pavana River at Cincvad. After performing the proper rituals in front of the devotees, he led his father to the cave, lighted the lamps and placed a copy of the *Gaṇeśa Purāṇa* in his lap there. Devotees sang songs of praise to Gaṇeśa; all were thrilled at the sight. Then Morayā Gosāvī sat in the lotus posture, meditated on Gaṇeśa, and then became Gaṇeśa himself [*Gaṇeśasvarūpa jhāle*]. While all chanted devotional songs, Cintāmaṇi and his two wives worshipped his father, and then placed a slab over the cave. (Deva and Bhingarkar, pp. 10–11)

The following year a temple was built over the cave. The center of religious focus at the Cincvad temple is shared by the *samādhi* of Morayā Gosāvī and the image of Gaṇeśa. The anniversary of Morayā Gosāvī's *samādhi* marks one of the major annual ritual events at the shrine.

Cintāmaṇi Deva, the son of Morayā Gosāvī, likewise obtained a reputation for disclosing Gaṇeśa's form through his own actions. Mahīpati (1715–90), in his hagiography of Tukārāma—the Maharashtrian poet-saint associated with the god Viṭṭhala and his shrine at Pandharpur—tells the story of Tukārāma, a low-caste devotee, and Cintāmaṇi Deva dining together at Cincvad:

> It was rumored that the lord Viṣṇu, in his image at Pandharpur, dined with Tukārāma, a *śūdra,* and so Cintāmaṇi Deva invited him to dine with him. Tukārāma challenged Cintāmaṇi to call Gaṇeśa to dine with them, insisting that if god does not manifest himself visibly to his devotees, then worship is in vain. Tukārāma composed two devotional songs [*abhaṅg*] to Gaṇeśa, and then the

deity appeared in [*saguṇa*] form in front of his plate and ate. Meditating again, Tukārāma brought Viṭhoba [Viṭṭhala] to that place also. Cintāmaṇi and the other Brahmins looked on with wonder at the forms of the two deities dining together before them. (Mahīpati, *Bhaktalīlāmṛta* 34.75–139 in Abbott, pp. 187–93; Sykes, pp. 67–70)

Cintāmaṇi Deva was succeeded by his son Nārāyaṇa (d. 1719). Nārāyaṇa's years as the reigning incarnate Gaṇeśa at Cincvad were a time of intense political turmoil that saw the demise of Moghul rule and the rise of the Maratha empire under Śivājī. At Cincvad the story is told that when one of Aurangzeb's military officers came to Cincvad to plunder the temple, Nārāyaṇa refused to let him enter the temple compound. The officer decided to send the temple a "gift" to be offered to the image of Gaṇeśa in the temple. When the tray bearing the gift was ceremoniously brought before the image and unveiled it turned out to be a piece of raw cow's flesh. However, when Nārāyaṇa Deva placed the offering before the image it miraculously turned into an offering of fresh flowers. So impressed were the Moghuls at this miracle that they gave the shrine a large grant of land (Moor 1801, pp. 381–82).

During Nārāyaṇa Deva's lifetime the temple at Cincvad grew into an important center for Gaṇeśa devotion in the region, equaling Moragaon in importance. Nārāyaṇa Deva became involved in Hindu resistance against the Moghuls during the waning years of their rule. In the *Rāja Vayahara Kośa*—a dictionary of administrative terms in Marathi, which Śivājī had prepared in order to change the terminology from Persian to Marathi—it is said that Śivājī received initiation [*anugraha*] from Nārāyaṇa Deva. By this time several of Nārāyaṇa Deva's brothers also served as temple priests in several of the *aṣṭavināyaka* shrines. Nārāyaṇa Deva was succeeded in turn by his son, Cintāmaṇi II, and his grandson, Dharanidar (d. 1772). Dharanidar Deva played a role in the political life of the Maratha empire and was influential in the management of a coinage mint that operated at Cincvad from the mid-eighteenth century until it was closed by the British East India Company after their conquest of the Peshwa empire in 1818. Dharanidar was succeeded in turn by his son, Nārāyaṇa II (d. 1802), and his grandson, Cintāmaṇi III, who was the seventh and last of the dynasty of incarnate Gaṇeśa at Cincvad. In 1800, Edward Moor, the British captain assigned to the Peshwa court in Pune, visited Cintāmaṇi III at Cincvad and skeptically noted his observations of this human incarnation:

> The actions of the Deo [Deva] . . . are also minutely watched; as his actions as well as words are but the transient manifestations of the Almighty will, totally unpremeditated, and unrecognized by the Deo, they are noted as prophetic. Should he remain the night through in peaceful repose, national repose is henceforth predicted; should his slumber or his waking moments be perturbed, similar mishaps threaten the public weal. If, as hath happened, he starts wildly from his seat or couch, seizes a sword or spear, or makes any movements indicating martial measures, a war, attended by circumstances deduced from the nature of such movements is foretold. Every circumstance of this kind is carefully noted by persons employed by the government; all is carefully considered, and reported accordingly, with appropriate inferences. (Moor 1801, p. 390)

Moor's observations about the divinatory character of this *āvatāra,* the living embodiment of Gaṇeśa at Cincvad, are instructive. The Cincvad center enjoyed the patronage of the Peshwa court at Pune. Twice each year the image of Gaṇeśa that Morayā Gosāvī had miraculously found in the Moragaon *tīrtha* and later brought to Cincvad was ceremoniously carried in pilgrimage to Moragaon and returned. When the procession of this pilgrimage passed through Pune, the Peshwa came out to receive its *darśana* personally and to feed the hosts of Brahmins who accompanied it. The city of Pune and its rulers were surrounded by Gaṇeśa shrines, for the *aṣṭavināyaka* complex may be viewed as a *maṇḍala* embracing and protecting the city and the empire that was centered there.

Although Gaṇeśa did not in the eighteenth and nineteenth centuries enjoy the same popular devotion that he does in contemporary Maharashtra, he benefited from the support of influential groups of people, principally the Brahmin castes of the Pune subregion—the Konkanastha or Citpavan Brahmins. Many of them worshipped Gaṇeśa as their family deity, their *kuladevatā.* G. S. Ghurye maintains that Gaṇeśa's rise to prominence parallels the emergence of Brahmin influence in the Pune region from the seventeenth to the twentieth centuries and that the Brahmins promoted the Gaṇeśa cult partly as a means to limit the influence of Jains in the region (p. 96). Geṇeśa received special attention from the Peshwa court. Several of the Peshwa rulers worshipped Gaṇeśa as their *iṣṭadevatā* (personal deity). Balaji Bajirao and Madhavrao I both visited the *aṣṭavināyaka* shrines at Moragaon and Theur on many occasions. They contributed substantially to the renovations of the temple properties. Madhavrao I moved the seat of government from Pune to Theur just prior to his death at Theur, and his wife committed *satī* there after his death (Preston, pp. 120–21). With the rise of the Brahmin Peshwa rulers in Pune in the eighteenth century, the *sampradāya* had not only a spiritual center at Moragaon and an administrative center at Cincvad but also the best friend at court one could hope for in Pune.

With the demise of the Peshwas in 1818, the Gāṇapatya tradition experienced a temporary eclipse that persisted during the remainder of the century. By 1894, however, Gaṇeśa would have a new champion in Lokamanya Tilak. Tilak saw the annual Bhādrapada festival as potentially a great national event in which the intellectual, religious, and political aspirations of Indians, under the leadership of the traditional Brahmin elites, would find new and potent expression under the banner of the overcomer of obstacles. Through Tilak's efforts at the end of the nineteenth century, Gaṇeśa's appeal was broadened to include more active participation by non-Brahmin castes. And Gaṇeśa's mythological character as the one who guarantees success in undertakings and removes obstacles that thwart them became identified with the nationalist aspirations for home rule in the early part of the twentieth century.

Gaṇeśa and the Lokamanya: Religious Symbols and Political Conflict

When the British defeated the Peshwa dynasty, they brought to a close a remarkable era in the history of Maharashtra. As Brahmins who espoused *kṣatriya* values and symbols, the Peshwa rulers had achieved a measure of integration of the political and religious worlds. They functioned as priests and kings in the minds and imaginations of Maharashtrians. The Citpavan Brahmin community, both the royal and priestly caste, had overseen the rise and fall of the Maratha empire. In displacing the Brahmin government of the Peshwa, the British "faced the task of assimilating, pacifying, or neutralizing the single community which had functioned both as the spiritual and temporal elite of the region most difficult for them to conquer" (Wolpert, p. 2). The new British administration under the leadership of Mountstuart Elphinstone recognized the power latent within Maharashtrian cultural and religious unity. He regarded it as a genuine threat to the effectiveness of British rule over this last and most resistent of conquests. Elphinstone wrote at the time:

> . . . one talisman that while it animated and united them all, could leave us without a single adherent. This barbarism is the name of religion, a power so obvious that it is astonishing our enemies have not more frequently and systematically employed it against us. (Quoted in Wolpert, p. 4)

Throughout the century that followed, the British remained deeply suspicious of the political fidelity of the Maharashtrian people and the loyalty of their traditional elite caste, the Citpavan Brahmins. Their main concern initially was to keeep things as calm as possible. They continued to pay the traditional *dakṣiṇā* (payment) the Peshwas had given the Brahmin pandits, to maintain grants of land and revenues to shrines and centers of traditional learning, and to discourage the spread of Christian missionary activity in the region. Historian Stanley Wolpert notes:

> The peasant majority would be pacified so long as they were assured a minimal return on their toil on the land, the nobility was a small enough class to be wooed or watched, paid off or punished, depending on the varieties of their individual temperaments, but the Brahmins were a persistent problem. As intellectuals their loyalty could really only be won and retained by capturing their minds. (p. 5)

Within a decade there began a fundamental change in the outlook of British rule regarding its cultural role in India. Thomas Babington Macaulay represented the new British civilizing mission: to transform India into a new and enlightened culture by bringing to it the fruits of Western science and wisdom. In Maharashtra British support shifted from the centers of traditional learning to those emphasizing Western ideas, methods, and values. In 1824 the Bombay Educational Society established an

English-language school, followed three years later by the founding of Elphinstone College. In Pune by 1840 the English language and Western learning had become available to selected students from the Sanskrit College. The old Brahmin elite provided the early recruits for the process of "Westernization," a process that deeply divided them. In sponsoring and financing these educational opportunities, the British attempted to win the loyalty of this displaced group and thereby preclude any serious challenges to its hegemony in the region. A consequence of these developments was that some members of the Citpavan elite became committed to social revolution and reform based on Western notions of individuality and society, whereas others became equally devoted to the necessity of protecting orthodox religion from further erosion by external forces. Both groups agreed their status under the British Raj had diminished, but they differed fundamentally on how to recover it and what role the British could or should play in that process.

A number of influential Brahmin families produced sons who enthusiastically endorsed British rule and pursued efforts at social reform according to Western models. Dadoba Pandurang (1814–52) advocated the abolition of caste and defended widow remarriage; Bal Gangadhar Jambhekar (1810–46) published the reform journal *Digdarśan.* Sardar Gopal Hari "Lokahitavadi" Deshmukh, from a former noble family under the Peshwas, argued that British rule had been sent by God to awaken Hindus from their terrible sleep, a sleep that had tolerated widow immolation, female infanticide, and other social abuses. His voice was echoed by Jyotiba Phule (1827–90) from the gardener [*Māḷi*] caste. For Phule the British had conquered India to lift the intolerable weight of Brahminic tyranny from the shoulders of the oppressed *śūdras.* Their loyalty to Britain did not go unrewarded. The reform efforts of these pioneers helped to create a new class of Westernized Hindus who enjoyed the appreciation of their rulers and received the angry condemnation of many of their orthodox fellow caste members.

Within less than a generation the voice of reaction against Western influence began to be heard. Vishnu Bhikaji Gokhale, known also as Vishnu Guva Brahmacari (1825–71), called for the return to Vedic religion, and Vishnushastri Chiplunkar (1850–82) wrote vigorous denunciations of missionary evangelism in his monthly Marathi journal *Nibhanda Mālā*. Beyond the battle of words, some defenders of the old order took more violent action. Insurrections against British rule in Maharashtra broke out in 1844, 1857, and 1876. In 1879 a Citpavan Brahmin named Vasudeo Balwant Phadke (1845–83) led a revolt from the hills in the name of Śivājī. By the mid-1870s not even the most daring of political extremists attempted revolt by force of arms against the British in the Marathi-speaking region. More effective means of asserting the traditionalist cause were used by Vishnu Chiplunkar, the son of Vishnushastri. After becoming a teacher in the Poona High School, he wrote a series of essays critical of British rule. For his efforts he received a transfer to an obscure village school in the coastal region of Konkan. He resigned this position and returned to Pune to start, together with Bal Gangadhar Tilak and other associates, the New English School as an educational institution run by and for Indians. It opened its doors to students on January 1, 1880. Within five years it enrolled over one thousand students and quickly achieved the highest rates of students passing the Bombay University examinations; all this without any financial aid from the British government in Bombay Presidency. Chiplankar and Tilak shared the view that Indians were slaves in their own country: slaves to foreign rulers and slaves to ignorance and superstition. Much of India's traditions—so quickly ridiculed by British scholars, missionaries, and Indian admirers of Western culture—contained within them much that was noble and worth preserving and building on for a uniquely Indian future. The question was which parts of the tradition were viable and how could they be reappropriated in the light of the current circumstances.

By the 1870s two identifiable groups emerged within the elite of Pune and Bombay (an elite made up in Pune predominantly of Citpavan Brahmins): the reformers, led by M. G. Ranade (1842–1901) and Gopal Krishna Gokhale (1866–1915); and the neo-traditionalists, led by Tilak (1856–1920). The reformers had the greater measure of support from the British administration. In pressing for fundamental changes in Indian social structure and thereby bringing it more into line with the values of Western culture, the reformers created a community that appeared to be more open and free than that of traditional Brahmanical culture. They saw themselves as the vanguard of a new and inevitable era of progress into the modern world, an era that would see an evolved relationship of equality with Britain.

The neo-traditionalists, on the other hand, held a different vision of what the direction India's future should take. The term "neo-traditionalist" is used by Robert Bellah to describe those persons and movements in Asian societies that "use modern ideas and methods to defend traditional cultural values, which are held to be superior to those of any other tradition" (p. 201). Tilak and his compatriots looked to India's past as the paradigm for its future directions. To them the British represented alien domination, and they saw efforts at reform advocated by the British and their Indian allies to be purely and simply a matter of cultural and political control. For this group the political imperative was to rid India of foreign rule and restore the essential character of its past. To displace this powerful alien rule, a rule whose power was so dazzling as to lead away the brightest and most able among the Brahmin elite, a revitalization of India's masses would be necessary. These masses of Indians would have to be taught the meaning and value of their ancient heritage. Formal institutions, such as schools and universities, could only hope to reach a tiny fraction of the populace; new, more fluid and less expensive institutions would have to emerge as the vehicles for educational and cultural revitalization. The challenge before the neo-traditionalists was to create a mass political movement, one that enabled Indians to feel solidarity with one another, one that would embrace the past and look to those classes of leaders that had created, in large measure, the greatness of that past—the Brahmins. The neo-traditionalists did not have access to the mechanisms of law and policy-making to change society as the reformers did; they had to rely on the more ambiguous areas of religion and popular sentiment to create a counterforce powerful and disciplined enough to prevail against the British and their Indian admirers.

Bal Gangadhar Tilak came from an orthodox Citpavan Brahmin family in the coastal Konkan region. He was the son of a schoolteacher and small landowner. Married at the age of fifteen and orphaned a year later, the young Tilak took his inheritance and, like many others from his subcaste during this time, moved to Pune. In 1872 he enroled as a student in Deccan College.

Tilak displayed remarkable talent for mathematics, astronomy,

Vedic studies, and law. The years of famine and political upheaval in Maharashtra from 1875–79 saw Tilak unemployed and searching for his own directions. In 1880 he joined with Chiplunkar in founding the New English School. A year later he launched two newspapers: the English-language *Mahratta* and the Marathi-language *Kesarī*. His papers relfected his strongly nationalist convictions. The tone and style of *Mahratta* was more subdued than that of *Kesarī*. The latter appealed to the anxieties, frustrations, and hopes of a mass audience and established Tilak as the most powerful and persuasive Marathi journalist of his time. His rhetorical skills from time to time got him into trouble. In 1882 he served four months in prison for libel against M. V. Barve, the divan of Kolhapur. Tilak had written that Barve conspired with the British to have the prince of Kolhapur judged insane. Tilak's imprisonment earned him no small measure of sympathy from the Maharashtrian populace. He had a volatile and awesome personality; it evoked passionate responses from admirers and critics alike. From his vantage point as a journalist and political leader, Tilak pursued his efforts to revitalize the social, religious, and political world of Maharashtra.

The burning issues for Tilak were not those of the status of widows, the disabilities of caste, unsanitary health conditions, inadequate public services, or religious superstition, all issues to which the reformers devoted so much attention. For him there was only one issue: foreign rule. The traditional social structure had its abuses in Tilak's judgment, but it represented the wisdom of thousands of years of experience and reflection. It was a manifestation of divine presence brought into being through the workings of *karma* and sustained according to the teachings and duties of *dharma*. The reformers, Tilak argued, had been seduced by British fraud and force into abandoning their worthy heritage of language, religion, and society in exchange for, at best, a second-class citizenship in a racist empire. As Stanley Wolpert observes, Tilak "refused to concede that India's body politic needed the plastic surgery of Western institutions grafted upon it" (Wolpert, p. 304). Tilak's constant criticism of British policy on a variety of issues made him a prime target. Although he always denied that he engaged in seditious activities, he spent a number of years in prison for them. To the British, Tilak represented everything about the Poona Brahmins they most feared and hated.

In the 1870s the Poona Sarvajanik Sabha (Poona Public Society) became one of the most vigorous political groups in India. It was the place where Western-educated Indians met to press for wider levels of participation in the British administration and greater influence in formulating policy. The benefits of expansions of British rule in this direction would fall primarily on them as the educated class. Although Phadke's revolt in 1879 was short-lived and politically ineffective, it spoke of the continuing Brāhmaṇical hostility toward British rule. William Temple, the Governor of Bombay at the time, saw little difference between the reformers and the neo-traditionalists. From his perspective it was the Citpavan community that was pressing its advantages on all fronts, from open rebellion to reformist social change. Even though the Citpavans had gained entry into the British administration in proportions far exceeding their actual population in Pune, Temple thought "they will never be satisfied until they regain their ascendancy in the country as they had it during the last century" (quoted in Cashman, p. 30).

In 1900 M. G. Ranade's widely read and influential book, *The Rise of Maratha Power,* was published. It presented a reading of Maharashtrian history that supported the neo-traditionalists' case that foreign rule was a dangerous folly for India. Ranade's vision of the past was one in which there was a solidarity of language, polity, and religion—at least among Hindus—guided by the benevolent hand of the Citpavan community and its Peshwa leaders.

Tilak also looked to the past for guidance in imagining the future. He turned to mathematics and astronomy to show that, on the basis of astronomical calculations and inferences, the Vedas must be far older than any Western scholars had thought. They antedated any texts written in the West by a wide margin. He also wrote an exhaustive commentary on the *Bhagavad Gītā* in which he argued that its central teaching was that of *karmayoga*—a vigorous and selfless effort in the protection of tradition rather than in an escape into personal devotionalism and renunciation (see Brown).

Tilak vigorously opposed any attempts at social change through law and public policy. In his editorials he led the fight against raising the minimal marriage age for women from ten to twelve. He did not defend the specific practice of child marriage as such but attacked the legitimacy of the British to legislate the social practice of various castes.

The year 1893 was one of frequent conflict between the Hindu and Muslim communities. In Bombay a movement made up primarily of Brahmins called the Gaupalan Upadeshak Mandali (Society for the Propagation of Cow Protection) conducted a series of public demonstrations to bring the issue of cow protection to the attention of the masses. For centuries the cow has been the quintessential symbol of feminine and maternal nurture. Cows are honored frequently at religious festivals. The British were the primary consumers of beef, and the butchers came from the Muslim community. For neo-traditionalists the cow became the symbol for "Mother" India; to protect the cow was to protect one's vision of what India meant.

In August of that year, a riot broke out among mill workers in Bombay. The proportions and ferocity of the episode surprised everyone. The moderate leadership attributed it to the isolated expressions of lower class passions. The British blamed the cow-protection advocates for stirring up latent hatred between Hindus and Muslims. Further communal violence erupted over the next year in several towns in Maharashtra, leaving a total of over twenty dead. Hindu reformers were deeply wounded by the British hostility to them over this issue, and they became increasingly apprehensive about the conduct of British administration and policy. This shift of opinion among the new elite of Westernized Indians was reflected in the polarization within in the infant Indian National Congress between those who wanted to work within the framework of British rule and those who argued for challenging it more vigorously. Lord Harris, Governor of Bombay at the time, had little sympathy for the Westernized elite, and Brahmin alienation from the British reached its highest level to date under his administration.

The levels of energy released so destructively during the riots over cow protection did not go unnoticed by Tilak. For some time he had been searching for a way to bridge the gap between the Brahmins and the non-Brahmins and find an appropriate context in which to build a new grassroots unity between them. Tilak believed that such a display of unity should be dramatic and take place under the guidance of the Brahmins as the tradtional and natural leaders of society.

At an open meeting on 10 September 1893, a few days after the Bombay riots, Tilak urged Hindus to withdraw their participation from the Muslim festival of Moharram, which was to be held that year in mid-September. The Moharram festival honors the martyrdom of Mohammed's grandson, Ali. It includes a procession accompanied by music and dancing in which devotees carry placards [*tābūts*] bearing images of the martyr's tomb through the streets. Traditionally many of the musicians and celebrants were Hindus. Tilak appreciated the social and religious power of the festival. He seized on the idea of holding a similar public festival in honor of Gaṇeśa that would serve as a religious rallying point for a revitalized Hindu community.

Since the fall of the Peshwa dynasty in 1818, the annual festival to Gaṇeśa had not enjoyed official recognition in Maharashtra although it continued to be observed with much éclat in Benares (Rousselet, pp. 538–39). It had, however, continued as a family tradition and neighborhood festival, particularly among Brahmins in Pune. The British *Gazeteer,* published in 1885, describes the festival as it was traditionally observed in Pune before Tilak's innovations:

> Sometime before Gaṇapati's birthday [*Gaṇeśa Caturthi*] the reception hall is whitewashed and painted, a wooden framework or other seat is made ready, and the room is filled with rich furniture and at night is brightly lit. On the morning of the feast day the head of the house and some children and servants, with music and a palanquin, go to the market to buy an image of the god, seat it on the palanquin and bring it home. . . . It is set in the shrine and with the help of the family priest verses are recited that fill the image with the presence of god. . . . At the end of the service sweetmeats are handed around among the guests and family. . . . According to the will and means of the family the image is kept in the house from one and a half to twenty-one days, in most cases about a week. So long as it is in the house the god is worshipped night and morning. When the time comes for the god to go, in the evening prayers and a palanquin are hired, and a priest is called in. After praying Gaṇapati to bless the family, to keep sorrow from its doors, and to give wisdom to its children, verses like those that brought the presence of the god into the image are said and its divinity withdrawn. Then waving a lamp around its face, laying a little curds in one of its hands, and seating it on a flower-decked palanquin, calling out the god's name as they go, they carry him to

> the side of the lake or river. At the water's edge they take the image out of the palanquin and seat it on the ground, and waving a lighted lamp around its face carry it to the water sorrowing that for another year they will not see the god again. (*Gazeteer of the Bombay Presidency,* vol. 18/3, pp. 246–47.)

In 1894 Tilak and his associates transformed the Gaṇeśa festival by adding a public dimension that lasted several days between the time the images were installed in the homes and when they were taken for immersion. Singing groups [*meḷās*] composed songs of political protest and social concerns to accompany the traditional devotional songs to Gaṇeśa that were sung in homes and temples. *Meḷās* were composed mainly by students who adopted similar dress and formed themselves into cadres. During the festivals they sponsored song sessions, dramas, political speeches, and lectures. Tilak and his followers spoke to many of the *meḷās* in Pune during the first year; later festivals took them to surrounding towns and villages to promote the festival and its message. On the day of the immersion of Gaṇeśa images, the *meḷā* groups, along with other more traditional gatherings of devotees, formed a common procession to the river. At the head of the festival, there was the image belonging to Kasba Peth Gaṇeśa temple in Pune (Gaṇeśa is the *grāmadevatā* of Pune, its guardian deity). The festival procession consisted of nearly a hundred *meḷā* groups, seventy-five bands of musicians, and about twenty-five thousand spectators and celebrants who flocked to the event. Non-Brahmin *meḷās* outnumbered Brahmin ones by two to one during that first year (Cashman, p. 80). The festival clearly drew support from a cross-section of Hindu society in the urban environs of Pune.

For Tilak this revitalized religious festival was a means through which the masses could be reached with his message of both renewed confidence in the traditions of the people and greater suspicion of and resitance to change imposed from the outside. The festival as a social, political, and religious structure seemed to offer the potential for creating a new sense of unity among Hindus. It was an occasion when rustic villagers and urban sophisticates could meet in a common context and affirm their solidarity as Hindus. Tilak also organized a festival in honor of Śivājī. It was an occasion for Maharashtrians to express their pride in their martial traditions. Like the Gaṇeśa festival, the

Śivājī festival was an instant success as a political and symbolic event. Tilak's enthusiasm for this potential of festivals came out clearly in an editorial he wrote in his Marathi newspaper, *Kesarī* on 8 September 1896.

> These festivals have two main roles. The first is mass recreation and the second is mass education. That nation which cannot spend eight or ten days in order to satisfy its spiritual desires, which cannot sing devotional songs to its deities and cannot become engrossed in listening to them, which cannot forget its life of slavery for a moment, and which cannot see or hear things which induce a spirit of competition and enthusiasm, that nation is ruined. Consequently, in order to be able to show that our lives are different from those of prisoners, that we are not as base as slaves, our inborn love for festivals should be encouraged to swell and overflow. (Quoted in Kelkar, p. 567)

In another editorial Tilak argued that festivals had been major events in the heroic Indian past, occasions when teachers and students and the learned and the illiterate gathered together for the purpose of common uplift and solidarity (Ibid., pp. 561–65). Tilak never believed, unlike his reformist and British opponents, that the religious and political realms of life could be separated into some kind of sacred and secular domains; he argued that political concerns among others were a legitimate part of festivals. He wrote:

> Why shouldn't the fairs organized in conjunction with festivals be used for political purposes? Just as men put up stalls all over the fair for games, the educated should put up a few tents and hold discussions on various subjects. This would not be as physically or financially demanding as holding national assemblies. Wouldn't this be an easier method for enlightening our bretheren in the villages about moral and religious matters? . . . On such occasions why shouldn't the educated people give the masses a clear picture of their real state? Why shouldn't those who call themselves educated remind the people of the atrocities committed by the government? Or, why shouldn't they awaken the religious sense in the people and as a result strengthen their national pride? Our ancestors have given us a place where people could gather, but the educated live as though it did not exist. That is because their education has filled them with false pride and they are reluctant to mix with the people. (Ibid., pp. 566–68)

What was it about Gaṇeśa as a deity and symbol that made him so appealing to Tilak and others as a vehicle for this new fusion of religious and political spirit? Gaṇeśa was a deity of the "great tradition" of pan Indian Hinduism who had regional and local status in Maharashtra and Pune. He was worshipped by many castes as the protector of beginnings and the remover of obstacles. Formerly he had been associated with the Peshwa dynasty as the deity of its lineage [*kuladevatā*], as was also the case with many prominent Citpavan Brahmin families in Pune. Hence Gaṇeśa could mediate the non-Brahmin masses who loved Gaṇeśa with the Brahmin elite who stood to gain the most in the revitalization of a revisionist traditionalism that emphasized the unity of Hindus and the intellectual and political leadership of the Brahmins. As the remover of obstacles, Gaṇeśa symbolized the Hindu resistance to the obstacle of British rule. His iconography combined the associations of virile warrior and enjoyer of the good life—a combination that resonated particularly well with Maharashtra's cultural traditions. Gaṇeśa's emergence into this new role gained him almost instant popularity and brought increasingly larger audiences to hear the political views expounded by Tilak and his associates during the annual Gaṇeśa festival. Within the framework of the traditional institutions of the festival and fair, institutions revitalized by a new awareness of their possibilities and occasions for political consciousness raising, the Brahmin elite had a new opportunity to educate and politicize non-Brahmins and involve them in the politics of dissent (see Cashman, p. 59).

In 1897 the number of public groups participating in the festival nearly doubled, spreading spontaneously from Pune to Bombay, Ahmadnagar, and a number of other cities in the region, helped in part by the publicity Tilak gave the festival in his newspapers. Within a decade over seventy towns outside Pune sponsored public Gaṇeśa celebrations along the lines advocated by Tilak. In the smaller towns the festival maintained a more traditional religious character, but after 1900 many of Tilak's political allies in the neo-traditionalist movement visited other cities and towns and gave lectures on topics of political and social interest. Tilak spoke to many such groups, admonishing them to recapture the strength and virtue known under the Peshwas and in ancient times. He stressed that education along British lines left students ignorant of their country's history and incapable of appreciating the strength of their own culture. Reform of society, he stressed, should come from within, out of the traditions and inclinations of the people, rather than borrowed from a foreign culture that held India in contempt (Karandikar, p. 564). Vishvanath Kashinath Rajwade, a noted historian, lectured in 1905 that the festival is a mode of traditional Hindu education, combining celebration with edification and that it brings together the pandit and the peasant in a common bond of worship and community. Hindu rulers in the ancient past understood this and made good use of the virtues of such events. Only with the advent of foreign rule had this tradition of festivals fallen into disuse (Ibid., p. 577). Lectures given during the early years of the festival included such topics as: "*Ahiṃsā* and Victory," "The Place of Hinduism in Politics," "Who Runs Maharashtra?", "Prohibition," and "Brahmins and Non-Brahmins" (Ibid., p. 595).

Gaṇeśa provided the neo-traditional elite with a symbol around which they could rally to express their concerns about the disrupting change brought about by British rule, a change they saw as undermining the integrity and position of the Hindu tradition and thereby giving advantage to the Muslim community. One of the songs sung by a voluntary association [*meḷā*] for the festival gave voice to these fears and frustrations (quoted in Cashman, p. 78):

Oh! Why have you abandoned today the Hindu religion?
How have you forgotten Gaṇapati, Śiva and Maruti?
What have you gained from worshipping tābūts?
What boon has Allah conferred upon you
That you have become Mussalmans today?
Do not be friendly to a religion that is alien,
Do not give up your religion and be fallen,
Do not at all venerate the tābūts.
The cow is our mother, do not forget her.

The songs of the *meḷā* singers offer insights into the merger of religious devotion and political protest during these turbulent years of the festival's initial revitalization. The majority of songs in the festival were traditionally religious, extoling the greatness of Gaṇeśa. Some of them celebrated his mythology (quoted in Agarkar, p. 143).

Underneath the mountain forest spread did Pārvatī come to bathe.
Away she wiped the scurf [mala] *from her limbs, and lo! Gaṇa(pati) was born from it.*
To worship Śiva he went forth, sitting on his mouse carrier-horse.
And with a whip he hit his carrier-horse, and down from it came Gaṇa(pati).
The moon laughed at his plight and this Gaṇa(pati)'s anger rose.
And he gave the moon a curse: "Anyone who sees you on caturthī *night shall be falsely accused of theft.*

Other songs brought the symbolism of Gaṇeśa into the political arena. Set to the tunes of traditional devotional songs [*bhajana*], many of these songs explicitly linked mythological categories with contemporary political circumstances. A few songs from the period of the festivals are most aggressively of a political character; collected by J. S. Karandikar, an associate of Tilak, they convey the tone and imagery of the songs:

> The noose of political dependence is strangling, us. Why, Gaṇeśa, aren't you merciful? Like Karpūrāsura [the demon who is the color of white mineral], the white people harass the land. Bhāratā [India, feminine gender] is cursed by the demon and is in pain. O giver of wealth and happiness, deliver us a counter-curse and bring us peace. (Karandikar, p. 442)

A second song draws more explicitly upon the ritual of the festival itself for its political metaphors:

> O Gaurī, son of Śiva and Gaurī, Gaṇeśa, bring an end to obstacles. Take away this illusion, for we are oppressed by the *kali yuga* [i.e., British rule]. We come to you to carry you [in procession] because our motherland calls to you. Do not abandon us, but ward off this peril. Give us the *modaka* of self-rule [*svarāja*] as your *prasāda.* Make us fearless, O Giver of Safety, this is my plea laid at your feet. (Ibid., p. 446)

Other songs stress the necessity of unity among the Indian population in the face of foreign rule. One song likens the conflict between reformers and neo-traditionalists within the Hindu community (or perhaps the conflict between Hindus and Muslims) to a quarrel within an extended family (Ibid., p. 523):

Until recently they lived as loving brothers, twins like
Rāma and Lakṣmaṇa.
How did this knife of division pierce their chests?
In the house they once lived as a happy family, but evil
fate hated their auspiciousness. Now the waters
in the stream have dried up.
Like a madman who has different views within himself, they
have become confused.
The tradition of the family was great and sumptuous, but
now all have been reduced to dust, and the minds of the
sons have become corrupted.
Fighting among themselves, they have burnt their glorious
past to ashes.
Those who were kings have become paupers, and the enmity
has reached to their bones.
O Ocean of Mercy, Supreme God, my prayer is that you pardon
them and put them on the right path.
O Gaṇanātha, give us rebirth to brotherly love.
Giver of Auspiciousness, I pray to you in all these
different ways.

One of the Pune *meḷās* that was drawn from the scheduled castes community sang a song in the festival that addressed the issue of social cquality as the form of a new unity among Hindus that would bring about the future fulfilment of the Hindu destiny (Ibid., p. 516):

Let us go to the court of Gaṇeśa. Let us weave our silk
*scarf [*goph*]**
of the different brothers among Hindus.
There is no distinction between the small and the great;
no room for distinction here.
Gentlemen and rogues have become one here.
Let us lose ourselves in this celebration. Come out, you
who lag behind, you who were untouchable in the past,
come all!
This Paṇḍari [town of Pandharpur] is beyond duality,
this city of Gaṇeśa.
This is the word of Śrīpād [the author], now let's prove
it to be true.

*also referring to a scarf dance performed during the festival procession in which dancers weave a series of scarves together, similar to a maypole dance.

This song makes explicit use of the spirit of unity that becomes possible during the liminal time of the festival procession when all boundaries of social and ritual hierarchy become blurred, and it offers this moment as the paradigm for a new kind of Hindu society. As the scarves are woven together around a single pole, so should society be woven in such a way that there is no distinction or duality of importance between the great and the small. Such a society would indeed be the "city of Gaṇeśa."

In addition to the *meḷā* songs, a number of dramatic performances, staged by individual *meḷās* (professional acting companies), became a highlight of the revitalized festival. One of the most popular plays performed during the period at the turn of the century when the festival was at its peak of political vitality was one by Krishnaji Prabhakar Khadilkar (1873–1948), a first generation Citpavan Brahmin resident of Pune and the editor of Tilak's Marathi newspaper, *Kesarī*. Khadilkar was among the more radical of Tilak's associates. After his mentor's death in 1920, he became a Gandhian and then retired from political life in 1930 and continued to have a distinguished career as a Marathi playwright.

Khadilkar's play *Kīcaka Vadh* (*The Murder of Kīcaka*) is based on the story in the *Mahābhārata* of Kīcaka's attempt to seduce Draupadī (MBh 4.13–23). As the play develops the story: after the Pāṇḍavas were exiled for twelve years because Duryodhana cheated Yudhiṣṭhira out of his kingdom, they came in disguise to the kingdom of Virāṭa. Draupadī, their wife, took the disguise of a chambermaid. Virāṭa's brother-in-law and commander of his army, whose name was Kīcaka, returned from a visit to Hastināpura, the former kingdom of the Pāṇḍavas. When he saw the disguised Draupadī, he became captivated by her beauty and demanded that Virāṭa give her to him for his harem. Eventually Bhīma slew Kīcaka when he attempted to seduce Draupadī and thus freed her. With their general defeated, Virāṭa's army retreated from the Pāṇḍavas' superior courage and virtue.

The play focuses on the events of Draupadī's abduction and rescue. Virāṭa is reluctant to give Draupadī to Kīcaka, but he fears the power of his commander-in-chief. He seizes on a compromise plan and sends her to a temple where she will be out of Kīcaka's control but not entirely safe from his lust for her. Yudhiṣṭhira and Bhīma argue over what course of action would be best to follow in setting Draupadī free. Yudhiṣṭhira counsels caution, hoping that some twist of fate will dissuade Kīcaka from his designs on Draupadī. Bhīma insists that Kīcaka must be slain for the honor of Draupadī and the Pāṇḍavas, no matter what the risk. Bhīma then takes the disguise of Bhairava, Śiva in his fierce form, and lies in wait for Kīcaka to come to the temple in search of Draupadī. When Kīcaka arrives and attempts to seduce Draupadī, Bhīma jumps down from the divine throne and slays Kīcaka, strangling him to death.

The allegorical meanings of the play were not lost on the audience or on some British observers. Kīcaka, the lustful and avaricious commander-in-chief resembled Lord Curzon, whereas Virāṭa, the weak monarch, was the ineffective home government that gave Lord Curzon a free hand. Draupadī was India. Yudhiṣṭhira resembled the moderate faction of the Brahmin elite, such as Ranade and Gokhale, whereas Bhīma stood for the neo-traditionalists, such as Tilak and his followers. The setting for the seduction and rescue shifts from the dance hall, as it appears in the *Mahābhārata* story, to the shrine. Bhīma incarnates himself, as it were, in the form of Śiva the mad warrior, and he comes to life at the moment of Draupadī's most intense distress. The slaying of Kīcaka, a deed with sacrificial overtones, brought cheers from the audience. Once Kīcaka was slain and his army dispersed, the exiled family is united again, which leads to a happy ending at the final curtain. The play's theme drew upon the classical mythological tradition and set it, allegorically, in a circumstance that the audience could well understand resembled their own. The play was first performed in 1907, and it was later banned. Khadilkar was convicted of the crime of sedition for it.

One of Tilak's harshest British critics, Valentine Chirol, reflected on what he took to be the omnious meaning of the play for the future of Indian-English relations:

> It may be said that all this [i.e., the play] is mere fooling. But no Englishman who has seen the play acted would agree. All his life he will remember the tense, scowling faces of the men as they watch Kichaka's outrageous acts, the glistening eyes of the Brahmin ladies as they listen to Draupadi's entreaties, their scorn of Yudhisthira's tameness, their admiration of Bhima's passionate protests, and the deep hum of satisfaction which approves the slaughter of the tyrant. (Chirol, p. 339)

The initial response of British authorities to the festival was one of noninterference, a response that was in keeping with their general policy of reluctance in restraining their subjects' practice of religion. Some Englishmen were not convinced that the festival was merely a religious event and therefore saw a more ominous dimension to it. To them, it represented one more example of the Pune Brahmins' attempts to regain their former positions of prestige by manipulating mass superstition and discontent. Chirol grudgingly admired Tilak's rhetorical and organizational skills of infusing the festival with its new significance and vitality:

> Tilak could not have devised a more popular move than when he set himself to organize annual festivals in honor of Ganesh, known as Ganpati celebrations, and to found in all the chief centers of the Deccan Ganpati societies, each with its *mela* or choir recruited among his youthful bands of gymnists. These festivals gave occasion for theatrical performances and religious songs in which the legends of Hindu mythology were skillfully exploited to stir up hatred of the "foreigner"—and *mlenccha* the term employed for "foreigner," applied equally to Europeans and to Mahomedans—as well as for tumultuous processions only too well calculated to provoke affrays with the Mahomedans and with the police, which in turn led to judicial proceedings that served as fresh excuses for noisy protests and inflammatory pleadings. With the Ganpati celebrations the area of Tilak's propaganda was widely increased. (Ibid., p. 44)

From the first year of its performance in 1894, the revitalized Gaṇeśa festival would be plagued to a greater or lesser degree by communal violence or the specter of it. In Pune, during the first year of the new festival, while the procession moved through a street past a mosque, a group of Muslims, angered by the clamor of the celebrants in the streets, rushed out of the mosque and a scuffle ensued that left one Muslim dead. The Pune police authorities placed restrictions on music and made modifications in the procession route in succeeding years. Tilak angrily protested the police response as an infringement on Hindus' free exercise of religion. Muslims found many of the *meḷā* songs offensive. In 1895 they boycotted the Pune municipal elections in protest over what they took to be inflammatory and provocative attacks on them at the time of the festival. The festival's strong emphasis on Hindu unity, the denunciation of *mlecchas* (foreigners)—a term that included Muslims—and the criticism expressed during the festival that the British government had instituted policies that gave preferential treatment to Muslims, could not help but arouse anxiety on the part of the Muslim community. To them, the unity called for in the songs and praise to Gaṇeśa as the lord of the people was an exclusive one.

The years from 1897 to 1900 were difficult ones for Pune and Maharashtra. Slight harvests followed by outbreaks of bubonic plague caused the festival to shrink in the number and enthusiasm of its participants. From 1900 to 1905 there returned a tendency toward greater politicalization of the themes and songs in the festival. By 1910 it had taken on such a militant tone that it was virtually surpressed by the police. Strict rules of censorship were invoked on the content of the *meḷā* songs and rosters of members of *meḷās* had to be submitted to the police in advance. Restraints on music and programs kept a tight lid on the festival for several years. A few of the *meḷās* evolved into more permanent institutions holding to extreme neo-traditionalist views, such as the Abhinav Bharat (Young India Society) in Nasik and the Chhatrapati Mela, a group of non-Brahmin radicals that pressed for greater awareness of their particular political interest. (Cashman, pp. 91–92; Omvedt).

After the institution of the reforms in 1910, which brought about increased representation for Indians in the British administration and expanded opportunities for Indians within the Raj, the festival lost some of its political edge and audience. By 1919 it was possible for the government to remove its censorship of songs and behavior during the festival altogether. During the next decade Gandhi would capture the Indian imagination and create a mass movement of his own on a national scale that gave opportunity for direct participation by great numbers of Hindus of various castes. Like the festival, Gandhi's noncooperation protests offered direct participation in events that closely resembled rituals; yet, their religious associations were more vague and nonexclusive, focusing on Gandhi the Mahatma than on a particular deity. Like Tilak, Gandhi saw the religious and political realms to be indistinguishable in principle; and both valued above all other concerns the necessity for self-rule as a political and religious necessity for India. But Gandhi, the Mahatma, took the mantle of religious associations onto himself and turned political struggle into a context for religious realization rather than making religious events into political ones.

When Tilak died in 1920, the charismatic center he had provided the neo-traditionalists was gone, and the Gaṇeśa festival as an occasion for political awakening would never again have as strong an edge as it did between 1894–96 and 1905–10. Even on a reduced scale, however, as we have seen in the previous chapter in our consideration of its contemporary forms, the festival continues to include political and social dimensions as important parts of its public celebration.

At a time when there were no other institutions of mass appeal and participation available to Indians, particularly Hindus, the Gaṇeśa festival served as a bold and relatively effective vehicle for religious and political unity. The festival succeeded in displaying the relevance of religious symbols for political life, it raised the status and perspectives of Tilak and the neo-traditionalists, and it demonstrated the potential of religious events for mass-movement politics. These were lessons not lost on Gandhi and the Congress during the decades that followed. Beyond this level of diffuse religious symbolism, the festival resisted attempts at institutionalization. The songs of the *meḷā* singers did not move the British to alter substantially the direction of their rule, nor did it persuade the non-Brahmins that their political and cultural welfare was best served by the Brahmins' nostalgia for the past reconceived as a heroic utopia.

There is something appropriate about the outcome of the political phase of the Gaṇeśa festival, given what we have seen to be its patron deity's character. Gaṇeśa did remove some obstacles to political awakening by showing Hindus the possibility of combining commitments to greater political autonomy with loyalty to the past and its religious roots. However, Gaṇeśa is much too clever to allow himself to be so easily captured by a single group or ideology. The non-Brahmins did not flock to the banners of Tilak's elite, but they did take up a new interest in Gaṇeśa as a religious figure and symbol appropriate to their own changing situation. This process continues into the present day, particularly in small towns and larger villages. Other festivals, particularly the Durgā Pūjā in Calcutta, Kātaragāma in Sri Lanka, and the Aiyappan festival of Kerala have demonstrated similar tendencies (Sarma). The festival to Gaṇeśa contributed to restoring Hindus' pride in their own religious traditions, a pride that had been under attack from the combined forces of the British government, Christian missionaries, and the new class of Hindu reformers. It told them that their religion had the capacity for self-renewal and could provide a basis for progressive change from within.

With the coming of political independence in 1948, the festival again became a vehicle for limited social and political expression. After the trauma of years of political struggle and communal violence and separation, many Hindus saw the festival as an opportunity to raise the awareness of the nation as a whole and enhance solidarity among various communities. A pamphlet detailing instructions for observing the festival published a year after independence shows this sentiment. After relating a few Gaṇeśa myths, giving instructions for *pūjā,* and collecting popular devotional songs, the author exhorts his readers to comprehend the relationship between the worship of Gaṇeśa and the realization of India's new national purpose:

> The public Gaṇapati means the national [*rāṣṭrīya*] Gaṇapati. To undertake this festival everywhere in the country and carry it out successfully is to bring progress to the nation. . . . In order for our country's progress to move forward, all people must come together in the worship of this Lord of the People [*Saṅghādipati*]. . . . The name Gaṇeśa means God of Assemblies. Therefore everyone should participate in his worship. But before undertaking it, everyone must remove any misunderstanding about one another they may have formed earlier, and must work toward achieving unity. In this way the Lord of the People will be pleased with us and fulfill all our desires. (Marathe, p. 10)

In a prayer at the beginning of the pamphlet, the editor echoes this statement: "Friends, awaken! Let us pray to this auspicious deity to take our nation of India to the pinnacle [*śikhara*] of splendor [*vaibhāva*]."

From the 1950s until the present time, the festival has continued to spread its presence beyond the urban areas of Maharashtra into its villages, frequently taking root in the village school and spreading into the village as a whole. It has adapted itself to changing cultural and political circumstances (see Barnouw). As we have seen in the previous chapter, the festival continues to exhibit enormous vitality and crossing over of boundaries, sacred and secular. It is too religious in character for Indians committed to specific social or ideological programs, and it is too secular for Hindus oriented toward traditional religious practices. The festival, like the deity it honors, stands on the boundaries among categories, eluding them all, and remaining lord of them all.

6

Gaṇeśa: The Protean God

Throughout this study we have been guided by the questions: Who is Gaṇeśa? Where does he come from? What does he do? What religious longings, anxieties, perplexities, and joys does he embody for his devotees? How does he shape and change peoples' lives?

His origins in the historical sense of the term are difficult, if not impossible to locate, and much is left to conjecture. Indeed, he appears to come from many places at once. Ancient texts link him with Śiva (or perhaps Indra) as the Gaṇapati, the lord of creatures. His elephant shape associates him with the vehicles of the gods, particularly Indra, and the guardian figures of shrines. His behavior regarding placing and removing obstacles links him to ancient demon figures, the vināyakas, who must be placated with food and rites. Gaṇeśa seems to be the result of a coalescing of these various patterns although precisely how this process occurred eludes us.

His origins in the mythological sense are much more accessible. Stories from the Purāṇas give us many variations on the themes of his birth and the acquisition of his elephant head. Born from Śiva's thought or laugh, born from Pārvatī's leftover bodily substance, Gaṇeśa emerges connected to one or both of them, but also separate from them. Following almost immediately upon his creation, Gaṇeśa undergoes some form of beheading through combat, cursing, or the machinations of fate. This removal of head from body takes away the first and primordial head to make room for the elephant head, the real head, the one he was destined to have, the only head his iconography ever portrays. This head heals the breach between him and his parents and them to one another. Through the process of creation, sacrifice and restoration the myth recalls the fundamental rhythm of the universe itself. Gaṇeśa is an embodiment of the macrocosm; he is both rent asunder and made whole. From that vantage point Gaṇeśa rules over the territory of beginnings. Beginnings of actions in time as devotees call upon his graceful supervision of their undertakings; beginnings of actions in space as his worshippers find him at the doorways of homes and temples, straddling the two orders of profane and sacred space.

Although Gaṇeśa's myths cover a relatively small number of themes, they are immensely popular and reach deeply into the Hindu psyche. His myths evoke the primal realities of life's earliest and most precarious experiences. The intense intimacy Gaṇeśa enjoys as the child made from Pārvatī's own substance—he alone is permitted entry into her sacred enclosure—gives mythic form to the forgotten traces of mother love that all can claim. Soon therafter, however, this idyll is broken, in part by the mother's doing, when Gaṇeśa must undergo the loss of his original head to his father's rage. Gaṇeśa must venture into the outside world in order to be broken, the head that knew the now-forbidden intimacy with the mother must be replaced by the head of another species altogether. According to some versions of the story, even that head must be broken again; the tusk, the remaining and perhaps competitive resemblance to the father must be surrendered. This tale of intimacy and violence gives shape at the human level to the life process of separation from the mother and the painful but necessary and inevitable experience of socialization into the larger world of family and society. Among the males of twice-born castes, this process also finds ritual articulation in the rite of *upanayana,* the investiture of the sacred thread, in which the young man leaves the nurture of his mother and submits to the requirements of the outside world represented by the father and the cultural representative of the superego, the guru.

This process of maternal intimacy followed by paternal rupture is not a tragic one in the Hindu scheme of things. Instead it is a necessary and ultimately redeeming one. In the act of submission to the father and his representatives, one finds power. Gaṇeśa is rewarded for his painful submission: he receives dominion over every new undertaking; he moves to the entrance of the world of the gods. From that vantage point, Gaṇeśa becomes the friend at court for all devotees seeking blessing on their efforts. The anxieties that humans inevitably feel in taking up new endeavors in an uncertain world find relief when they are laid, along with offerings of food, flowers, and sacred speech, at Gaṇeśa's feet. Through this process of creation, sacrifice, and surrender, Gaṇeśa comes to know his *svadharma,* that is, the particular work he has to perform in the cosmic scheme of things. His work is the regulation of success and failure, his territory that of obstacles. He thereby becomes a model for all Hindus as they pass through the various thresholds of life's demands and challenges. Gaṇeśa knows their sorrows and desires; he is their best hope.

A central recurring theme in Gaṇeśa's character is that of mediation. Spatially this theme is symbolized by the threshold, Gaṇeśa's dwelling place, and temporally by the beginning, the potent moment when all outcomes are still possible. Mythically Gaṇeśa mediates between his mother and father; he stands between them as the source of both conflict and reconciliation, as children frequently do in the human world. He stands between the gods and their adversaries, both human and demonic. He stands between success and failure, the sacred and the profane. As the one who stands on the boundary, Gaṇeśa not only plays out his special *dharma* by creating and removing obstacles, he is himself an obstacle. He is the one whom Śiva must overcome to reach Pārvatī, he is the one the devotee must get past in order to reach the precious territory of the inner region of the shrine. He is the lord of the first plane of meditation for the yogi, the *mūlādhāra cakra,* through which consciousness must pass on its way to freedom.

Gaṇeśa's physical form signals these mediatorial roles and powers. His physical appearance is one of junctures and boundaries. Half animal/half deity, broken/joined together, half wild/half tame, son of the lord and lady of the universe, yet acquainted with demons, he is made up by joining together that which at other times and places stands apart. He does not reconcile these oppositions, he holds them together in dynamic tension. Hinduism does not seek resolution of extremes into a golden mean; it seeks to push each opposition to its outermost limits and then to gain a precious glimpse, a *darśana,* of that universe so fully and contradictorily extended. It is appropriate that Gaṇeśa's form be that of an elephant, the largest of animals, the one whose sheer size makes room for so many oppositions at once.

During the turbulent times of India's modern history, Gaṇeśa has stood on his mediatorial ground. A symbol of the traditional past, yet the bringer of success in the future, the god of all Hindus, yet the special deity of a displaced elite, Gaṇeśa has served as a symbol of a revitalized traditionalism in the face of rapid and uncertain change. Like the festival that annually honors him, Gaṇeśa has been an occasion for unity within Hinduism, and the source of fear and suspicion on the part of religious minorities in India. For the people of Maharashtra, themselves dwellers on the cultural boundary between the Aryan north and Dravidian south, Gaṇeśa enjoys special affection as the patron deity of the Marathi-speaking people. In paying homage to Gaṇeśa they not only honor the deity, they assert their common bond as Maharashtrians, a bond that unites them beneath the divisions of class and caste.

From the vantage point of our examination of Gaṇeśa's character and impact on Hindu culture, it is clear that Gaṇeśa is not finished. His protean nature continues to give forth vitality. He has not been displaced by the conditions of modernity in India, quite the contrary. His mythology and symbolism adapt well to the novel circumstances brought about by a culture undergoing rapid change. In his capacity as the Lord of Beginnings, he lends religious meaning to new undertakings, and as the Lord of Obstacles he stands as a reminder of the precariousness of all human adventures. For India's Hindus, standing on the threshold between tradition and modernity, Gaṇeśa stands there with them. He spreads out his massive body and dances at the door.

APPENDIX

The Śrī Gaṇapati Atharvaśīrṣa

The *Śrī Gaṇapati Atharvaśīrṣa* is a upaniṣad that celebrates Gaṇeśa as the embodiment of the ultimate principle *brahman.* It is the most widely recited Sanskrit text among sectarian devotees of Gaṇeśa in Maharashtra. The entire text is lettered over the doorway to the temple hall [*maṇḍapa*] in the *aṣṭavināyaka* Gaṇeśa shrine at Ranjangaon, and it was the first Sanskrit text to be published in the prestigious Ānandāśrama Sanskrit Series, in Pune, at the end of the last century.

There is some dispute as to the dates of origin of this text. It was probably composed during the sixteenth or seventeenth centuries. It received the attention of Śrī Upaniṣad Brahma Yogin in his commentary on one hundred eight upaniṣads in 1751, as well as others (Bühnemann 1983, p. 103). G. S. Ghurye locates its emergence in the early nineteenth century, corresponding to the rise in the Gaṇapati cult in Maharashtra among Brahmins centered in Pune (pp. 101–2). The text traces its own lineage to the *Atharva Veda.* My translation is taken from the edition by J. R. Sartha (Bombay, 1969). A heavily edited and abbreviated translation was done in the early nineteenth century by Vans Kennedy (pp. 493–94). A critical edition and translation has been published recently by Gudrun Bühnemann (1984).

Homage to Lord Gaṇeśa. *Oṃ,* Reverence to Gaṇapati. You are indeed the visible "That Thou Art" [*tattvamasi*]. You indeed produce the universe. You indeed sustain it. You indeed destroy it. You indeed are the all pervading reality. You are the manifestation of the eternal self [*ātman*]. I speak what is fitting. I speak the truth. I describe your form. I listen to [the description of] your qualities. I give you my worship. I devote myself to your study. From the west, the east, the north, the south, from above, from below, from wherever calamity may come during your worship, please give me protection.

You are the essence of sound. You are pure consciousness [*cit*]. You are pure bliss [*ānanda*]. You are *brahman.* You are the form of truth, consciousness, and bliss [*saccidānanda*]. You are the visible *brahman.* You are knowledge [*jñāna*] and insight [*vijñāna*]. This entire world is born from you. Through you this entire world is maintained. Through you this entire world is dissolved. This entire world returns to you again. You are earth, water, fire, air, and space. You set the places for the four classes [*varṇa*].

You are beyond the three qualities [*guṇa,* i.e., *sattva, rajas,* and *tamas*]. You are beyond the three states of consciousness [i.e., waking, dream, and dreamless sleep]. You are beyond the three bodies (i.e., corporal, subtle, and blissful [*sthūla, sūkṣma, ānandamaya*].) You continually dwell in the sacral plexus at the base of the spine [*mūlādhāra cakra*]. You embody the creative power. Yogins constantly meditate on you. You are Brahmā, Viṣṇu, and Rudra [Śiva]. You are Agni, Vāyu, and Sūrya. You are Candrama. You are earth, space, and heaven. You are the manifestation of the *mantra* "*Oṃ.*"

Having uttered the first letter of the word *gaṇa, ga,* then I utter the nasal sound *ṇa* which follows and appears beautifully like the crescent moon. This is your form. The *ga* forms the initial letter, the *a* forms the middle letter and the *ṇa* forms the final letter. To utter this sound [i.e., *gaṃ*] is to utter all sounds together.

I give recognition to the one having the single tusk, I meditate on the one having the twisted trunk, that trunk which inspires me. To him who holds the single tusk, your hands: the upper right holds the noose, the upper left holds the goad, the lower left holds an elephant's tusk, the lower right gestures blessing, to him whose color is red, whose belly is large, whose ears resemble a grain-winnowing basket, whose garments are red, upon whom sandal paste is applied, to him I offer my worship [*pūjā*] with red flowers.

He is the deity who renders compassion to those who are devoted to him. He is the one who gave birth to these worlds. He is imperishable, he was produced before this universe was formed. He is beyond the principles of spirit and matter [*puruṣa* and *prakṛti*]. Whoever meditates on him will become the most excellent yogin among yogins.

Homage to the leader of the *gaṇa* of the gods. Homage to the lord of the divine group. May my praises go to him who is the primier lord, who has the large belly, and the single tusk. To the one who destroys obstacles, the son of Śiva, to the one whose sight brings blessings, may my praises be offered repeatedly.

Whoever studies this *Atharvaśīrṣa* will obtain the whole of Brahmā in this age [*kalpa*]. He will realize all happiness. He will not receive affliction from any calamity. He will obtain freedom from the five great sins [i.e., murdering a Brahmin, drunkenness, adultery, stealing, and associating with evil persons]. Whoever recites this in the evening becomes free from sins committed during that day. Whoever recites this in the morning becomes free from the sins committed during the previous night. Hence, whoever recites this text morning and evening becomes free from all sins, and obtains the goals of right conduct [*dharma*], success [*artha*], sensual enjoyment [*kāma*], and release [*mokṣa*].

One should refrain from teaching this *Atharvaśīrṣa* to anyone who lacks faith in it. Whoever teaches it only for money commits the highest sin. One who recites this *Atharvaśīrṣa* one thousand times will find all his desires fulfilled.

Whoever, along with this *Atharvaśīrṣa,* performs the rite of bathing the image of Gaṇapati becomes a good orator. Whoever utters this on the fourth day of each half of the month [*caturthī*] while fasting becomes well-endowed with knowledge [*vidyā*]. This text was told by the Atharvan sage, and through it one recognizes the veil covering *brahman* and becomes fearless. Whoever offers *dūrvā* grass [to Gaṇeśa] obtains the riches of Vaiśravaṇa [Kubera]. Whoever offers parched grain becomes honored and endowed with wisdom. Whoever offers one thousand *modakas* gains the fruit of his undertakings. Whoever offers burning wood with clarified butter obtains all happiness and gains all worthwhile things.

Whoever teaches this *Atharvaśīrṣa* to eight Brahmins attains vital power like that of the sun. Whoever utters this during a solar eclipse in a sacred place obtains the power of the fulfillment of *mantra.* He becomes free from great obstacles. He becomes free from great fault. He becomes free from great sins. He gains all knowledge. This is, indeed, the Veda. This is the Upaniṣad. May it be auspicious!

BIBLIOGRAPHY

1. Primary Texts in Indic Languages

Agni Purāṇa. AAS, no. 41. Poona, 1957.
Aitareya Brāhmaṇa. With commentary of Sāyaṇa. Bib. Ind. Calcutta, 1896.
Āśvalāyana Śrauta Sūtra. Bib. Ind. no. 49. Calcutta, 1874.
Atha Gaṇeśacaturthī—pūjākathā prārambh. See Javadekar in secondary sources.
Atharva Veda. With commentary of Sāyaṇa. Bombay, 1895.
Baudhāyana Gṛhya Sūtra. Ed. R. S. Shastri. Mysore, 1920.
Baudhāyana Gṛhyapariśiṣṭa Sūtra. Selections ed. and trans. by Pieter N. U. Hartung. Amersfoort, Neth., 1922.
Bhagavad Gītā. Ed. and trans. Franklin Edgerton. HOS, nos. 38–39. Cambridge, Mass., 1946.
Bhāgavata Purāṇa. With commentary of Śrīdhara. Bombay, 1832.
Bhaviṣya Purāṇa. Bombay, 1959.
Brahmāṇḍa Purāṇa. Delhi, 1973.
Brahmavaivarta Purāṇa. AAS, no. 102. Poona, 1935.
Bṛhaddharma Purāṇa. Bib. Ind. Calcutta, 1888–97.
Bṛhaddevatā of Śaunaka. HOS, no. 5. Cambridge, Mass., 1904.
Bṛhatsaṃhitā of Varāha Mihira. Bib. Ind. Calcutta, 1865.
Buddhacarita. See Johnston 1937, 1972.
Caturvargacintāmaṇi of Hemādri. Bib. Ind. Calcutta, 1873.
Devī Purāṇa. Ed. P. K. Sharma. Delhi, 1978.
Devībhāgavata Purāṇa. Benares, 1960.
Gaṇeśa Gītā. See Yoroi in secondary sources.
Gaṇeśa Purāṇa. Bombay, 1892.
Garuḍa Purāṇa. Benares, 1963.
Gopatha Brāhmaṇa. Leiden, 1919.
Harivaṃśa. Ed. V. S. Sukthankar et al. Pune, 1969–71.
Jaiminīya Brāhmaṇa (Talavakāra). Sarasvatī-vihara Series, no. 31. Nagpur, 1954.
Jātakas. Ed. V. Fausbøll. 7 vols. London, 1877–96.

Jñāneśvarī. Ed. S. V. Dandekar. Poona, 1967. See also Pradhan in secondary sources.

Kāmasūtra of Vātsyāyana. Bombay, 1856.

Kathāsaritsāgara of Somadeva. Bombay, 1930. See also Penzer in secondary sources.

Kumārasambhava of Kālidāsa. Bombay, 1955.

Kūrma Purāṇa. Ed. A. S. Gupte, Benares, 1972.

Liṅga Purāṇa. Calcutta, 1812.

Mahābhāgavata Purāṇa. Bombay, 1913.

Mahābhārata. With commentary of Nīlakaṇṭha. Bombay, 1862.

Mahābhārata. Ed. V. S. Sukthankar et al. Poona, 1933–69.

Maitrāyaṇī Saṃhitā. Ed. L. von Schroeder. Wiesbaden, 1881 (reprint, 1970).

Mānavadharmaśāstra. With commentary of Medhātithi. Bib. Ind. Calcutta, 1932.

Mānavagṛhyasūtra. Trans. Mark J. Dresden. Groningen, 1941.

Mārkaṇḍeya Purāṇa. Bib. Ind. no. 29 Calcutta, 1862.

Mātaṅgalīlā. See Edgerton in secondary sources.

Matsya Purāṇa. ASS, no. 54. Poona, 1907.

Mudgala Purāṇa. Bombay, 1976.

Nāmadeva Gāthā. Bombay, 1970.

Padma Purāṇa. ASS, no. 131. Poona, 1893.

Pāraskaragṛhyasūtra. Ed. A. F. Stenzler. *Abhandlungen für die Kunde des Morgenlandes*, 6/2, 1876.

Rāmāyaṇa of Vālmiki. Ed. G. H. Bhatt, et al. Baroda, 1960–75.

Ṛg Veda. With commentary of Sāyana. Ed. F. Max Müller. 2nd ed. London, 1890–92.

Śabdakalpadruma of Raja Sir Radhakant Deb Bahadur. Calcutta, 1886.

Śaiva Upaniṣads. Ed. A. M. Shastri. Madras, 1950.

Śaṅkaravijaya of Ānandagiri. Ed. J. Tarkapanchanana. Bib. Ind. Calcutta, 1868.

Śatapatha Brāhmaṇa. Ed. Albrecht Weber. Bib. Ind. Calcutta, 1903.

Śiva Purāṇa. Benares, 1964.

Śiva Purāṇa, Dharmasaṃhitā. Bombay, 1884.

Skanda Purāṇa. Bombay, 1867.

Śrī Gaṇeśa Ārādhanā. See N. Joshi.

Śrīsamartha Rāmadāsāṃce Samagra Grantha. Ed. A. C. Bhat. Poona, 1916.

Subhāṣitaratnakoṣa of Vidyākara. Ed. D. D. Kosambi and V. V. Gokhale. HOS, no. 42. Cambridge, Mass., 1957. See also Ingalls in secondary sources.

Taittirīya Āraṇyaka. With commentary of Sāyana. ASS, no. 36. Poona, 1897–1898.

Taittirīya Brāhmaṇa. With commentary of Sāyana. Bib. Ind. Calcutta, 1859.

Tāṇḍya Mahābrāhmaṇa (Pañcaviṃśa). With commentary of Sāyana. Trans. W. Caland. Bib. Ind. Calcutta, 1931.

Tukārāma Gāthā. Bombay, 1950.

Upaniṣads. One Hundred and Eight Upaniṣads. 4th ed. Bombay, 1913.

Vāmana Purāṇa. Ed. A. S. Gupta. Benares, 1968.

Varāha Purāṇa. Bib. Ind. no. 110. Calcutta, 1893.

Vāyu Purāṇa. ASS, no. 49. Poona, 1860.

Viṣṇu Purāṇa. With commentary of Śrīdhara. Calcutta, 1972.

Viṣṇudharmottara Purāṇa. Bombay, n.d.

Yājñavalkyasmṛti. ASS, no. 46. Poona, 1903–4.

2. *Secondary Sources*

Abbott, Justin E. 1930. *Tukārām: Translations from Mahīpati's* Bhaktalīlāmṛta, chapts. 25–40. Poet-Saints of Maharashtra, no. 7. Poona.

Agarkar, A. J. 1950. *Folk-dance of Maharashtra*. Bombay.

Agrawala, P. K. 1966. Skanda in the Purāṇas and Classical Literature. *Purāṇa* 7/1:135–88.

———. 1978. *Goddess Vināyakī: The Female Gaṇeśa*. Benares.

Agrawala, V. S. 1963. Meaning of Gaṇapati. *Journal of the Oriental Research Institute, Baroda* 13:1–4.

Apte, V. S. 1975. *The Practical Sanskrit-English Dictionary*. Delhi.

Aravamuthan, T. T. 1949. Gaṇeśa: Clue to a Cult and a Culture. *Journal of Oriental Research* 18:221–45.

Ayyar, P. V. Jagadisa. 1982. *South Indian Customs*. New Delhi.

Babb, Lawrence A. 1975. *The Divine Hierarchy*. New York.

Bedeker, V. M. 1969. Kubera in Sanskrit Literature with Special Reference to the *Mahābhārata*. *JGJhRI* 25:425–51.

Banerjea, J. N. 1956. *The Development of Hindu Iconography*. Calcutta.

Barnouw, Victor. 1954. The Changing Character of a Hindu Festival. *AA* 56:74–86.

Beck, Brenda E. F. 1969. Colour and Heat in South Indian Ritual. *Man N.S.* 4:553–72.

———. 1974. The Kin Nucleus in Tamil Folklore. In Thomas R Trautmann, ed., *Kinship and History in South Asia*. Michigan Papers on South and Southeast Asia, no. 7. Ann Arbor. Pp. 1–22.

Bellah, Robert N., ed. 1965. *Religion and Progress in Modern Asia*. New York.

Berkeley-Hill, Owen, 1921. The Anal-Erotic Factor in the Religion,

Philosophy and Character of the Hindus. *International Journal of Psycho-Analysis* 2:306–38.

Berkson, Carmel. 1983. *Elephanta: The Cave of Śiva.* Essays by Wendy D. O'Flaherty, George Michell, and Carmel Berkson. Princeton, N.J.

Bhandarkar, R. G. 1913. *Vaiṣṇavism, Śaivism, and Minor Religious Systems.* Strausberg, Ger.

Bharati, Agehananda. 1970. Pilgrimage Sites and Indian Civilization. In J. Elder, ed., *Chapters in Indian Civilization.* Dubuque, Iowa. Pp. 88–126.

Bhat, A. C. 1916. Śrīsamartha Rāmadāsāṃce Samagra Grantha, Poona.

Bombay Presidency. 1885. *Gazeteer of the Bombay Presidency,* vol. 18/3. Bombay.

Brown, D. McKenzie, 1958. The Philosophy of Bal Gangadhar Tilak: *Karma* vs. *Jñāna* in the *Gītā Rahasya. JAS* 17:197–208.

Brubaker, Richard L. 1977. Lustful Woman, Chaste Wife, Ambivalent Mistress. *Anima* 3:59–62.

———. 8 November 1979. The Uses of Decapitation. Paper presented at annual meeting of the American Academy of Religion, New York.

Bühnemann, Gudrun. 1983. *Budha-Kauśika's Rāmarakṣāstotra.* Publications of the De Nobili Research Library, vol. 10. Ed. Gerhard Oberhammer. Vienna.

———. 1984. Some Remarks on the Structure and Application of Hindu Sanskrit Stotras. *Wiener Zeitschrift für die Kunde Südasiens* 28, pp. 73–104.

Carstairs, G. Morris. 1958. *The Twice-Born.* London.

Cashman, Richard I. 1975. *The Myth of the Lokamanya: Mass Politics in Maharashtra.* Berkeley, Calif.

Cendavankar, Sadanand. 1964. *Śrī Aṣṭavināyaka.* Bombay.

———. 1965. *Mahārāṣṭratīl Mahāgaṇapati.* Bombay.

Chattopadhyaya, Debiprasad. 1959. *Lokāyata: A Study in Ancient Indian Materialism.* Delhi.

Chirol, Valentine. 1910. *Indian Unrest.* London.

Clothey, Fred. 1978. *The Many Faces of Murukan.* The Hague.

Coomaraswamy, A. K. 1928. Ganesha. *Bulletin of the Museum of Fine Arts* [Boston] 34:30–31.

———. 1928a. *Yakṣas.* Smithsonian Miscellaneous Collections, vol. 80/6. Washington, D.C.

Courtright, Paul B. 1974. Gaṇeśa and the Gaṇeśa Festival in Maharashtra: A Study in Hindu Religious Celebration. Ph.D. dissertation, Princeton University.

———. 1980. The Beheading of Gaṇeśa. *Purāṇa* 22:67–80.

Crooke, William. 1928. *Popular Religion and Folklore of Northern India.* 2 vols. Oxford.

Danielov, Alain. 1964. *Hindu Polytheism.* Bollingen Series, no. 73. New York.

Das, Veena, 1977. On the Categorization of Space in Hindu Ritual. In Ravindra Jain, ed., *Text and Context: The Social Anthropology of Tradition.* Philadelphia.

Deleury, G. A. 1960. *The Cult of Viṭhoba.* Poona.

Della Valle, Pietro. 1892. *The Travels of Pietro Della Valle.* 2 vols. Ed. Edward Grey. London.

Dessigane, R., P. Z. Pittabiramin, and Jean Filliozat. 1960. *La Légende des jeux de Çiva à Madurai.* Publications de l'Institut Français d'Indologie, no. 19. Pondicherry.

———. 1964. *Les légendes Çaivites de Kāñcipuram.* Publications de l'Institut Français d'Indologie, no. 27. Pondicherry.

———. 1967. *La légende de Skanda selon le Kandapurāṇam tamoul et l'iconographie.* Publications de l'Institute Français d'Indologie, no. 31. Pondicherry.

Deva, Vighnahari and K. Bhingarkar. n.d. *Moragāvīcī dev Ciṇcvāḍī āle.* Cincvad.

Diehl, Carl Gustave. 1956. *Instrument and Purpose.* Lund, Sweden.

Douglas, Mary. 1966. *Purity and Danger: An Analysis of Concepts of Pollution and Taboo.* London.

Dube, S. G. 1967. *Indian Village.* New York.

Dubois, Abbe J. A. 1959. *Hindu Manners, Customs, and Ceremonies.* Ed. and trans. Henry Beauchamp. 3rd. ed. Oxford.

Dundes, Alan. 1962. Earth-Diver: Creation and the Mythopoeic Male. *AA* 64:1032–1105.

Eck, Diana L. 1978. Kāśī: City and Symbol. *Purāṇa* 20/2:169–92.

———. 1982. *Banāras, City of Light.* New York.

Edgerton, Franklin. 1931. *The Elephant Lore of the Hindus: The Elephant-Sport (Mātaṅgalīlā) of Nīlakaṇṭha.* New Haven, Conn.

Eichinger Ferro-Luzzi, Gabriella. 1977a. The Logic of South Indian Food Offerings. *Anthropos* 72/3–4:529–56.

———. 1977b. Ritual as Language: The Case of South Indian Food Offerings. *Current Anthropology,* 18/3:507–14.

Eliade, Mircea. 1959. *The Sacred and the Profane.* Trans. Willard R. Trask. New York.

Elwin, Verrier. 1949. *The Myths of Middle India.* Oxford.

Freud, Sigmund. 1965 (reprint). *The Interpretation of Dreams.* Trans. James Strachey. New York.

Gadgil, Amarendra. 1968. *Śrī Gaṇeśa Kośa: Upāsaka āṇi abhyāsaka aśā sarvāṃsaṭhī Gaṇeśa daivataviṣayaka sādhanagrantha.* Pune.

Gennep, Arnold van. 1960. *The Rites of Passage.* Trans. Monika Vizedom and Gabriella Caffee. Chicago.

Getty, Alice. 1936. *Gaṇeśa: A Monograph on the Elephant-faced God.* Oxford.

Ghurye, G. S. 1962. *Gods and Men.* Bombay.

Goldman, Robert P. 1978. Fathers, Sons and Gurus: Oedipal Conflict in the Sanskrit Epics. *Journal of Indian Philosophy* 6:352–92.

Gonda, Jan. 1954. Pratiṣṭhā. *Studia Indologica Internationalia* 1:1–37.

———. 1963. On Mantra. *Oriens* 16:247–97.

Grierson, G. A. 1914. Gāṇapatyas. *ERE* 6:175–76.

Gupte, B. A. 1901. Harvest Festivals in Honour of Gauri and Ganesh. *Indian Antiquary* 25:60–64.

———. 1919. *Hindu Holidays and Ceremonials.* 2nd rev. ed. Calcutta.

Hanchett, Suzanne L. 1972. Festivals and Social Relations in a Mysore Village: Mechanics of Two Processions. *Economic and Political Weekly* 8:1517–22.

Hara, Minoru. 1958. Nakulīśa-Pāśupata-Darśanam. *Indo-Iranian Journal* 2:8–32.

Hazra, R. C. 1948. Gaṇapati Worship and the Upapurāṇas Dealing with It. *JGJhRI* 5:263–76.

———. 1951. The Gaṇeśa Purāṇa. *JGJhRI* 9:79–99.

Heesterman, Jan. 1967. The Case of the Severed Head. *WZKSO* 11:22–43.

Heras, H. 1954. The Problem of Gaṇapati. *Tamil Culture* 3:152–213.

Herbert, Jean. 1944. *Ganesha: Précédé d'une étude sur dieu chez les Hindous.* Lyon.

Hiltebeitel, Alf. 1976. *The Ritual of Battle: Krishna in the Mahābhārata.* Ithaca, N.Y.

———. 1980. Śiva, the Goddess, and the Disguises of the Pāṇḍavas and Draupadī. *HR* 20:147–98.

———. 1982. Sexuality and Sacrifice: Convergent Subcurrents in the Firewalking Cult of Draupadī. In Fred Clothey, ed. *Images of Man: Religion and Historical Process in South Asia.* Madras.

Hospital, Clifford. 1978. The Enemy Transformed: Opponents of the Lord in the *Bhāgavata Purāṇa. JAAR* (*Supplement*) 44:199–215.

Howell, Catherine H. 1975. "Discovering" the Goddess: An Analysis of the *Vrat Kathā.* MA thesis, University of Virginia.

Hynes, William J. and Thomas J. Steele, S. J. 1981. Saint Peter: Apostle Transfigured into Trickster. *Arché: Notes and Papers on Archaic Studies,* No. 6: *Transformations of Archaic Images.* Ed. William G. Doty, pp. 112–28.

Inden, Ronald B., and Ralph W. Nicholas. 1977. *Kinship in Bengali Culture.* Chicago.

Ingalls, Daniel H. H., trans. 1965. *An Anthology of Sanskrit Court Poetry* [Vidyākara's *Subhāṣitaratnakoṣa*]. HOS, no. 44. Cambridge, Mass.

Jacobi, H. 1914. Brāhmaṇism. *ERE* 2:799–813.

Javadekar, A. Y., trans. 1969. *Now Begins the Worship and Story for the Fourth Lunar Day of the Lord of Troops* [*Atha Gaṇeśacaturthī—pūjākathā prārambh*]. Ed. by McKim Marriott with suggestions from J. A. B. Van Buitenen and Jean Varenne, 2nd ed. Committee on Southern Asian Studies, University of Chicago. Chicago.

Johnston, E. H. 1937. The Buddha's Mission and Last Journey: *Buddhacarita* 15–28. *Acta Orientalia* 15:26–62; 85–111.

———. trans. 1972 (reprint). *The Buddhacarita: or Acts of the Buddha.* New Delhi.

Joshi, M. Y. 1975. *Śrī Gaṇeśa Darśana.* Pune.

Joshi, Narayanashastri. 1969. *Śrī Gaṇeśa Ārādhanā.* Bombay.

Jouveau-Dubreuil, G. 1937. *Iconography of Southern India.* Paris.

Kaelber, Walter O. 1978. The "Dramatic" Element in Brāhmaṇic Initiation: Symbols of Death, Danger and Difficult Passage. *HR* 18:54–76.

Kakar, Sudhir. 1978. *The Inner World: A Psychoanalytic Study of Childhood and Society in India.* New Delhi.

Kane, P. V. 1968–75. *History of Dharmaśāstra.* 2nd ed. 5 vols. Pune.

Karandikar, J. S. 1953. *Śrīgaṇeśotsavācī Sāṭh Varṣe.* Pune.

Karve, Iravati. 1962. On the Road—A Maharashtrian Pilgrimage. *JAS* 22/1:1–17.

———. 1968a. *Kinship Organization in India.* Bombay.

———. 1968b. *Maharashtra, Land and Its People.* Bombay.

Kelkar, N. C., ed. 1922. *Lokamānya Ṭiḷakāce Kesarītīl Lekh.* Pune.

Kennedy, Vans. 1831. *Researches into the Nature and Affinity of Ancient and Hindu Mythology.* London.

Knipe, David M. 1977. *Sapiṇḍīkaraṇa:* The Hindu Rite of Entry into Heaven. In Frank Reynolds and Earle Waugh, eds., *Religious Encounters with Death: Insights from the History and Anthropology of Religions.* University Park, Pa. Pp. 111–124.

Kosambi, D. D. 1962. *Myth and Reality.* Bombay.

Kramrisch, Stella. 1975. The Indian Great Goddess. *HR* 15:235–65.

———. 1981. *The Presence of Śiva.* Princeton.

Leach, Edmund R. 1962. Pulleyar and the Lord Buddha: Aspects of Religious Syncretism in Ceylon. *Psychoanalysis and the Psychoanalytic Review* 49:80–102.

Mani, Vettam. 1975. *Purāṇic Encyclopedia.* Delhi.

Mann, Thomas. 1941. *The Transposed Heads: A Legend of India.* Trans. H. T. Lowe-Porter. New York.

Marathe, Anant Vasudev. 1947. *Śrīgaṇeśotsav.* Bombay.

Marriott, McKim. 1966. The Feast of Love. In Milton Singer, ed., *Krishna: Myths, Rites and Attitudes.* Chicago. Pp. 200–212.

Mate, M. S. 1962. *Temples and Legends of Maharashtra.* Bombay.

McKenzie, John. 1938. *The Mahar Folk: A Study of Untouchables in Maharashtra.* Calcutta.

Miller, Barbara Stoler, trans. 1978. *The Hermit and the Love Thief: Sanskrit Poems of Bhartrihari and Bilhana.* New York.

Mitra, Haridas. n.d. *Gaṇapati.* Shantiniketan.

Monier-Williams, Monier. 1964 (reprint). *An English-Sanskrit Dictionary.* Oxford.

Moor, Edward. 1801. An Account of an hereditery living Deity, to whom devotion is paid by the Brahmins of Poona and its neighborhood. *Asiatic Researches* 7:383–97.

———. 1968 (reprint). *Hindu Pantheon.* Benares.

Mukherji, Abhay Charan. 1916. *Hindu Fasts and Feasts.* Allahabad.

Narain, A. K. 1978. On the Earliest Gaṇeśa. In L. P. K. Indrapala and J. E. van Lohuizen-De Leeuw, eds. *Senarat Paranavitana Commmemoration Volume.* Leiden. Pp. 142–44.

Navaratnam, Ratna Ma 1978. *Aum Ganesa: The Peace of god.* Jaffna.

Obeyesekere, Gananath. 1984. *The Cult of the Goddess Pattini.* Chicago.

O'Flaherty, Wendy D. 1973. *Asceticism and Eroticism in the Mythology of Śiva.* Oxford.

———. 1975. *Hindu Myths.* Baltimore.

———. 1976. *The Origins of Evil in Hindu Mythology.* Berkeley, Calif.

———. 1980. *Women, Androgynes, and Other Mythical Beasts.* Chicago.

———. 1981. *The Rig Veda: An Anthology.* New York.

Omvedt, Gail. 3 May 1971. The Non-Brahman Challenge in Poona, 1922–26. Paper presented at the Maharashtra Study Group, Minneapolis.

Östör, Ákos. 1980. *The Play of the Gods.* Chicago.

Pandey, Raj Bali. 1968. *Hindu Saṃskāras.* Delhi.

Parker, H. 1909. *Ancient Ceylon: An Account of the Aborigines and Part of the Early Civilization.* London.

Penzer, N. M., ed. 1924. *The Ocean of Story.* 10 vols. Trans. C. W. Tawney. London.

Pfaffenberger, Bryan. 1977. Pilgrimage and Traditional Authority in Tamil Sri Lanka. Ph.D. dissertation, University of California, Berkeley.

Pradhan, V. G., trans.; H. M. Lambert. ed. 1967. *The Jnaneshvari.* 2 vols. London.

Preston, Laurence W. 1980. Subregional Religious Centers in the History of Maharashtra: The Sites Sacred to Ganesh. In N. K. Wagle, ed., *Images of Maharashtra: A Regional Profile of India.* Toronto. Pp. 102–28.

Radin, Paul, 1956. *The Trickster: A Study in American Indian Mythology*. New York.
Ramasubramaniam, V. 1971. The Gaṇapati-Vināyaka-Gajānana Worship: Analysis of an Integrative Cult. *Institute of Traditional Cultures Bulletin* 97–153.
Ramanujan, A. K. 1972. The Indian Oedipus. In Arabinda Podder, ed., *Indian Literature, Proceedings of a Seminar*. Simla. Pp. 127–37.
Ranade, M. G. 1900. *The Rise of Maratha Power*. Bombay.
Rao, T. A. Gopinatha. 1914. *Elements of Hindu Iconography*. 4 vols. Madras.
Rao, U. Venkatakrishna. 1949. The Gaṇapati Cult. *Quarterly Journal of the Mythic Society* 41:92–99.
Rassat, Hans-Joachim. 1955. Gaṇeśa: Eine Untersuchung über Herkunft, Wesen und Kult der Elefantenköpfigen Gottheit Indiens. Ph.D. dissertation, University of Tübingen.
Renou, Louis, 1937. Note sur les origines Vediques de Gaṇeṣa. *Journal Asiatique* 229:271–74.
Risley, Herbert H. 1969 (reprint). *The People of India*. 2 vols. Delhi.
Riviere, Juan Roger. 1962. The Problem of Gaṇeśa in the Purāṇas. *Purāṇa* 4/1:96–102.
Rousselet, Louis, 1878. *India and Its Native Princes*. London.
Russell, R. V. and Hira Lal. 1963 (reprint). *The Tribes and Castes of the Central Provinces of India*. 4 vols. Delhi.
Sarma, Jyotimoyee. 1969. Pūjā Associations in West Bengal. *JAS* 28/3:579–94.
Sartha, J. R., ed. 1969. *Śrī Gaṇapati Atharvaśīrṣa*. Bombay.
Sastri, H. Krishna. 1974 (reprint). *South Indian Images of Gods and Goddesses*. Delhi.
Shastri, A. Mahadevi. 1950. *The Śaiva Upaniṣads*. With the Commentary of Śrī Upaniṣad Brahmayogin. Madras.
Shulman, David D. 1980. *Tamil Temple Myths: Sacrifice and Marriage in the South India Śaiva Tradition*. Princeton, N.J.
Sivaramamurti, C. 1974. *Nātarāja in Art, Thought and Literature*. New Delhi.
———. 1977. *The Art of India*. New York.
Sontheimer, Gunther-Dietz. 1976. *Birobā, Mhaskobā, und Khaṇḍobā: Ursprung, Geschichte und Umwelt von pastoralen Gottheiten im Mahārāṣṭra*. Wiesbaden, W. Ger.
Spratt, Philip. 1966. *Hindu Culture and Personality: A Psychoanalytic Study*. Bombay.
Srivastava, M. C. P. 1972. Gaṇeśa and Jyeṣṭhā. *Journal of the Bihar Research Society* 58/1–4:165–70.

Stanley, John. 1977. Special Time, Special Power: The Fluidity of Power in a Popular Hindu Festival. *JAS* 37/1:27–43.

Stevenson, R. 1845. Analysis of the Gaṇeśa Purāṇa, with special reference to the history of Buddhism. *JRAS* 8:3:19–24.

Sykes, W. H. 1823. An Account of the Origin of the Living God at the Village of Chinchore, Near Poona. *Transactions of the Literary Society of Bombay* 3:64–72.

Trautmann, Thomas R. 1981. *Dravidian Kinship*. Cambridge, Eng.

Tulpule, S. G. 1979. *Classical Marāṭhī Literature*. History of Indian Literature, vol. 9/4. Wiesbaden.

Turner, Victor W. 1969. *The Ritual Process*. Chicago.

———. 1974. *Dramas, Fields, and Metaphors*. Ithaca, N.Y.

Tyler, Stephen A. 1973. *India: An Anthropoligical Perspective*. Pacific Palasades, Calif.

Underhill, M. M. 1921. *The Hindu Religious Year*. Calcutta.

Varadpande, M. L. 1973. Ganesh in Indian Folk Theatre. *Sangeet Natak* 27:64–75.

Vaudville, Charlotte. 1973. Paṇḍharpur, the City of Saints. In H. M. Buck and Glenn Yocum, eds., *Structural Studies on South India*. Chambersburg, Pa. Pp. 137–161.

Winternitz, Maurice. 1898. Gaṇeśa in the *Mahābhārata*. *JRAS* 3:380–84.

Wolpert, Stanley A. 1962. *Tilak and Gokhale: Revolution and Reform in the Making of Modern India*. Berkeley, Calif.

Yoroi, Kiyoshi. 1968. *Gaṇeśa Gītā: A Study, Translation with Notes, and a Condensed Rendering of the Commentary of Nīlakaṇṭha*. The Hague.

Ziegenbalg, Bartholomaeus. 1869. *Geneology of the South Indian Gods*. Trans. G. J. Metzger. Madras.

Zimmer, Heinrich. 1946. *Myths and Symbols in Indian Art and Civilization*. Bollingen Series no. 6. New York.

———. 1955. *The Art of Indian Asia*. 2 vols. Bollingen Series, vols. 39–40. Princeton, N.J.

Index